KING *of the* PIRATES

The Swashbuckling Life
of Henry Every

KING *of the* PIRATES

The Swashbuckling Life of Henry Every

E.T. FOX

In memory of my grandfather, Ken Fox, whose tales instilled in me a love of history which I have never lost.

Acknowledgements

I am indebted, in no particular order, to David Moore and Elisabeth Shure for their help supplying a number of source documents, to Craig Long for his excellent cover painting depicting the battle between the *Fancy* and the *Gang-i-Sawai*, to Jeremy Fox for taking me off at tangents, to friends and family for their enthusiasm and encouragement, and above all to the record keepers of the past whose work provided the material for this book.

Frontispiece: Pirates ransacking chests and trunks.

First published 2008

The History Press
Cirencester Road, Chalford
Stroud, Gloucestershire, GL6 8PE
www.thehistorypress.co.uk

British Library Cataloguing in Publication Data.
A catalogue record for this book is available from the British Library.

ISBN 978 0 7524 4718 6

Printed and bound in Great Britain

Contents

Introduction

All the best stories begin at the end, and this story is no exception. In 1695 Henry Every, a thirty-six-year-old master mariner from the south coast of Devon, led one of the most powerful pirate crews in history on a short but spectacularly successful cruise in the Red Sea. Their capture of the Grand Moghul's ship the *Gang-i-Sawai* was one of the most successful crimes ever committed, and while it made the fortune of Every's pirates, it plunged the nascent British Empire into turmoil.

Were it not for the capture of the *Gang-i-Sawai* the world might never have remembered Henry Every: as it is his name ranks alongside those of Bartholomew Roberts and Jack Rackham in the annals of piracy. Even so, in modern times his fame has been eclipsed by men like Captain William Kidd and the notorious Blackbeard, despite their comparative lack of success, and in spite of the fact that both those men were probably inspired in part by Henry Every – though in very different ways.

In his own time though, Henry Every was the most famous pirate of them all. Had such a term existed in the 1690s he would undoubtedly have been 'Public Enemy Number One', top of the 'Most Wanted' list. Within a generation or so of his capture of the *Gang-i-Sawai* theatregoers watched his story played out on the stage in *The Successful Pirate*, and alehouse patrons thumped their tankards and jugs on the tables in time with whichever of the several ballads about Every and his men was popular that week. Printers set their plates to turn out sensationalised accounts of Every's life and career. Readers with more ghoulish appetites might already have read the printed account of the trial of six of Every's crew. In 1724 a semi-accurate account of Every's piracy formed the first chapter of London's new best-seller *A General History of the Robberies and Murders of the Most Notorious Pirates*, by Captain Charles Johnson.

But it was not just the public at large who took note of Every's successes. The government and the powerful East India Co. both had an interest in Every's apprehension. The capture of the *Gang-i-Sawai*, and the reports of the atrocities which followed, threatened to split asunder the already delicate relationship between the East India Co. and the Great Moghul of India, Aurangzeb. Without the Moghul's support the East India Co. would have been forced from the sub-continent, irreparably damaging the world's largest empire before it had blossomed. Every earned the moniker 'arch-pirate' for his success, and the government in Whitehall offered a reward of £500 for his capture, an unprecedented amount for a pirate.

The manhunt which followed took place over four continents, and was certainly the largest of the seventeenth century. Every agent of the law in Britain was on the lookout for Every and his men. Throughout the colonies of North America and the Caribbean they were chased. Ships calling at Madagascar sought news of the pirates there, and in India and the Red Sea area the Moghul's authorities and the East India Co. were on the hunt.

But in spite of the immense efforts, not to mention the very attractive reward on offer, only a handful of Every's men were arrested, and most of those were allowed to go free. Every himself disappeared with his double share of the loot and was never captured.

This last fact is what really sets Henry Every apart from his contemporaries. Almost all of the most famous pirates of the so-called 'golden age of piracy' (roughly 1690-1730) met sticky ends. Many were captured and executed like Captain Kidd; others, like Bartholomew Roberts and Blackbeard, were killed in battle with the Royal Navy; some died alone, marooned on a desert island or murdered by their mutinous crew. The pirate captains of this era who survived to accept a pardon or live out their days on a lush tropical island were few and far between, and not one of them was as successful as Henry Every. Of all the pirates who make up the subject matter of that 1724 publication of the *General History*, Every is the only one who lived to enjoy his wealth.

Perhaps it is the almost complete obscurity concerning Every's eventual fate that has dissuaded previous historians from attempting a full-length biography of the arch-pirate. In fact, Every's final years are not as devoid of evidence as it would first appear. From the tangle of theories and suppositions surrounding the end of Every can perhaps be gleaned some salient information. This information can then be compared to what is known of Every's early life, and the comments of his shipmates. After a gap of more than three centuries it is impossible to determine with any certainty what happened to Every and his wealth, but perhaps enough shards of light can be seen through the gloom to allow us to create a workable theory, a credible account of what might have happened.

I first became particularly interested in Henry Every while researching for a book and television series about pirates of the West Country. During the course of that research I came across a little-known publication of 1734 entitled *The History and Lives of all the Most Notorious Pirates and Their Crews*. At first glance it appeared to be a much-condensed cheap edition of Captain Johnson's *General History*, and indeed the vast majority of the text was taken verbatim from the *General History*. There was, however, one extra chapter which had never appeared in any edition of the *General History*. Having ascertained that at least part of the *History and Lives* represented original work I began to check the other chapters more thoroughly to see if any significant changes had been made. Only two chapters differed materially from their counterparts in the *General History*: those of Mary Read and Henry Every. In both cases, although the main part of the story followed the same lines (and often the same words) extra biographical information was added.

There might be several reasons for these additions, but it is difficult to imagine what they could be. Authors, publishers, and readers of the early eighteenth century had much more relaxed views on plagiarism than we do today, and the anonymous author of the *History and Lives* shows clearly that he was quite happy to use the work of others. His anonymity itself shows that he did not make the additions in an attempt to prove himself a better scholar than the equally anonymous Captain Johnson. Neither Every's nor Read's stories are noticeably improved from the point of view of being good yarns, so the additions can hardly have been made for artistic reasons.

What if the reason for the additional information was that it was true? Did the author of the *History and Lives* manage to find extra information unavailable to Johnson and other previous biographers? I decided to test the hypothesis by checking some of the extra information against the historical record. Initially some of the checks produced positive results, and in turn an increased enthusiasm. However, continued research showed the *History and Lives* to be no more or less accurate than any other account, as many of the extra details turned out to be wrong. By that time though my interest was aroused, and the more I looked into Every's life and career the more interesting it was revealed to be, so after 300 years the hunt was on once more.

In any work of history the author faces a number of difficulties, particularly when it comes to things like place names, which may have changed over the intervening centuries. In this book I have tried to follow certain conventions which I have arbitrarily set myself.

Place names I have tried to keep consistent with the names the pirates would have used. Where a place name has changed significantly between the seventeenth century and today I have, on the first occasion of using the name, noted its modern name, but thereafter have reverted to the older name.

The names of people might have several different spellings in different documents, so I have chosen to use one version of each name consistently throughout the book. This is particularly important when considering the name of the arch-pirate himself. Charles Johnson spelled his name 'Avery', a spelling which was certainly used by others at the time, and which has become the most commonly used spelling today. However, there are plenty of other spellings to choose from: Every, Evorie, Ivory, Avory etc. Most official documents relating to the case use the spelling 'Every', and more importantly that was the spelling that Every himself used. It is, therefore, the version which I have used throughout.

By the end of the seventeenth century several European nations had opened trade links in the East, and there were thus several rival East India Co.'s operating in the area. This book is most concerned with the English East India Co., though the companies of other nations are occasionally mentioned. For simplicity's sake anywhere that an East India Co. is mentioned without nationality it can be assumed to be the English company. The companies of other nationalities are clearly noted as such.

When quoting at length from period sources I have modernised and standardised the spelling. To the casual reader I do not feel that the vagaries of seventeenth-century spelling add anything to the feel of the text, and in many cases can make the text difficult to read and understand. Punctuation can be similarly erratic in period writing, but in this case I have tried to retain as much of the original punctuation as possible because, unlike spelling, I think the character of the text is changed by modernised punctuation.

Dates throughout are written in their original form, taking no account of the switch from the old calendar to the new. When the calendars were changed in the eighteenth century ten days were lost, thus an event which took place on, say, 1 January 1695 would have its anniversary on 10 January today. Since the actions described in this book all took place before the change to the new calendar I see no reason to alter dates. However, under the old calendar the new year was seen in on Lady Day, 25 March – thus what we would describe as 1 January 1695 might be written in a period document as 1 January 1694, or sometimes 1 January 1694/5. To avoid any confusion I have taken the new year to begin on 1 January.

Where sums of money are mentioned in the text I have made no attempt to give a modern equivalent of value. Many historians have devised complex methods of calculating the modern worth of period sums, each based on different criteria, and each giving a different value for the same sum. The truth is that the buying power of money can be based on so many things that there can never be a 'right' answer. For example, the cost of a loaf of bread when compared with the average weekly wage for a labourer was considerably higher in the seventeenth century than it is today. If we compare sums based on a typical weekly wage we will get one figure; if we use the 'bread index' we will get a completely different figure.

To avoid this veritable minefield of financial confusion all sums mentioned in the main text are seventeenth-century figures. For the interested reader I have provided a section in the Appendices listing the important sums mentioned in the text and offering various other period sums and prices so that the reader can make their own comparisons.

Finally, there have been several biographies of other pirates written in recent years, and more than a few of them have adopted a dramatic narrative style. There is nothing wrong with this approach *per se*, but it presents the problem that the reader cannot know where historical fact finishes and author's imagination begins. I am well aware that my imagination, vivid though it can be at times, is no substitute for historical truth. I have not, therefore, included any imagined conversations between people, or tried to assign motivations to the people involved. Where spoken words are quoted in the text they are drawn from actual records. If occasionally I have made a guess at someone's motivation I hope I have made it clear that I am guessing. Partly this is because when it comes to history I am a student of the truth – as far as it can ever be ascertained – and partly it is because I feel no need to invent things for the story: Henry Every and his men are interesting enough without my help.

E.T. Fox,
Brixham,
October 2007

Prologue

The little port of Dunfanaghy in the north of Ireland was a quiet sort of a place. Most of the vessels that called there were coasters: they were familiar to the inhabitants and their crews were well known. Occasionally a strange ship arrived, making its way perhaps from Scotland to America. One summer day, towards the end of June, just such a strange vessel arrived, but this ship had all the marks of being homeward bound, not outbound. Her crew were well tanned, and her sails bleached white from weeks at sea. Twelve men, a couple of boys, and one woman stepped ashore. After bidding farewell to the ship's skipper they set off together on the road inland. Six miles or so from Dunfanaghy the woman and one of the men split off from the group and turned down the road towards Derry. Perhaps the rest of the party gave them a wave to cheer them on their way. It was the last time any of them saw the most famous man in the world: Henry Every.

Like so many interesting historical characters, very little is known about Henry Every's birth, childhood, and early life; two books, published in the early eighteenth century, purport to be the biography and autobiography of Every, and contain some information about Every's youth. Unfortunately both of them contain a fair mix of fact and fantasy, with the emphasis on the fantasy, and so are most unreliable. What can be ascertained about the origins of the man who would one day become 'the arch-pirate' must be reconstructed and supposed from snippets of information provided much later in his life.

For example, in 1696 one of Every's men, William Phillips, described the captain as being 'aged about forty years' and from 'near Plymouth'. Examination of the records of baptisms in south Devon for the relevant year suggests that the pirate was the boy Henry, son of John and Anne Evarie, who was born on 23 August 1659 in Newton Ferrers, a small village in the South Hams a little over seven miles east along the coast from Plymouth.[1]

There are no portraits or engravings of Every drawn from life, so we cannot know what he looked like, though William Phillips thoughtfully provided the authorities (and subsequent researchers) with a physical description of the pirate: 'wears a light coloured wig most commonly, pretty swarthy, grey eyes, [and] a flattish nose'.[2]

More important than his physical attributes, though, are his personal ones. Unfortunately neither Phillips nor anyone else left descriptions of his personality so we can only make assumptions based on his actions.

We know that many of Every's pirate crew were literate enough to sign their own names, some with neat and well-formed signatures, others with barely legible scrawls which perhaps represent the limit of their ability. On the whole though, literacy was surprisingly high at the end of the seventeenth century, and especially so amongst the officer classes to which, we shall see, Every belonged. The best-known document connected with Every personally is a letter which he left at the Indian Ocean island of Johanna. It is possible that he dictated it, but he certainly signed it. Furthermore, we also know that during the time Every waited at anchor at Corunna in 1693-4 he wrote home to his wife, so it seems most likely that he was at least functionally literate. In fact, to have performed his practical duties as an officer would have required some degree of literacy, so the matter can be in little doubt.[3]

Every's character is harder to determine. That he must have been charismatic is undeniable: for almost two years he managed to retain command of a band of ruffians of different nationalities, many of whom had already committed one mutiny and can hardly have feared the consequences of a second, and during that time there was no attempt to oust Every or replace him. On a smaller scale, it took him less than a month to tempt a young newly-wed away from her husband and into his arms.

Some of Every's actions seem to indicate a quiet caution coupled with a strong resolution. He did not rush to make decisions, and once they were made he awaited the best time to put them into practice. He understood just how much leeway to give his men, without giving them too much. Foresight and planning went into his actions, but he also had the ability to make good choices when faced with the unexpected. In short, whatever else might be said of the arch-pirate, he was an ideal leader of men.

Every grew up in the most interesting of times. Before he was a year old the Commonwealth rule of England was brought to an abrupt end. Cromwell had died and his son had proven himself incompetent, so in May 1660 Charles II was invited to return to England as king. Some commentators have seen Charles' reign as one of the worst in English history: Charles has been described as arrogant, self-ish, hedonistic, and ineffectual. This may be true, but against that must be balanced the enormous strides in scientific discovery which were made during his reign, the flowering of the arts, and the expansion of English colonies the world over.

The Royal Society was founded in the year of Charles' Restoration and its early members included such scientific luminaries as Sir Christopher Wren, Robert Boyle, Robert Hooke, and Sir Isaac Newton. Its members carried out experiments and listened to lectures on varied subjects, from the semi-successful attempts by Christopher Huygens to develop a sea-going chronometer almost a century before William Harrison to Captain Robert Knox's account of his experiences of the narcotic qualities of cannabis.

In the same year the theatres were reopened after their closure by Cromwell, Mrs Hughes became the first stage actress, and the diarist Samuel Pepys drank his first cup of tea. Two years later Charles married Catherine of Braganza, who brought with her as part of her dowry the colony of Bombay, thus ensuring a plentiful supply of tea into England for years to come. Pepys, meanwhile, was being entertained by Punch and Judy.

Although most of the major European nations had tried their hand at colonisation in the early decades of the century the English Civil War and the Thirty Years War had diverted much money and interest away from such projects. The 1660s and following decades saw the growth of overseas European colonies on an unprecedented scale: amongst others the colony of New Jersey was founded, New York was surrendered by the Dutch to England, and the French East India Co. was founded. It was not long before the first serious colonial revolt occurred in 1676 when Virginian farmer and militia officer Nathaniel Bacon rebelled against Governor Sir William Berkeley in opposition to new taxes and Berkeley's policy towards the Native Indians.

In 1665 English expansion in Africa led, in part, to the second Dutch War – which was fought entirely at sea and culminated in a Dutch fleet sailing up the Medway, torching much of the English fleet (which was taking shelter there), and briefly landing forces on the coasts of Kent and Essex. Charles II signed the Treaty of Dover with the French King Louis XIV, and in 1672 declared war once more on the Netherlands in support of his French ally. The Dutch fleet scored several victories and forced peace in 1674.

In 1665 the Great Plague broke out in London and to a lesser extent in the provinces, though in London at least it was effectively ended by the Great Fire which destroyed much of the capital in the following year. The destruction caused by the Great Fire gave Wren a blank canvas from which rose St Paul's Cathedral and other famous monuments.

The greatest fear in England during Every's early years was the perceived threat to the established Church. Charles had married a Catholic, and it was widely believed that his brother, the Duke of York (later James II), had strong Catholic tendencies until he openly converted to that religion in 1676. Meanwhile, Charles had tried to introduce religious tolerance with the Declaration of Indulgence in 1672, but public outcry led to the replacement of the Declaration with the Test Acts the following year which required anyone entering public office to take the Anglican sacrament. William Penn was among the most prominent Quakers and was arrested and tried in 1670 before helping to found the colony of Pennsylvania in 1677.

The village of Newton Ferrers in 1659 was a quiet little place whose principal industries were fishing and agriculture. In Every's day around 125 adult males lived in the village, so in the absence of any formal census it seems reasonable that the population consisted of somewhere in the region of 100 family units. The village had suffered a little in the years leading up to Every's birth from the Civil War which was fought in the 1640s between Charles I and his Parliament. As a county Devon largely supported the Royalist cause, but the cities of Exeter and Plymouth were strongly Parliamentarian, and this conflict brought the war into the very heart of the county.

Newton Ferrers escaped any actual fighting, but when the Royalists laid siege to Plymouth a number of fishing vessels from the village were lent in support.

The conflict ended with Parliament's victory and the execution of Charles I in 1649, and the whole country (including the areas loyal to Charles I) found itself under Cromwell's rule. In Newton Ferrers the influence of Parliament was most strongly seen in the operation of the Church of the Holy Cross. In 1644 the rector, Edward Elliot, died. He was succeeded by Anthony Clifford, but it was not long before Clifford was replaced by a Parliamentarian, and no sacrament was said until Clifford's reinstatement in 1661 following the Restoration. This perhaps explains the lack of any record of Henry Every's baptism in the village.[4]

By contrast with Newton Ferrers, where life went on slowly in the traditional rural Devon way, Plymouth was a buzzing centre of trade and industry in the seventeenth century. Although the city had existed since the Anglo-Saxon period, and was granted its charter in the medieval era, it was really put on the map in the sixteenth century when it became the centre of English expansion into the New World as well as an important base for naval ships and privateers thanks to the influence of Queen Elizabeth's sea-dogs such as Drake and Hawkins as well as its natural advantages as the best deep-water harbour in the West.

There had been a corn market in the city since 1605, a yarn market since 1653, and the city was also blessed by butter, poultry, meat, and fish markets. Fresh water had been pumped into the city from Dartmoor since the sixteenth century, a result of Sir Francis Drake's tenure as mayor. A stone wall ran around the city and was extended and provided with outworks prior to and during the civil war siege. A medieval castle had once stood, but by the beginning of the seventeenth century had fallen into disuse and was replaced with the Royal Citadel overlooking the harbour which was completed in 1670.

Devon itself is a county dominated by the great expanses of Dartmoor and Exmoor, large areas of fairly uninhabited rock and scrub which have resulted in the majority of the settlements in the county being situated in the more coastal regions. This, coupled with Devon's unique status as the only English county with two separate coastlines, has made the area an important breeding ground for sailors. Throughout the centuries a large proportion of Devon men have been mariners, so it is no surprise to find that the young Henry Every chose a career at sea.

The first thirty years of Every's life are something of a mystery. Between his birth and 1689 nothing is known of his movements and activities, but some things can be reasonably guessed. We can say with some certainty that he was a professional seaman. Most seamen in the seventeenth century started at an early age, probably in their middle teens. Although there were exceptions in which men went to sea in their twenties after trying at another profession, Every entered the Royal Navy at the age of twenty-nine as a midshipman – which strongly implies considerable former experience and skill. Several of the pseudo-historical biographies of Every of the eighteenth century state that he learned his trade aboard men-of-war and merchantmen, but since no early record of Every serving in the Royal Navy has yet been found it seems likely that he spent most of his early years as a seaman aboard merchantmen.[5]

Living next to the sea as Every did when he was a child, it is likely that he went to sea young, probably aged between twelve and sixteen. He may have started his career as a young hand on one of the many fishing vessels which sailed from Newton Ferrers or the neighbouring village of Noss Mayo, but it is equally possible that he first went to sea on a coastal trading vessel, or on an ocean-going ship. He may have been signed on as a grommet, or ship's boy, a young lad literally learning the ropes and receiving a small wage in return. Alternatively he might have been apprenticed to the sea, serving a master for a specified time (usually seven years), and receiving no wages but finishing his apprenticeship qualified to serve as an able seaman or junior petty-officer.

There is only one real clue as to the nature of Every's employment during these missing years. At the trial of some of his pirate crew it was implied that Every was a 'true cock of the game, and an old sports man'. What exactly was meant by this statement is unclear, but the context suggests some previous experience of piracy.[6]

At first glance it would appear that this is at odds with Every's later known service in the Royal Navy, but in fact there is no mystery about it. During the 1670-80s the world centre of piracy was in the Caribbean where buccaneer strongholds had been firmly established at Jamaica and Tortuga. What made the Caribbean buccaneers of the seventeenth century different from the cut-throat villains who roamed the seas a generation later was their preference for sailing under some pretence of legality. For the most part they understood and accepted amongst themselves that they were pirates, but for the sake of their public image they deliberately sought out letters of marque which legiti-mised their activities as privateering rather than piracy. They usually referred to themselves as privateers, and if they were generally indiscriminate about their choice of targets they rarely attacked shipping of their own nation or its allies. Frequently their letters of marque were worthless; one buccaneer band, for example, took commissions from the rebel king of a small South American tribe to allow them to plunder from the Spanish.

Tempting though it is to imagine Every attacking the Spanish in the Caribbean, crossing Panama and sailing the Pacific, his life remains a mystery until a few months before his thirtieth birthday.

CHAPTER ONE

Going to Sea

In early 1688 the political and religious dissatisfaction caused by the accession of the Catholic King James II to the throne of Protestant England three years earlier reached crisis point. In January of the year it was announced that James' Queen, Mary, was expecting a child, and it was widely feared that she would provide him with a Catholic heir to the throne. James had already made himself unpopular with many of the leading politicians and noblemen by a series of political blunders, mostly designed to increase tolerance of Catholicism, and increase the power held by his own Catholic cronies. Those who spoke out against James' policies risked arrest and prosecution.

Various plots were mooted in Protestant circles, but little was actually done about them in the early months of 1688. Then, on 10 June, Queen Mary gave birth to a healthy boy, James. Three weeks later seven prominent Protestants signed a letter known as the 'Invitation to William', in which they invited Prince William of Orange to come to England with an army and depose James II. William of Orange was James' nephew, and in 1677 had married his cousin, James' daughter Mary. William and Mary therefore both had independent claims to the English throne, and indeed Mary had been heir until the birth of James' son. Most importantly, they were Protestants.

The letter was signed by the Earls of Danby, Shrewsbury, and Devonshire; Viscount Lumley; the Bishop of London; former Navy officer Edward Russell (later Lord Orford) whose father had been executed for his part in a plot to ensure James' exclusion from the throne in 1683; and Henry Sydney (later Earl of Romney), a politician whose brother had been executed following the Rye House Plot, the same plot in which Russell's father had been involved. Henry

Sydney actually composed the letter, which was to be delivered to William by Arthur Herbert, until recently a Rear-Admiral. Herbert disguised himself as a seaman and smuggled the letter to the Hague.

William was at that time anticipating war with France. The Holy Roman Emperor and leaders of several German states had already formed the League of Augsburg, an alliance against Louis XIV of France. William joined the League, principally for reasons of military expedience, and so became committed to a war which had not yet begun, but which was imminent. The invitation which Herbert presented to him thus represented a great gamble: on the one hand he could scarcely spare the troops and ships required for an invasion of England, but on the other hand if the invasion could be carried out quickly and success-fully before Louis XIV could begin the war William would be able to draw on the military might of England in his coming campaigns.

Although William had been considering an invasion of England since news of the Queen's pregnancy was announced he had not had the support of his own politicians, but King Louis' continuing attacks on the Dutch merchant classes converted them and gave William the support he needed. It would take time to assemble the troops and fleet needed to invade England, and the approaching autumn was hardly the best season to mount a large sea-borne operation. The time of year also worked in William's favour though, for the bulk of the French Army was committed elsewhere and could not be diverted against the Netherlands, while the main French fleet was concentrated in the Mediterranean, and the oncoming season meant that they could not possibly hope to mount their own sea-borne attack until the following year.

In October the fleet was ready to depart, and command was given to Admiral Herbert, under whom sailed a number of other disaffected English Navy offic-ers. On the nineteenth day of that month they set sail, north through the North Sea, destined for a landing place somewhere on the north-east coast of England. Contrary winds forced them back into harbour, and they did not set sail again until 1 November.

While the Dutch fleet remained in harbour the English fleet left theirs and sailed down to the Gunfleet, an anchorage at the eastern end of the Thames estuary. The Gunfleet is famously difficult to sail from when an east wind blows, and at the end of October just such a wind was in the air. The wind forced Herbert to reconsider the fleet's landing place, and so when he set sail once more he directed a course for the West Country. The English fleet watched the Dutch pass, but were unable to bring their ships up to stop them – and so, on 5 November, William made a triumphal landing at Brixham in Devon.

The English fleet only managed to sail as far as Portsmouth, where they received a message ordering them to cease fighting, as the Army had already gone over to William. James fled the country in December, and in February

1689 Parliament formally offered the throne to William and Mary, who were crowned on 11 April by the Bishop of London, one of the signatories to the invitation carried by Herbert.

William immediately went about formalising an alliance between England and the Dutch Republic, and succeeded in creating an Anglo-Dutch fleet under the command of Herbert. James, meanwhile, had found refuge in France, and more importantly the recognition and support of Louis XIV. Most of Ireland remained loyal to James, and while William was consolidating his gains James and the French were sending a fleet carrying a large number of troops and numerous supplies to augment the Irish Jacobite troops. Herbert met the French fleet off Bantry Bay on 1 May and fought an inconclusive action in which both sides claimed victory. Some days later war between England and France was declared.[1]

The earliest definite information about Every's sea-going career can be found amongst the pay books and related documents of William III's Royal Navy. In March 1689 Every was in Portsmouth, where he signed aboard HMS *Rupert* as a midshipman.[2]

The rank of midshipman had been established in 1643, but did not become commonplace until the reforms of the Cromwellian Commonwealth Navy in 1653. In 1655 it was determined that nobody should be admitted to the rank of midshipman who could not perform the duties of an officer.

By Every's time the role of a midshipman had not quite evolved into the familiar one of a young man of good family entering the Navy to learn seamanship. Originally the rank of midshipman was given to experienced seamen who were thought fit to become officers, so that they might learn leadership as well as seamanship. In the years following the Restoration Charles II instigated a scheme whereby each ship was to carry one less midshipman, and his place be filled by a young man or boy starting on the road to a naval commission. Thus in 1689 some of the midshipmen to be found aboard a man-of-war might be young men of good family who had recently entered the Navy, while the rest were old hands whose skill was thought sufficient to enable them to progress to become officers.

Since the Navy of Elizabeth I debate had raged over the wisdom of appointing experienced seamen of low birth into positions of command rather than well-bred men of noble birth, and vice versa. Nathaniel Knott, in his *Advice of a Seaman*, summed up the argument in favour of 'tarpaulin officers', as those who had worked their way up from the lower decks were called:

> It is apparent that every creature is most able in his own element: how easily is the fiercest beast overcome when he is in the water; on the other side, how quickly are the strongest and most cruel fishes dead when they are on dry ground! The element of a land captain is the land; the sea, of a sea captain...

I dare look lawfully back to the times of our fathers, but not compare them. What was the reason that in the reign of that famous Queen (whose memory shall live into eternity) the English were lords of the seas, but that seamen were lords of the ships? Who sees not the other part of this comparison? I will give you an emblem of a late captain, better known to others than to himself, who, being a fresh-water soldier, was sick with the savour of the sea; and his men pumping the ship in their watch, it gave a noisome smell (which notwithstanding is a good sign of a tight ship), whereof this young Neptune in a fume demanding the reason, reply was made that it was the pump. 'Why,' quoth he, 'cast it overboard, for if it stink so, I will have none in my ship!'[3]

The Earl of Halifax stated the case for the need for 'gentleman officers':

…in case the officers be all tarpaulins, it would be in reality too great a tendency to a Commonwealth… In short, if the maritime force, which is the only thing that can defend us, should be wholly directed by the lower sort of men, with an entire exclusion of the nobility and gentry, it will not be easy to answer the arguments supported by so great a probability, that such a scheme would not only lead toward a democracy, but directly lead us into it.[4]

Samuel Pepys, the diarist and tireless secretary of the Navy Board, was caught in the middle of the arguments, but was in no doubt about the importance of good seamanship over gentle upbringing. In 1679 he wrote to Sir Robert Holmes:

You are greatly right in what you observe and wish touching that distinction so much laboured to be kept up by some between Gentleman and Tarpaulin commanders, and the liberty taken by the first of thinking themselves above the necessity of obeying orders and conforming themselves to the rules and discipline of the Navy, in reliance upon the protection secured to them therein through the quality of their friends at court. And as long as I have the fortune of remaining in the place I am, I will continue to do my part towards the rectifying of it…[5]

It was Pepys, in fact, who provided the solution to the problem in 1677 when he regulated the requirements for a man to be commissioned lieutenant. Henceforth, naval lieutenants, whatever the pedigree of their birth, must be over twenty years of age, have served at least three years at sea including at least one as a midshipman, and have passed a rigorous examination. Powerful patronage still played a part in the appointment of officers, but no longer could a landsman ignorant of the sea demand a place in the command of a vessel by virtue of nobility alone. Lieutenants must first serve as midshipmen, and midshipmen, like Every, were expected to be proficient in a wide range of skills including the abilities to, 'produce a good journal… knot a shroud, splice rigging, shift his tides [know and understand their movement], bring a ship to sail and tack her in sailing, take up a reef in a sail, and take observations [measure the position the sun or stars for the purpose of navigating].'[6]

HMS *Rupert* was a third-rate ship, the smallest group of ships which was thought suitable to fight in line of battle, launched in 1666. Her crew of 400 was commanded by Sir Francis Wheeler, an ambitious officer. Gabriel Hughes and Joseph Bankes assisted Wheeler as first and second lieutenant, while the business of actually sailing the *Rupert* was overseen by her sailing master John Fletcher, assisted by master's mates Edward Cole and Henry Washington.

HMS *Rupert* had been laid up for the previous winter, and so with the crew all signed aboard the first job was to make the ship ready to go to sea. Yards, topmasts, sails and most of the rigging had been removed to protect them from the winter weather, so from 19 March the next month was spent at this work. As a junior officer and experienced seaman, able to knot and splice, Every would doubtless have been in the thick of the work, probably directing a small working party. Though the ship was not yet at sea the whole crew's pay began from that day, and they were put on an allowance of 'petty warrant' victuals.[7]

Petty warrant was the name given to a short allowance of food given to men whose ships were in harbour. At sea the crew would have to rely entirely on whatever stores were carried aboard, but in harbour it was reckoned that the men's diet could be supplemented with food and drink bought from shore. Edward Barlow described the quality and quantity of petty-warrant victuals as, 'a little brown bread made of the worst of their wheat, a little small [weak] beer, which is as bad as water bewitched… and a little old, tough beef, when all the best was picked out leaving us poor seamen the sirloin next to the horns; and a little fish.'[8]

On 19 April HMS *Rupert* sailed from Portsmouth harbour and two days later the crew were put on to 'sea victuals'. As noted, sea victuals were considerably better than petty warrant. In theory at least, and often in practice, seamen received a ration each day of:

1 lb… of good, clean, sweet, sound, well-baked, and well-conditioned wheaten biscuit.

1 gallon… of beer, brewed with good malt, and very good hops, and of sufficient strength.

2 lb… of beef… for Sundays, Mondays, Tuesdays and Thursdays; or, instead of beef, for two of those days, 1 lb of bacon or salted English pork and a pint of peas.

[On Wednesdays, Fridays and Saturdays] 1/8 part of a full-sized North Sea cod of 24in. long; or 1/6 part of a habardine [salted or dried cod], 22in. long; or ¼ part of a habardine 16in. long; or 1lb… of well-savoured Poor John [salted or dried hake]; 2 ounces of butter; 4 ounces of Suffolk cheese or 2/3 of that weight of Cheddar. [9]

When men are packed into the close confines of a ship they risk the spread of disease. Although naval surgeons and physicians were forever coming up with new ideas to prevent epidemics, and while some (indeed many) of these ideas were based on good sense and had a positive effect, the knowledge of germs at the end of the seventeenth century was nothing like sufficient for even the wisest doctors to really succeed at preventing disease spreading through a ship.

Ships known to be carrying contagious diseases were often put into quarantine, but by the time many diseases showed themselves it was already too late. In the summer of 1689 the English fleet was ravaged by disease of almost epidemic proportions, so that by September Admiral Torrington had to report that 599 men from his fleet were dead from illness, and 2,588 were sick. [10]

Henry Washington, master's mate of HMS *Rupert*, may well have been one of the men who fell sick that summer, for on 28 July he was discharged. The same day Henry Every was promoted into his place. [11]

With his promotion Every's wages increased from £1 17s 6d per month to £2 16s 2d. [12] The promotion also brought an increase in responsibility, for the master's mates were expected to be almost as skilled as the master himself, and to be able to act in his stead when he was off-duty or otherwise not present. Writing earlier in the century, Admiral Monson described the duties of a master:

His place and charge is to undertake to conduct the ship safe from port to port, and to direct at sea to and fro as the captain shall require him…; he is also to give chase, manage a fight, or retreat by the captain's directions. He has the power to command the mariners and all the company to perform the ordinary labours in the ship and to keep due watch in their turns at the helm; and may by himself, or the boatswain and his mates, correct and punish, according to the custom of the sea, such as refuse his command for the service of the ship, wherein I conceive no man is exempted respectively. He must likewise be acquainted what furniture [equipment], ground tackle, and sea stores belong to the ship, and to justify the needful expenses of sea stores in the boatswain's or carpenter's charge during the voyage, to the end there may be warrant for supply while the ship is under his charge.

There are six things necessary and requisite in a master or mariner that takes charge, viz. the card [record of the ship's movements], the compass, the tides, the time, the wind, and the ship's way. [13]

There was little action in the Channel during the summer of 1689, as most of the efforts of the French Channel squadron were directed towards supplying and reinforcing the Jacobite Army in Ireland. After the early battle at Bantry Bay there were no major engagements for the rest of the year. The French continued to send occasional convoys to Ireland, and occasionally these were attacked by patrolling English warships. Early in the summer HMS *Rupert* was involved in an action against one of the convoys sailing from Brest, but for the most part the purpose of the fleet was simply to retain strategic command of the Channel. For his services before and since William and Mary's accession to the throne, Admiral Herbert was knighted and made Earl of Torrington.

On 24 June 1690 Sir Francis Wheeler was promoted to command the second-rate HMS *Albemarle*. In the Navy of the late seventeenth century it was common for men to volunteer to serve under a particular officer rather than on a particular ship, and when a captain changed ship it was usual for him to take some of his personal followers along with him. When Wheeler went to take over command of HMS *Albemarle* he noted in his log: 'I removed Lt. Hughes from the *Rupert* to be first lt. of this ship Lieut. Pomeroy going to command the *Rupert*, Mr Fletcher to be master, a master's mate, and sixty... men.'[14] The master's mate who followed Wheeler was Henry Every.

At the beginning of 1690 Louis XIV determined that his war with both England and the Netherlands required a large French fleet to take control of the English Channel. By commanding the Channel he would be able to launch an invasion either of England or the Netherlands, whichever seemed more suitable at the time. The threat of invasion galvanised the Admiralty into increasing the size of Torrington's Channel fleet. The ongoing war in Ireland had forced the Admiralty to divert fourteen ships under Admiral Shovell into Irish waters; fifteen ships under Admiral Wright had been sent to protect England's colonies in the West Indies, and seventeen ships commanded by Admiral Killigrew were despatched to try to prevent Louis' Mediterranean fleet leaving that sea and joining the main fleet assembling at Brest. These squadrons, while tactically necessary, had left the main Channel fleet woefully undersized with only sixty-six ships of all sizes (including seventeen fireships and three small dispatch boats), of which only forty or so were ships of the line.[15]

A squadron of Dutch ships augmented the English fleet, but it still only numbered somewhere in the region of fifty-five ships of the line. In May the French Mediterranean squadron managed to slip past Admiral Killigrew and succeeded in reaching Brest. On 13 June, the whole French fleet set sail from Brest and entered the Channel; on the 23rd, the English fleet left its anchorage at Portsmouth and also sailed out into the Channel, anchoring off the Isle of Wight, first at Culver and then off Dun-nose. In the small hours of the 25th the English fleet weighed anchor and formed a line of battle. In the early light a few French scout ships were spotted, and as the morning wore on the whole French fleet came into view. Estimates of the size of the fleet varied, but Captain Wheeler on the *Albemarle* reckoned it at 100 ships.[16]

The French ships were to windward of the English, which meant that they had more control over the action than the English, an advantage known at sea as 'having the weather gauge'. Around noon the leading English squadron was a little ahead of the French fleet, and Torrington ordered them to tack to windward in an attempt to steal the weather gauge from the enemy. The French fleet tacked at the same time, thus diffusing the English attempt, and for the rest of the day the two fleets sailed up the Channel trying to outmanoeuvre each other, each Admiral weighing up his adversary. In the afternoon the wind shifted a little, robbing the French of the weather gauge and giving a little of it to the English, but by this time the French fleet was some way ahead and all Torrington's ships could do was use the slight advantage to try to catch up.

Early in the morning of 26 June, Admiral Torrington called a council of war consisting of all the Admirals in his fleet, Dutch and English. It was resolved that since the French fleet was so much larger than their own it would be unwise to engage the enemy until Admiral Killigrew's squadron, which was making its way up Channel, was able to join them.[17]

Torrington wrote that day to the Privy Council, in the person of the Earl of Nottingham, explaining his actions over the previous days:

> It is unaccountable why the French shunned us [the previous day]; for though they had many ships to leeward and scattered, they had enough in a body to have given us more than sufficient work. I do acknowledge my first intention of attacking them a rashness that will admit of no better excuse, than that, though I did believe them stronger than we are, I did not believe it to so great a degree. I find by their manner of working that, notwithstanding their strength, they act with some caution, and seem to be willing to add to the advantage of force that of wind too. Their great strength and caution have put soberer thoughts into my head, and have made me very heartily give God thanks they declined the battle yesterday. And indeed I shall not think myself very unhappy if I can get rid of them without fighting, unless it may be upon equaller terms than for the present I can see any prospect of... We have now had a pretty good view of their fleet, which consists of near, if not quite, 80 men-of-war fit to lie in a line, and 30 fire-ships, a strength that puts me besides the hopes of success if we should fight, and really may not only endanger the losing of the fleet, but at least the quiet of our country too; for if we are beaten, they, being absolute masters of the sea, will be at great liberty of doing many things they dare not attempt whilst we observe them, and are in a possibility of joining Vice-Admiral Killigrew and our ships to the westward.[18]

Torrington's strategy was sound. His job, and that of his fleet, was to prevent the French gaining enough control in the Channel to make a landing in England. The French could not invade while a strong English fleet was in existence, so since Torrington could not hope to inflict a defeat on the superior enemy his best hope of preventing an invasion was to keep his own fleet intact while he shadowed the French. Unfortunately his prudence was seen as timidity by some in high circles, and the presence of a large French fleet patrolling off English shores was too much to stand.

Torrington had also raised the possibility of retiring the fleet to the Gunfleet, where it could re-arm and wait for more ships to be ready, while preventing the French from entering the Thames as the Dutch had done in 1667. Only two years previously Torrington had successfully used the wind to stymie an English fleet stationed at the Gunfleet, and had used his advantage then to launch a successful invasion of England. He must have forgotten his first success as William III's Admiral, but others had not, and his suggestion of using the Gunfleet had alarmed his superiors in London. James II, who had been Lord High Admiral himself during Charles II's reign, made it a point never to interfere with his Admirals' decisions. Queen Mary (who was ruling alone during William's absence in Ireland) had never been an Admiral, and was quite happy to interfere.

On 29 June the Queen wrote to Torrington ordering him, in velvet terms, not to retreat to the Gunfleet, but to keep a close eye on the French fleet at all times. The orders went on, 'We choose rather that you should upon any advantage of the wind give battle to the enemy, than retreat farther than is necessary to get an advantage upon the enemy.' In short, Torrington could retreat if his purpose was to get into a better position to fight the enemy, but for no other reason. He must have known that any further posturing on his part would lead to his replacement, so he had no real choice but to fight the French.[19]

By now the two fleets were off Beachy Head, and a few more ships had managed to join the English fleet. Torrington called another council of war, which agreed that they had no choice under the Queen's orders but to fight. There are no minutes of that council, but subsequent events suggest that Torrington's plan was to use the weather gauge to his advantage and engage the French in a long-range artillery duel, thus fulfilling his orders but without exposing his ships to the dangers of close combat. He was thus doing his best to obey his sovereign while maintaining his own cautious but prudent plan of conserving the fleet. HMS *Albemarle* was in the Red squadron, the squadron commanded by Torrington himself and in the centre of the Anglo-Dutch line.[20]

Many writers have since written of the Battle of Beachy Head which took place the following day, but when looking at a large battle as a whole it can be difficult to understand what it was like to see the battle from a participant's viewpoint. Henry Every left no account of the battle he fought in, but we can perhaps get a glimpse through his eyes from the account left by his commander, Sir Francis Wheeler.

…at 9 last night with the flood the fleet weighed, the wind at ENE and lay driving all night with our heads to the westward.

About 4 this morning Beachy bore NNE when we bore down on the enemy in the order of battle, the body of their fleet bearing SSW about 4 leagues off. We found them braced to and their line formed and drawn up in three squadrons, viz.

Their General, Monsieur Tourville in the centre with a square white flag at his fore-topmast head, his vice-admiral whom we took for Monsieur Amsreville astern of him with a square white flag at the topmast head, and his rear-admiral ahead with a swallow tailed flag at the same place. The second squadron was D'Estrées in the rear of the line with a square white and blue flag at the foretopmast head, and his vice-admiral with that flag at the mizzen, and his rear-admiral with a swallow tail at the same place.

The third squadron led the van commanded by Chateau-Renault [who had brought the Mediterranean squadron to Brest] with a blue square flag, both him and his admirals carrying their flags on the same masts as the others did.

…Their fleet consisted of a hundred twenty two sail, small and great, of which I reckoned seventy-three in the line, the Dutch reckoned eighty.

The Dutch consisting of twenty men-of-war and four fireships were divided into three divisions and led our van with the starboard tacks onboard commanded by Evertson as admiral, Callenburgh as rear-admiral, and Van der Putting as rear-admiral. About 8 o'clock our general put out his red flag of battle.★ The Dutch some time after began to engage, being much out of musket shot [range], the Blue [squadron] next and at half an hour past, the Red.

The first of our misfortunes was the Vice-Admiral of the Red and the *Expedition*, his second, losing their fore-topmast, which occasioned their and part of their division's falling out of the line to repair.

The next to our view was Vice-Admiral Van der Putting, with Rear-Admiral Dyke, his second, and several of that division losing their masts, and becoming an unhappy and irresistible mark to the enemy's shot.

The third piece of ill fortune was by the Dutch permitting eleven sail of the enemy's van to stretch out ahead, and weather Vice-Admiral Callenburgh and our

---

Amongst pirates and privateers the 'bloody flag' was usually a signal that no quarter would be given or accepted, and often this practice spread into naval ships of various nations fighting small engagements. As a signal for a fleet it usually simply meant an order to begin fighting.

van, which occasioned our general's keeping his wind to avoid being weathered by the whole van of the enemy. Between eleven and twelve it fell dead calm and about two we came to be out of shot so that the engagement with us ceased, though not till 4 with the Dutch, and Blue, about which time the tide of ebb being made, after the general had drove between the enemy and the Dutch crippled ships, we all let go our anchors…

In this fight I judge the Dutch fought nearest, being about half cannon shot off, next to them Vice-Admiral Ashby's division, and then the Blue.

The Admiral's division was about half cannon shot when we began and continued so about an hour, the which I judge by the distance of the shot that flew over us. I am positive that we steered NW and NW by N most part of this time, and that the French in the centre of the line towing to leeward, to avoid a Dutch fireship that took fire brought us out of distance.

In this unfortunate battle the Dutch had a ship of 64 guns taken, having first lost all her masts, commanded by Captain Van der Goose.

Admiral Van der Putting's main and mizzen masts shot by the board, the ship torn to pieces.

Rear-Admiral Dyke killed and all his masts shot by the board and his ship's hull terribly shattered.

Rear-Admiral Brackle and Captain Norther killed, and a few other of the Dutch ships lost their topmast.

The English Captain Botham in the *Restoration*, and Captain Pomeroy in the *Rupert* were killed, and two marine captains. The *Sandwich*, the *Expedition*, the *Rupert*, and the *Berwick* lost their topmast, and the admiral her foremast.

In this ship there was ten men killed and about twenty men wounded, five and forty great shot in the hull, of which twelve between wind and water. Fore-yard and mizzen-yard dangerously wounded, all the sails and some of the rigging cut… about half out ammunition shot away and the upper deck shot.

And to give everybody their due, our officers, seamen, and soldiers behaved themselves very well. [21]

Torrington's worst predictions had come to pass. The Anglo-Dutch fleet had been crippled, several of the ships were afloat on prayers and good luck, and a number of important and senior officers had been killed. The French fleet, on the other hand, was virtually undamaged – they had lost no ships, and now had complete command of the Channel. The one small ray of hope was that the Anglo-Dutch fleet still existed. The defeat might have been much worse, and although most of the English and Dutch ships needed repairs to a greater or lesser degree, they were not completely destroyed.

It was not long before the blame began to be apportioned, and most of it was laid on Torrington. This was distinctly unfair since his motives for avoiding battle had been sensible, and had his advice been heeded at court the French might not have been left in possession of the sea. One of the principal charges laid against him was that he had left a gap in the line between the Dutch squadron and the English ships. His own defence was that he had done so to extend his own line in order to deny the French fleet a chance to outflank him. Interestingly, the French were full of admiration for this manoeuvre:

> There are those who commend Admiral Herbert's method of drawing up his fleet, when he bore down on the French in the battle [Beachy Head], 1690. Being inferior in number he resolved to make his main effort against our rear. He accordingly ordered the Dutch, who formed the van, to attack our second division, then he opened his fleet in the centre, leaving a large gap abreast of our centre; after which he opposed his [rear] in very close order, to our rear, and lay off slightly with his own division, so as to prevent the French from taking advantage of the gap he had left… In effect this rendered our leading division almost useless. [22]

Whoever was to blame for the disaster, the campaign did not end that day. The officers present at a council of war called on the evening of the battle all agreed that they were beaten, and decided to retreat and 'avoid the enemy all we could'. When dawn broke the following morning Wheeler could see the bulk of the French fleet some distance away, with a few ships closer by. The crippled ships of Torrington's fleet were taken in tow and for most of that day the two fleets cautiously shadowed each other. That evening two of the crippled Dutch ships which were slowing the fleet down were destroyed.

The Anglo-Dutch fleet was making for the Thames where the damaged ships could be repaired. For several days the French fleet followed them, and though they had several good opportunities to force a second, perhaps decisive battle, they chose not to. On 4 July the weather turned bad and 'dirty', and eventually the French fleet broke off and sailed for home, while the Anglo-Dutch fleet limped into the Thames. On 9 July they reached the Nore; on the 11th some of the ships were moved into the relative safety of the Swale, the stretch of water separating the Isle of Sheppey from the Kentish mainland.

Aboard HMS *Albemarle* the officers and men set about repairing their battle-damaged vessel. On 15 July ballast and guns were shifted to one side of the ship, heeling her over to expose more of one side of her hull above the water. The carpenter and his mates, assisted by other seamen, then went over the side to remove the enemy cannonballs from the timber and repair what damage they could. When they were done, the ballast and guns were shifted to the other side and the process repeated. On the same day they replaced the damaged fore-yard.

On 19 July the broken mizzen-yard was replaced, and on the same day a group of five Navy commissioners arrived. Torrington had struck his flag and left the fleet on 12 July, and had travelled to London to make his reports. The commissioners who now arrived had come to interview all of the captains and 'examine' them regarding the battle.

Over the next few weeks the ships took in supplies and readied themselves for sea again. The Battle of Beachy Head and the subsequent repairs must have been thirsty work, for the only commodity Wheeler mentioned taking aboard in his log was beer. On 6 August Admiral Delavall, who had commanded the Blue squadron at Beachy Head, sailed down to the Gunfleet with the third- and fourth-rate ships. Admiral Ashby followed the next day with the larger ships, including HMS *Albemarle*.

While the fleet waited at the Gunfleet, disease once again ran through the ships. Within a week fifty of the *Albemarle*'s crew fell sick. Two days later the number had risen to 200. Three days later, on 19 August, Wheeler wrote that he had no more than 250 well men aboard, out of a compliment of almost 600. The *Albemarle* was one of the worst-affected ships, along with HMS *Windsor Castle*, so when the rest of the fleet sailed for the Downs these two ships were sent back to the Nore.

On 23 August, in the Swale, 123 sick men of the *Albemarle*'s crew were sent ashore. Two days later the order arrived for her to sail up to Chatham, there to be laid up for the winter. With the campaign season almost at a close and the French fleet apparently gone home there was little need to keep too many of the biggest ships at sea, and since it would be some time before the *Albemarle* could recruit enough new men to replace her ailing crew, there was no sense in keeping her in commission any longer. On 28 August fifty of her healthy men were transferred to HMS *Wolf*, and the following day, amidst the unloading of guns, Henry Every was discharged.[23]

Henry Every was definitely married by the summer of 1693, and it may be that his marriage took place on 11 September 1690 in the Church of St James, Aldgate, to Dorothy Arther. Thirty-one was perhaps a little older than the normal age for marriage, but seamen who often spent years away from home in their teens and twenties were apt to marry late. Life was hard for the wives of seamen: with their menfolk often away from home for protracted periods, and wages often in arrears, most were forced to earn their own living until their husbands returned home. Many kept victuallers or alehouses; some went into service. Mrs Every earned her living selling wigs on Ratcliffe Highway, a famous haunt of sailors in London, little more than a good cannon-shot away from St James, Aldgate.[24]

One of the great difficulties with trying to piece together the lives of historical characters is that often little or no record of them was kept until after they became famous. The evidence concerning Every's movements and activities over the next three years is almost non-existent, and is far from reliable, but is perhaps enough for us to draw some conclusions.

In 1693 the slave trader Thomas Phillips wrote that he 'never found the negroes so shy and so scarce, which he attributes to kidnapping tricks having been played on them by Long Ben, alias Every, and others of his kidney who had seized upon them and carried them off without any payment'. Henry Bruce, a West Indian merchant, wrote in his memoirs that between 1690 and 1694 Every operated under the protection of the Governor of the Bahamas, Sir William Jones. Bruce must have been mistaken in his dates for, as we shall see in the next chapter, Every was in England by the summer of 1693.[25]

Nevertheless, from these two snippets of information we can assume that in the opening years of the 1690s Henry Every was working as master of a slave ship, transporting slaves between West Africa and the Caribbean. We can further assume that Every was not working for the Royal African Co. who had a monopoly on the African trade. If he had been, he would not have risked the Company's trade and reputation by acting in the manner described by Phillips, nor would he have needed the protection of Governor Jones.

There is also just a possibility that Every supplemented his slave-trading income with a little piracy or privateering, for it may be that when John Guy described Every as a 'true cock of the game, and old sports-man' he was referring to Every's activities during this period. By the 1690s piracy in the Caribbean was not the thriving industry it had been in earlier years under Henry Morgan, or would become again in the first decades of the next century, but privateering was rife. The War of the League of Augsburg was fought in the colonies as well as at home, and the Caribbean contained a large number of both French and English colonies, as well as some Dutch colonies. The English government sent a squadron of warships for the defence of their interests in the region, but the force was hardly sufficient to keep a watch on all of England's far-flung territories, which were numerous and well spread. Colonial governors therefore found it expedient to commission privateers for their own defence, and these privateers also served the useful purpose of bringing some measure of stolen wealth to the impoverished colonies. It would be quite in keeping with Every's experience and general way of life for him to have served on one of these privateers, but since the evidence for it is so slim further speculation would be out of place here.

While in the Caribbean Every may also have met an old colleague. In 1692 Sir Francis Wheeler was promoted temporarily to Rear-Admiral and given command of a squadron of eighteen ships with which he was instructed to attack French possessions in the Caribbean before sailing north to attack the French settlements in Canada. Wheeler's squadron arrived in the Caribbean in the early months of 1693 and remained there until May. There is no reason at all to suppose that Wheeler did come across Every during his months in the region, and indeed if Every had not already left before Wheeler arrived he must have done so by the time Wheeler left.[26]

The Royal African Co., originally known as 'the Company of Royal Adventurers Trading to Africa', was founded shortly after the Restoration by a group of London merchants, heavily supported by the Prince of Wales (later James II) and his cousin, Prince Rupert of the Rhine. Their original plan was to exploit the continent's supply of gold, but it was soon realised that the trade in European commodities and slaves was more profitable than prospecting. The Royal African Co. was granted a monopoly on English trade in Africa, and the power to confiscate the cargoes of any non-Company ships found trying to break the monopoly. The slave trade had always been an underhand business, and from the first English forays of Hawkins and Drake (who themselves had illegally traded slaves in Spanish colonies, against Spanish laws of monopoly) traders had flouted the rules. Henry Every was just one of many.

Sailing from Bermuda to Africa, Every would have carried a cargo of the kinds of trade goods which were popular on the African coast and which could command a high price: red and blue cloths, pewter dishes, old sheets, large knives, iron bars, and strong spirits 'seldom or never fail of a good market'[27]

In Africa the slave traders then met with local kings and arranged to exchange these goods for slaves. Thomas Phillips, who was a contemporary with Every in the slave trade and perhaps even knew him personally, described the slave markets:

When we were at the trunk [the market], the king's slaves, if he had any, were the first offered for sale, which the cappasheirs [African courtiers and slave dealers] would be very urgent with us to buy, and would in a manner force us to it ere they would show us any other, saying they were the *Reys Cosa*, and we must not refuse them, though as I observe they were generally the worst slaves in the trunk, and we paid more for them than any other, which we could not remedy, it being one of his Majesty's prerogatives; then the cappasheirs each brought out his slaves according to his degree and quality, the greatest first etc and our surgeon examined them well in all kinds, to see that they were sound wind and limb, making them jump, stretch out their arms swiftly, looking in their mouths to judge of their age, for the cappasheirs are so cunning, that they shave them all close before we see them, so that let them be never so old we can see no grey hairs in their heads or beards, and then having liquored them well and sleek with palm oil, 'tis no easy matter to know an old one from a middle-aged one, but by the teeth's decay; but our greatest care of all is to buy none that are poxed, lest they should infect the rest aboard; for though we separate the men and women aboard by partitions and bulkheads, to prevent quarrels and wrangles among them, yet do what we can they will come together, and that distemper which they call the yaws, is very common here, and discovers itself by almost the same symptoms as the *Lues Venerea* or clap does with us; therefore our surgeon is forced to examine the privities of both men and women with the nicest scrutiny, which is a great slavery, but what can't be omitted. When we had selected from the rest such as we liked, we agreed in what goods to pay for them, the prices being already stated before the king, how much of each sort of merchandise we were to give for a man, woman, and child, which gave us much ease, and saved abundance of disputes and wranglings, and gave the owner a note, signifying our agreement of the sorts of goods, upon delivery of which the next day he received them, then we marked the slaves we had bought in the breast, or shoulder, with a hot iron, having the letter of the ship's name upon it, the place being before anointed with a little palm oil, which caused but little pain, the mark being usually well in four or five days, appearing very plain and white after.[28]

Every, of course, did not pay for all the slaves he transported, but he probably found the African slave markets much as Phillips did. It is likely that Every sometimes came upon a stretch of African coast and simply grabbed the first natives who came to talk with him, but it would have been difficult to fill a ship with enough human cargo that way, so it is reasonable to assume that he also visited the markets. Since Phillips' experience of the market, described above, took place in 1694, the year after he noted how shy the inhabitants were as a result of Every's perfidy, it is possible that the cappasheirs' insistence on receiving payment before they handed over their slaves was a result of Every and 'his kidney'. Perhaps Every had found it easier to dupe the dealers.

Once the slaves had been gathered the next task was to get them all safely aboard the ship:

When our slaves were come to the seaside, our canoes were ready to carry them off to the longboat, if the sea permitted, and she conveyed them aboard ship, where the men were all put in irons, two and two shackled together, to prevent their mutiny, or swimming ashore.

The negroes are so wilful and loath to leave their own country, that they have often leapt out of the canoes, boat and ship, into the sea, and kept underwater till they were drowned, to avoid being taken up and saved by our boats, which pursued them, they having a more dreadful apprehension of Barbados than we can have of Hell, though in reality they live much better there than in their own country, but home is home etc. We have likewise seen diverse of them eaten by the sharks, of which a prodigious number kept about the ships in this place, and I have been told will follow her hence to Barbados, for the dead negroes that are thrown overboard in the passage. I am certain in our voyage there we did not want the sight of some every day, but that they were the same I can't affirm.

We had about 12 negroes did willfully drown themselves, and other starved themselves to death, for 'tis their belief that when they die they return home to their own country and friends again.

I have been informed that some commanders have cut off the legs or arms of the most wilful, to terrify the rest, for they believe if they lose a member they cannot return home again. [29]

Once the slaves were all aboard the ship would set sail, either for the plantations in the Caribbean or for another port to buy more slaves. If the latter, the crew of the slave ship would have to take extra precautions in sight of land, for the imprisoned slaves were likely to mutiny given the chance:

…to prevent which we always keep sentinels upon the hatchways, and have a chest of small arms, ready loaded and primed, constantly lying at hand upon the quarter-deck, together with some grenade shells [hand grenades], and two of our quarter-deck guns, pointing on the deck thence, and two more out of the steerage, the door of which is always kept shut, and well barred. They are fed twice a day, at 10 in the morning and 4 in the evening, which is the time they are aptest to mutiny, being all on deck; therefore all that time, what of our men are not employed in distributing their victuals to them, and feeding them, stand to their arms, and some with lighted matches at the great guns that yawn upon then, loaded with partridge [fine ammunition, much like buck shot], till they have done and gone down to their kennels between decks… When we come to sea we let them all out of irons, they never attempting then to rebel, considering that should they kill or master us, they could not tell how to manage the ship, or must trust us, who would carry them where we pleased. [30]

Once at sea it might take several weeks to reach the Caribbean, and during that time the ever-present threat of ship-board disease was magnified by the close confines in which the slaves were kept:

The negroes are so incident to the smallpox, that few ships that carry them escape without it, and sometimes it makes vast havoc and destruction among them; but though we had 100 at a time sick of it, and that it went through the ship, yet we lost not a dozen by it. All the assistance we gave the diseased was only as much water as they desired to drink, and some palm oil to anoint their sores, and they would generally recover without any other helps but what kind nature gave them…

But what the smallpox spared, the flux swept off, to our great regret, after all our pains and care to give them their messes in due order and season, keeping their lodgings as clean and sweet as possible, and enduring so much misery and stench so long among a parcel of creatures nastier than swine, and after all our expectations to be defeated by their mortality. [A total of 320 slaves and fourteen white crew died on the voyage.] No gold-finders can endure so much noisome slavery as they do who carry negroes, for those have some respite and satisfaction, but we endure twice the misery, and yet by their mortality our voyages are ruined, and we pine and fret ourselves to death, to think that we should undergo so much pains to so little purpose.

I delivered alive at Barbados 372, which being sold, came out at about nineteen pounds per head...[31]

Once he had seen the slaves safely to their purchaser the slave-ship captain, such as Every, would perhaps spend some time enjoying the profits of the voyage while his ship was made ready to return to Africa. How many slaving voyages Every made is not known, but perhaps he tired of the hard and unpleasant work for after a while, probably towards the end of 1692 or in the first months of 1693, he returned to London.

CHAPTER TWO

Mutiny

In 1692 a group of London merchants led by Sir James Houblon met to discuss a proposed private venture which became known as the Spanish Expedition. Houblon himself was one of the founder members of the Bank of England, and he had strong family ties to the East India Co. Other merchants involved in the venture had similar interests.

The plan of the Spanish Expedition was to send a squadron of strong privateer ships to aid the Spanish Guarda Costa (a 'coast guard' whose duties included the protection of Spanish territory and the guarding of her trade rights in the West Indies). The profits from the voyage would be augmented by also using the ships to mount treasure-hunting expeditions on the wrecks of Spanish bullion ships in the region. The English economy was ailing in the closing years of the seventeenth century, and it was hoped that the profits from the Spanish Expedition would inject some seriously needed cash into England's finances.

King Carlos II of Spain welcomed the plan as a way for him to increase the strength of his forces in the Caribbean with little outlay of his own, and in early 1693 the English government gave permission for the expedition to go ahead. Four ships were purchased for the squadron; the *James* (sometimes called *St James*), the *Dove*, the *Seventh Son*, and the squadron's flagship, the *Charles II*, named after the expedition's royal Spanish patron.[1]

Don Arturo O'Bourne, an Irishman who had seen long service in the Spanish Navy, was selected to be Admiral of the squadron. The choice of O'Bourne seems a little strange on the face of it. William III had only acceded to the English throne five years before the Spanish Expedition's setting out, and support for the exiled Stuarts was still strong. Irish and Scottish Jacobites had only been defeated in 1691, and although the infamous Glencoe massacre in 1692 had encouraged dilatory Jacobites to swear their allegiance to King William, it had done little to increase the king's popularity. O'Bourne, if not openly a Jacobite, had strong ties with the exiled Stuart court.

Recruiting men for the expedition would not have been difficult. Privateering was a popular career amongst seamen, for it held the promise of wages far in excess of those to be had in the Royal Navy or merchant services if the voyage was successful. Conditions aboard a privateer would depend entirely on the nature of the commanders and the generosity of sponsors, but since privateers tended to carry larger crews than most merchantmen at least a recruit could hope for a lighter workload as the shipboard tasks would be shared out over a greater number of men.

The attraction of the Spanish Expedition to the common seaman was increased greatly in February 1693 when the Admiralty gave orders for 100 men of the expedition to be exempted from impressment. The Royal Navy had the right to press seamen from private ships, so a man who had signed aboard a merchantman or privateer might yet find himself hauled off into the Navy. Certificates of exemption were highly prized, and might be given for a number of reasons, so the news that a proportion of the men signed on to the Spanish Expedition would be given such certificates would have been most welcome. [2]

. The investors' choice of captain for the flagship was perhaps more inspired than their choice of Admiral. Captain John Strong was an experienced seaman, but more than that, he also had experience of dealing with the Spanish authorities in the New World, and had been an officer on one of the most celebrated treasure-hunting expeditions of the seventeenth century. In 1686 Strong shipped as first mate of the *James and Mary* under the command of William Phips. Phips had already led one expedition in search of sunken Spanish treasure ships which had nearly been disastrous, but nevertheless he managed to find wealthy and influential backers for a second voyage.

Early in 1687 Phips' divers located the wreck of the *Nuestra Señora de la Concepción*, a fabulously wealthy ship which had sunk in 1641 carrying perhaps as much as 100 tons or more of silver. Over the course of several weeks Phips' divers recovered silver believed to be worth somewhere in the region of £210,000. Within a very short time of his return to England Phips set out on a third voyage to try to recover some of the treasure which was known to still be on the *Concepción*. Encouraged by his earlier success, Phips' backers provided a larger squadron, and Strong was given command of the *James and Mary*. Sadly, news had spread of Phips' success and when the third expedition reached the wreck site they found it crawling with dozens of vessels, all seeking the silver. In England the accounting of the initial treasure was still going on, and on his return John Strong, along with four other officers of the first expedition, was taken into custody accused of privately landing £1,000, thus defrauding the King and the expedition's investors. There was little or no evidence against Strong and he was released without charge.[3]

Strong's reputation cannot have been too badly damaged by the accusations of embezzlement, for shortly afterwards he set sail in command of the *Welfare* (or *Farewell*) on a privateering and treasure-hunting expedition to the Pacific. In 1692 the *Welfare* returned to London having had little success at treasure hunting, and only moderate success at privateering. The most important result of the voyage was Strong's rediscovery and naming of the Falkland Islands. Nevertheless, Strong's experience as an officer under Phips and as a treasure-hunting captain in his own right made him a good choice for the Spanish Expedition.[4]

Another of the officers who appears to have been carefully chosen was the second mate of the *Dove*, William Dampier. Dampier is well known today as an explorer, naturalist, and meteorologist thanks to the publication of his 'Voyages' which recounted his travels around the world. The first book, published in 1697, was *A New Voyage Round the World*, in which he told of his adventures circumnavigating the globe between 1679 and 1691 in the company of various bands of buccaneers.

In Jamaica in 1679 Dampier joined a buccaneer crew led by Bartholomew Sharp. They sailed for Porto Bello on the Panamanian mainland and sacked the town before marching on foot across the Isthmus of Panama with the intention of capturing the fabulous Panama City, as the famous Henry Morgan had done some years earlier. When they reached the Pacific the buccaneers easily captured a ship and some large canoes, but sailing down the coast to Panama City they discovered the harbour well guarded by eight Spanish warships. Sharp himself had sailed off in the buccaneers' ship after another prize, leaving only the men in the canoes to fight the Spanish men-of-war. Many of the buccaneers had grown up hunting livestock in the wilds of the Caribbean islands, and with their characteristic long-barrelled muskets had become proficient marksmen. This skill – and the courage of desperation – carried the day and the buccaneers defeated the far superior enemy force.

Heavy losses sustained in the battle forced the buccaneers to abandon any hope of capturing the city, and disagreement broke out over what to do next. A small band, including Dampier, elected to march back across the Isthmus. After a short time with another buccaneer gang in the Caribbean Dampier made his way to Virginia where he met up with another of Sharp's old men, John Cook.

In August 1683 Cook led a crew which included Dampier on a second voyage into the Pacific, sailing first to the Cape Verde islands and the African coast before rounding Cape Horn in February 1684. Bad luck dogged the buccaneers as they roved the Pacific, visiting the island of Juan Fernandez, the Galapagos Islands, and several points of the South American mainland. Cook died on the voyage and the buccaneers failed to make any significant captures. In March 1686 Dampier and his colleagues set sail across the Pacific and reached Guam two months later. From Guam they sailed to the Philippines and thence to Australia. Dampier later quitted the buccaneers and remained in the Indian Ocean, working several trading voyages there. Eventually he joined an East India Co. ship and arrived back in England in 1691.[5]

In England, Dampier had little to show for his experiences: he had almost no money, and although his book would later bring him fame he needed employment to enable him to survive while he worked on the manuscript from the journal he had carried with him for the past twelve years sealed up in a length of bamboo. His experience of privateering, and the long years he had spent in the Caribbean, made him an ideal man to join to the Spanish Expedition. Another man whose experience would hold him in good stead in the proposed voyage was the chief mate of the flagship *Charles II*, Henry Every.

Having been a mate aboard two large Royal Navy ships, Every was certainly qualified to act in that capacity on the *Charles II*, and his years of slaving experience would have qualified him for a voyage to the West Indies. There is no need to look any further into Every's past to see why he was given the job of chief mate on the expedition's flagship, but a little further speculation might be interesting. Patronage was often very important in the acquisition of posts at sea in the seventeenth century, and it seems likely that Every was recommended to Houblon's consortium. At the very least he was probably able to present testimonials from some respected former commander or associate, but who that may have been is uncertain.

The most likely person though was probably John Strong, who, as captain of the flagship, would have had some say in the appointment of his subordinate officers. There is no proof that Strong knew Every, and since no complete crew lists from Phips' expeditions exist it is impossible to say whether or not Every sailed on them. However, a possible string of patronage can be established into which Every fits nicely: in 1679 it was Sir John Narborough who ordered the promotion of Francis Wheeler from second to first lieutenant of HMS *Rupert*,[6] and it was the same Narborough who was in nominal command of Phips' second expedition to the *Concepción*. Narborough died in 1688 during that expedition, but it was shortly after the return of Strong and his crew to England that Every secured a post as midshipman under Wheeler. It remains nothing more than speculation, but it is entirely possible and not at all unlikely that Every had sailed under John Strong on the second expedition (and possibly the first as well) to the *Concepción*, and used his connection with Sir John Narborough to gain employment under that officer's former protégé Sir Francis Wheeler, then used the contact with John Strong made at the same time to obtain the post of his chief mate in 1693.

In May 1693 the Commissioners for Sick and Wounded Seamen were ordered to provide fifty or sixty men to be distributed amongst the ships for the Spanish Expedition. These would be men who had been invalided out of the Royal Navy, but were now sufficiently recovered to go to sea once more. The squadron was assembled at Gravesend and the crews began to go aboard their ships.[7]

On 1 August the crews were paid their wages up to that time and a one-month advance which was customary, preparatory to putting to sea. The ships flew Spanish colours, indicating to any passers by, and to the crews themselves, that they were in the service of the Spanish crown. On 10 August the squadron unfurled their sails and went downriver, arriving at the Downs a short while later.[8]

No detailed description of this first part of the journey survives, but based on similar occurrences it is likely that amid the bustle of preparations many of the seamen's wives had been staying aboard ship with their husbands and now left the vessels. Some perhaps remained aboard for the voyage to the Downs, and it is even likely that some stayed aboard while the ships lay at anchor there. Once in the Downs the ships would have been surrounded by bumboats, small boats put out from the shore carrying luxury commodities such as drink and tobacco to sell to the outward-bound seamen for their voyage. Bumboats were usually crewed by women, often sailors' wives scratching a living while their men were away at sea, and as well as carrying supplies often acted as ferries for officers wishing to step ashore if their captains allowed it. The third commodity that bumboats often transported was a human one – prostitutes hoping to earn a few nights' wages from the young male population of the ships at anchor. Prostitutes were often not officially tolerated aboard ships, but wives were, so a common ploy was for the seamen aboard ship to call out their names to the women in the approaching boats, who would then claim to be married to the men when questioned. The presence of prostitutes increased dramatically the danger of disease aboard ship, but there was little that officers could do to effectively police the trade, and in many cases the officers were just as eager for companionship as their men.

In the Downs the ships had to wait for a favourable wind to carry them down the Channel, and for the essential supplies of food, drink, gunpowder and the like to be brought aboard. Then, on 25 August, disaster struck the expedition when Admiral O'Bourne was detained on suspicion of treason. Finally the government had realised the potential danger of allowing an Irish officer, with possible pro-Jacobite tendencies, to assemble a powerful squadron of well-armed ships. Although England and Spain were at peace in 1693, and in fact were allies against France, a general suspicion of Catholicism was prevalent in England. Indeed, when King William's ministers first gave approval to the Spanish Expedition in January 1693 they required that monetary bonds be given by the consortium to guarantee that they would 'do nothing against the subjects of their Majesties or of their allies which is not warrantable by the laws of England and the treaties made with such allies.'[9]

But O'Bourne had friends with influence, and a great clamour erupted that a man with such good intentions as the Admiral should be besmirched with such accusations. In addition to the glory of the nation, not to mention the aid to the economy which the Spanish Expedition was expected to produce, O'Bourne had also shipped aboard a large number of Irish dissidents who were to be landed in the West Indies. The great expense which the investors had gone to to finance the expedition was also mentioned, and O'Bourne was allowed to continue without any new stain on his character.[10] With its Admiral free and supplies and crews aboard, the squadron set sail from the Downs on 8 September 1693.[11]

The wind was not the best they could hope for and the ships did not reach Corunna until early 1694. Corunna, often called 'The Groin' by Englishmen in the seventeenth century, was (and is) a busy port in the north-west corner of Spain. Portugal makes up most of the Atlantic coastline of the Iberian Peninsula, so Corunna was the best port for ships travelling via Spain from northern Europe to the Caribbean. Ships entering the port would be guided by the famous 'Tower of Hercules', a lighthouse standing 185ft high and built during the second century. Once in harbour ships were protected by two castles and two smaller forts. Like all sea ports, the town itself held a number of attractions to the seaman away from home.

Because of the international nature of the Spanish Expedition the squadron was required to put in to Corunna to receive official passes and instructions from the Spanish court. However, the orders were not ready for the English ships when they arrived at the port, and the ships were forced to lie at anchor while they waited for them to be written and sent up.

Sailors left idle are apt to grumble, and it was not long before the first signs of discontent began to show. According to the contracts signed at Gravesend, wages were to be paid out of the stock of the Spanish Expedition, but no provision was made in the contracts as to when or how often wages were to be paid. Many of the sailors were under the impression that wages were to be paid every six months, and there is some evidence that Sir James Houblon himself had promised this verbally to the men at Gravesend.[12]

By the time of their arrival at Corunna the men had been almost six months without wages, and so believed that they were due to be paid. At sea there is little need for ready cash, but left to amuse themselves ashore the seamen desperately wanted money. John Fishley was the Spanish Expedition's agent at Corunna and it was to him that the men applied for their pay.

However, even if Fishley had wanted to pay the men he had no funds to do so, and turned them away. Some of the men who had gone to Fishley had evidently been vocal in their demands and were imprisoned. Amongst men with already low morale the news that their employers were putting men in prison only for asking for what they believed to be their rights was devastating.

In the midst of this disagreement the Spanish Expedition was dealt another blow by the death of Captain Strong, the expedition's expert on wreck diving and commander of the flagship. Captain Charles Gibson, who had begun the voyage as commander of the *James* was transferred to the *Charles II*.

Eventually, after some months in port, the dispatches arrived which enabled the squadron to set sail for the West Indies, but there was mutinous feeling running below decks and the men refused to set sail until they had been paid their wages. Admiral O'Bourne, perhaps sympathising with his sailors, but more likely sensing that his command was in tatters, wrote to Sir James Houblon and the other investors, begging them for enough money to pay the crews and enable him to set sail.

To add weight to their argument the men wrote to their wives, asking them to go and see Houblon in person and beg for their wages. Some of the wives banded together and pressed at Houblon's door with their demands. Like Fishley, Houblon was in no financial position to hand out the wages, and so told the wives that their husbands were now in the service of the Spanish king, and must look to him for their pay. Carlos II could, Houblon told the wives, 'pay them, or hang them if he pleased.'[13]

When word of Houblon's response was relayed back to the seamen the news began to spread throughout the squadron. The ships had lain together at the Downs, sailed together to Spain, and now lay together at Corunna. The men went freely ashore and mingled together in inns and brothels when they were not visiting one another's ships. Rumour and bad news spread easily in a squadron where 'the masters and company of one of the… ships knew the master, and the majority of the company of the others there.'[14]

The men began to say that the whole purpose of the Spanish Expedition was not the eighteen-month privateering cruise that they had signed on for, but that from the beginning Houblon's consortium had planned to sell the ships and men into the service of Spain. Since their contracts were apparently worthless they had no idea how long they might be kept in Spanish service, and they feared that it might prove to be 'all the days of their lives'.

Matters did not improve when Richard Chapman, boatswain of the *Charles II*, met with Fishley. After a brief altercation Fishley drew his sword and threatened Chapman. Chapman responded that Fishley would not kill an Englishman, a loyal subject of William III. Fishley answered that 'he was none of King William's subject, he was the King of Spain's servant.'[15]

The men's minds now began to turn towards their Irish Admiral, and his connections to prominent Catholics in the Spanish and exiled Jacobite courts.

Rumours began to circulate that the English seamen in the squadron were to be turned out of their ships by the Spanish and Irish, and left on shore to make their own way home if they could. They accordingly kept a stricter watch on their ships, but the breaking point was close.[16]

William May, steward of the *Charles II*, approached Admiral O'Bourne ashore on 6 May and begged to be released from his contract. He would happily forego the £30 back pay that was owed to him if he could just go home. The Admiral, his temper no doubt shortened by the events and frustration of the previous few months, responded curtly. If May did not return to the ship and perform the duties which he was contractually obliged to, he would be thrown into prison and would rot there.[17] There were many seamen from the Spanish Expedition on shore that day, some of whom were perhaps witnesses to the meeting of William May and Admiral O'Bourne; others doubtless heard about O'Bourne's sentiments later in the day. Some of the men, 'finding they were betrayed', gathered together, probably in one of the taverns, to discuss what could be done. We do not know who these men were, but it seems likely that they included Robert Richie and Henry Adams, petty officers of the *Charles II*, and Anthony Track of the *James*.* Perhaps they were encouraged by one Benjamin Gunning 'belonging to a pirate then at Corunna'.[18]

Whoever they were, a small band of men approached Henry Every, who was also ashore that day, and proposed that they should 'carry away the ship.' Mutiny was rarely a crime committed on the spur of the moment. Usually a series of incidents, or prolonged poor conditions, led to a planned mutiny. Once the captain of a ship had been deposed somebody would be required to lead the mutineers, and more importantly handle the ship, so for a successful mutiny the support of at least some of the officers was required. Every was an obvious choice for the would-be mutineers: he was suffering from lack of wages as much as any of them; he was born in their class and was very much a 'tarpaulin' officer; he had previously been a captain so was experienced at commanding a ship; and the lack of scruples which had marked his earlier career (if the other

---

Whether the former buccaneer William Dampier knew of, or had anything to do with, the mutiny is open to speculation. Dampier later showed himself very sympathetic towards the mutineers, and he admitted personal friendship with several of the crew of the *Charles II*, so he almost certainly knew Every quite well. Dampier's experience would have been known to Every, and considering the forethought which Every gave to the events which would follow the mutiny it would not be at all surprising if he had quietly sought information from Dampier. Neither would it be surprising if Dampier had given him the information he asked for, for he was rarely reticent about his adventures. Nevertheless, Dampier played no active part in the mutiny and did not join Every, so speculation it must remain.

conspirators knew of it) perhaps suggested just the kind of moral ambiguity needed in the leader of a mutiny. The mutineers undoubtedly saw their actions as just, but it was a big step for a man in the seventeenth century to openly defy his superiors, and without a strong leader the mutiny would surely founder.

Every listened to their proposal and readily agreed. They then made contact with other men from the squadron ashore and recruited more conspirators. As the evening wore on their plans were laid. Captain Gibson had developed an illness and was lying sick in his cabin; the following evening, Monday 7, Admiral O'Bourne would be sleeping ashore. With their senior commanders both out of the picture it seemed like the best opportunity for the conspirators to strike. Everyone agreed, and swore to the plan; the party then broke up. The following day Every went from ship to ship, sought out his friends, and brought them in on the plan, so that as the day wore on everything was in readiness.

In the late afternoon Every sent word ashore for Thomas Joy, the *Charles II*'s cooper, to come aboard as there were some casks which needed attention. Whether or not Joy knew of the conspiracy at that time is uncertain, but Every's insistence that the cooper come aboard shows great foresight. Almost all the victuals carried by a ship in the seventeenth century, as well as the gunpowder and a great deal of the cargo, were stored in wooden casks. The cooper was thus an essential member of the crew, for without his expertise they could not hope to sustain themselves for any great length of time at sea.

That evening, after Admiral O'Bourne had gone ashore, several of the officers of the *Charles II* dined with Captain Gibson in his cabin. Every and the carpenter, John Guy, were among them, the steward, William May, was almost certainly present, and they were joined by David Creagh. John Gravet, the second mate, was officer of the watch.

After dinner Every, May, Guy, Creagh, and some others left the Captain's cabin and settled down for a drink together. William May proposed a toast to 'the captain, and prosperity to their voyage'. David Creagh, assuming May meant Captain Gibson and the Spanish Expedition, joined in the toast. The others present knew that May had meant a different captain and a new voyage.

Before 9 p.m. the company broke up and retired to their cabins. At about the same time a boat containing some of the conspirators was making its way around the squadron, collecting men from the *Seventh Son* and the *Dove*. When asked where they were going, some of the men from the *Dove* foolishly confided that they were going to run away with the *Charles II*.

When the boat reached the *James* someone aboard called out the password which had been pre-arranged, 'Is your drunken boatswain aboard?' Mr Druit, mate of the *James*, was naturally confused, and asked what they meant. The men in the boat were in turn confused not to be greeted with the pre-arranged response and revealed some of the plan to Druit. Druit in turn rushed to tell

Captain Humphreys, commander of the *James*. Almost simultaneously, word reached the captain of the *Dove* that some of his men had deserted, and he hailed the *James* with the news. Realising that their plan was about to come undone, the conspirators in the boat quickly made for the *Charles II*, leaving their co-conspirators on the *James* stranded.

Captain Humphreys ordered a boat to be manned and sent to try and prevent the mutiny on the *Charles II*. Improvising somewhat, the conspirators from the *James* contrived to get themselves into the boat which was ordered out by Druit. When Druit realised that the men in the boat were not going to quell the mutiny but to join it he ordered them to return to the *James*. The mutineers ignored the mate and pulled towards the *Charles II*, so Druit fired a shot at them and made a hole in the boat, but as they went off in to the darkness there was little more he could do to stop them. Meanwhile, the first boat reached the *Charles II* and the men in her swarmed aboard the ship. Every was on deck by this time and directed operations. The wind was fair to leave the harbour, but they were now racing to be away before the other ships could make sail after them or damage the *Charles II* with gunfire.

John Gravet, no doubt confused by this swift and unexpected activity, was grabbed around the throat by John Guy, the carpenter, who thrust a pistol into his chest and told him that he would be shot if he resisted the mutineers. Two more men grabbed hold of Gravet and dragged him below to his cabin where he was kept under armed guard.

Men ran aloft and began to loose the sails while John Guy went forward with his broad-axe and began to cut the anchor cables. Thomas Joy, who was at supper below decks, wondered what the commotion above was about. As he came up from below he saw Guy cutting the cables, and claims to have tried to prevent him. Guy threatened to hack his leg off if he got in the way, and Joy backed away.

Just as the cables were cut the boat from the *James* arrived alongside and the men in her boarded the *Charles II*. Captain Humphreys, unaware of the pace at which events had progressed, hailed the *Charles II* and called to Captain Gibson that some of his men had run away with his boat. Gibson was in his cabin under guard, but Every on deck replied, 'I know that well enough'.

David Creagh, hearing the bustle on deck, left his cabin to investigate. Every, Guy, and two others met him and sent him back down to his cabin where he remained, probably under guard, for the next few hours.

Captain Humphreys, realising that the mutiny was a *fait accompli*, and seeing the *Charles II* slip slowly from her moorings, fired two shots at her but did no damage. Alerted by the gunfire in the harbour the Spanish garrisons of some of the forts looked out to see the English ship under sail and leaving the harbour. Perhaps unsure of what was going on, the fire from the Spanish guns was minimal and ineffective, but the mutineers nevertheless had no wish to remain in range long enough for the Spanish to score a hit. The ship's boats were acting as a drag on the *Charles II*, so all but two were cut loose and the ship sailed safely out to sea.

Once the *Charles II* was well out of range of the guns, about two leagues from Corunna, Every went into the captain's cabin and informed Gibson of the mutiny. What passed between the two men went unrecorded, but since the mutineers had no complaints against Gibson personally, and going by Every's behaviour towards the other officers who did not join the mutiny, it seems likely that the meeting was at least polite. When he had finished with Gibson Every went to the cabin of the second mate.

'I suppose you do not intend to go with us?' asked Every. Gravet replied that he would not, and Every returned to the deck.

David Creagh then left his cabin and made his way to the quarter-deck where he was met by Every and John Guy. Every was directing the steering of the ship, but at Creagh's approach broke off. He took Creagh's hand and asked if he would join them. Creagh replied that since he did not know what they intended he could not answer. Every told him that very few people knew his true intentions, and Creagh asked him who those people were so that he might ask one of them. Every said that by the morning everyone would know his plans, but Creagh objected that it might be too late by then.

John Guy, overhearing the conversation, became angry at Creagh's wavering and inquisitiveness. He marched up to the two men and threatened to beat Creagh about the head if he did not go back down to his cabin. On the way to his cabin Creagh passed William May.

'What do you do here?' demanded May.

Creagh ignored him and continued on his way to his cabin.

'God damn you!' said May, raising a pistol to Creagh's face, 'You deserve to be shot through the head.'

Creagh retreated to his cabin and presently orders were circulated throughout the ship that anyone who did not wish to be a part of the mutiny could go ashore in the ship's pinnace, one of the boats that had not been cut adrift under the forts at Corunna.

The loyal seamen and officers assembled on deck. One of the mutineers claimed that they were 'Spanish and Irish', but at least some of them were English. William Dampier later stated that John Carverth, the master, Richard Chapman, the boatswain, Benjamin Whithall, third mate, James le Grange, the barber, Richard Roberts, the purser, and the seamen James Tull, John Reynolds, Richard Herbert, Richard Chapman junior, and John Cook, 'all refused to run away with the *Charles*'.[19] John Gravet and David Creagh also joined Captain Gibson's party.

Captain Gibson himself was brought up on to the deck, where Every addressed him again, 'I am a man of Fortune, and must seek my fortune.'

'I am sorry this happens at this time,' replied Gibson.

Then Every made a last attempt to reconcile Captain Gibson, 'If you will go in the ship, you shall still command her,' he offered.

'No,' answered Gibson, 'I never thought you would have served me so, who have been kind to all of you. And to go on a design against my owners' orders, I will not do it.'

As Gibson and his men prepared to board the pinnace one of the mutineers noticed that the ship's doctor was among them. When Every realised the doctor's intention he ordered that he remain aboard the *Charles II*. Nobody else was forced to remain, though many later claimed they were,⋆ but the doctor would be indispensable to the mutineers in the voyage ahead and they could not allow him to leave.

John Gravet had come on deck without his sea-chest, and begged to be allowed to go back down below to retrieve it. The mutineers would not let him, but Every found him a coat and waistcoat to put on. Every also gave Gravet his commission as chief mate, signalling his absolute resignation from the Spanish Expedition. William May shook Gravet's hand and asked him to give his regards to his (May's) wife at home in England.

About seventeen or eighteen men entered the pinnace, and were given four oars to row with. As the boat pushed away from the *Charles II* those that were in it noticed that it was leaking and cried out to the mutineers for a bucket to bail with. A bucket was accordingly sent down to them and the pinnace set off back towards Corunna, where they were picked up by the *James*. The *Charles II* set out to sea and by morning was well over the horizon.[20]

It is interesting to note that William May was thinking of his wife at the time of the mutiny, for he, along with many other mutineers, had committed an act which would leave their wives destitute. Jane May and other wives had been tirelessly working on the seamen's behalf to secure their wages at home. As news of the mutiny filtered back to England Jane May led a petition directed to Queen Mary herself, begging the Queen to intercede with Sir James Houblon on their behalf. They argued anew that their husbands had

---

Of all the men who later claimed to have been forcibly kept aboard the *Charles II* only Thomas Joy tells a convincing story. Apparently, as he went to board the pinnace one of the mutineers noticed him and quietly asked Every if he should be allowed aboard. Every replied in the negative and Joy was denied entry into the boat. As the cooper it would be quite believable that the mutineers refused to part with him were it not for the overwhelming testimony given both by the men who left in the pinnace, and by several of the mutineers themselves, that no man was forced to remain except the doctor.

been betrayed, that Houblon's consortium had not fulfilled their obligations in respect of the men's wages, in short that the mutiny was entirely justified. They also believed, as did many others, that the intention of the mutineers was to return to England. They were not criminals, they argued, but wronged men asserting their rights. Moreover they argued that not all of the men had been actively involved in the mutiny: many, their husbands included, had simply been swept along by it.

The Privy Council considered the case and on 2 August 1694 a copy of the petition was sent to Sir James Houblon who, with his partners, replied eight days later. With both sides of the argument presented to them the Privy Council referred the case to the Committee for Trade and Plantations on 16 August. A meeting was called for 10 a.m. on Saturday 1 September, but was postponed until the afternoon of the 11 September. The petitioners were subpoenaed to attend, as were Sir James Houblon and other investors in the Spanish Expedition. Among the witnesses called were several eye witnesses in the form of Captain Gibson and some of the men who had gone in the pinnace with him, some other seamen's wives not named in the petitions, and the wife of Henry Every himself, who was instructed to bring 'her books and letters'. The committee rejected the petition.

Houblon's answer to the petition had been that he and his partners had acted entirely within their rights as laid down in the seamen's contracts. The men should not have been surprised to find themselves dependent on the Spanish crown since they had been under Spanish colours since they had lain at anchor at Gravesend. They maintained that they did not know of any men having been imprisoned, but that if it were truly the case then it had been as a punishment for their mutinous and disreputable conduct ashore. Finally they argued that since Every and his men had gone off to be pirates they had forfeited all of their wages.

The evidence that the mutineers intended to turn pirate was slim. Every and his companions had been reluctant to talk about their intentions with Gibson and his loyal seamen, so even if they suspected Every's intentions they were unlikely to have known for certain. Neither had any of the mutineers written home. In fact, the only evidence to support the supposition that Houblon could present was a copy of a broadside ballad which had appeared shortly after news of the mutiny had reached England, and which purported to have been written by Every himself:[21]

Come all you brave boys whose courage is bold
Will you venture with me? I'll glut you with gold
Make haste unto Corunna; a ship you will find
Now called the *Fancy*, which will pleasure your mind

King of the Pirates: The Swashbuckling Life of Henry Every

Captain Every is in her, he calls her his own
He'll box her about before he has done
French, Spaniard, the Portuguese, the heathen likewise
He has made a war with until he dies

Her modle like wax and she sails like the wind
She is rigged and fitted and curiously trimmed
And all things convenient has for his design
God bless his poor *Fancy*, she is bound for the mind

Fair Plymouth farewell and Cat-down be damned
I once was part-owner of most of that land
But as I am dissolved so will abdicate
My person from England to attend on my fate

Then away from this frigid and temperate zone
To one that's more torrid you'll hear I am gone
With 150 brave sparks of this age
Who are fully resolved their foes to engage

These northern parts are not fitting for me
I'll raise the Antarctic which some men shall see
I am not afraid to let the world know
That to the South Seas and at Persia we'll go

Our names shall be blazoned and spread through the sky
And many a place I hope to descry
Where ever one Englishman never was seen
Nor any proud Dutchman can say he has been

My commission is large for I have made it myself
And the capstan shall stretch full larger by half
It was dated in Corunna, believe it, my friend
From the year ninety-three to the world's end

I honour St George, and his colours I wear
Good quarters I give, but no nation I spare
The world must assist me with what I do want
I'll give them my bill when my money is scant

Mutiny

Now this I do say and solemnly swear
He that strikes to St George the better shall fare
But he that refuses shall suddenly spy
Strange colours aboard of my *Fancy* to fly

Four cheveralls of gold in a bloody field
Environed with green, now this is my shield
Yet call but for quarters before you do see
A bloody flag out, which is our decree

No quarters to give, no quarters to take
We save nothing living, alas it's too late
For we are all sworn by the bread and wine
More serious we are as any divine

Now this is the course I intend for to steer
My false-hearted nation, to you I declare
I have done thee no wrong: thou may'st me forgive
For the sword shall maintain me as long as I live[22]

CHAPTER THREE

On the Account

As day dawned on 8 May 1694 the town and castle at Corunna lay several leagues astern of the *Charles II*. Sometime during the morning Henry Every called all hands onto the deck and addressed them for the first time as captain.

Although in later years piratical democracy evolved to a state where captains and other officers were routinely elected by ballot, it is doubtful whether such a state of affairs existed aboard the *Charles II* at this time. Some authors have suggested that Every was voted into command on the morning following the mutiny, but it seems more likely that any democratic decisions made that morning were more in the nature of a ratification. As we have seen, Every was chosen as the leader of the conspirators before the mutiny took place, and he was certainly the ringleader during the mutiny. Furthermore, of the original appointed officers of the *Charles II* Every was the senior of those who still remained aboard, and with his previous long seafaring experience he was probably the best choice for captain.

Whatever the case, Every was undoubtedly in command by the morning following the mutiny. When the men were assembled on the deck he outlined his plans. Although most of the crew were probably aware of the piratical intent of the mutiny, there were also those who probably genuinely believed still that the *Charles II*'s intended destination was home to England. If that were the case then they were shortly to be disabused of the idea.

The ship's destination, the crew were told, was the Indian Ocean. Every announced that each man would 'share alike', i.e. that each man would receive an equal part of any plunder they took. Only Every himself was to be excepted from this, and even then he would only reward himself with two shares, and this at a time when privateer captains could often expect four or five times the amount received by a common crewman.

With a new captain, a new destination, a new pursuit in mind, and a new system of dividing plunder, the mutineers decided that their ship needed a new name. Carlos II of Spain, the anglicised form of whose name adorned the stern of the ship, was hardly popular amongst the men. We cannot know who suggested the new name or how it came to be chosen, but from that day the *Charles II* would be known throughout the world as the *Fancy*.[1]

The crew of the *Fancy* now faced a journey of several thousand miles. The feat of navigation and seamanship which followed tends to be overlooked since it was not uncommon for vessels to make the voyage from Europe to the Indies. Nonetheless, no experienced seaman would be complacent about such a voyage, and even if Every was only one of many to navigate the route it does not detract from the achievement.

The first concern for the mutineers was to gather the supplies they would need to see them through the long months ahead. As the *Fancy* cut through the sea on a southward course, Every's experience gained aboard the slave ships must have stood him in good stead. The *Fancy* sailed first for the Cape Verde Islands, a Portuguese colony which was frequently visited by ships heading for the Cape of Good Hope and beyond. Thomas Phillips of the *Hannibal* visited the islands in 1693 and later wrote an account of the place:

> This island of St Jago is the largest of the Cape de Verdes, or, as they were anciently called, the Gorgades, the rest of the islands, which are nine, being subordinate to this governor [of St Jago]. They were discovered, according to Dr Heylin, in the year 1440 by a Genoese whose name was Antonio de Noli, employed thereto by and at the charge of duke Henry, a younger son of John the I King of Portugal. The town of St Jago was taken first by Sir Francis Drake in 1585 and by Sir Anthony Shirley in 1596. The main trade of these islands is salt, and that chiefly at Santo Mayo [the Isle of May], where our ships bound to Newfoundland generally go to load it for curing their fish. Also some ships call, in their way for our American plantations, at this island, Bonavista, St Nicholas, St Vincents etc where they purchase asses very cheap, and come to a good market for them at Barbados, where all sorts of brutes go off well. They lie very convenient for the refreshment of shipping in their way to Guinea or the East Indies, and few English, Dutch, or French East-Indiamen but call here outward bound. Their own [i.e. the Portuguese] Brazil fleet never fails. The negroes here go naked, except a cloth about their middles, and a roll of linen the women wear about their heads. The clothes they wear are of cotton, and chequered or striped with blue.[2]

At Bonavista the mutineers took on salt, essential for the preservation of meat and other foodstuffs that the crew would need to hoard. From Bonavista they sailed to the Isle of May, 100 miles or so to the south west, arriving around the 6 June with plenty of water and bread, but only one barrel of beef and a small quantity of fish.[3]

At the Isle of May they found three English ships, the *James and Thomas* and the *Rebecca*, both of Plymouth, and a third ship from London. To Paul Bickford, captain of the *James and Thomas*, the *Fancy* looked like a French privateer, large but poorly armed. When the pirates entered the road only the upper tier of guns was run out, and Bickford mistakenly assumed that that was her entire armament. The *James and Thomas* was armed with sixteen guns, and so would have stood a reasonable chance against a ship armed with only about twenty guns or less (as the *Fancy* appeared to be), particularly if the captains of the other two English ships were inspired by Bickford's show of bravado to join in the fight. The odds seemed fair, and Bickford ordered his men to make ready for battle.

As the *Fancy* glided into the road and came to anchor, someone aboard hailed the three English ships, commanding them to send their boats across. This was a common practice when ships came together in an anchorage, so that the officers of the ships could exchange news and supplies.

There must have been something curious about the *Fancy* which made Bickford uncomfortable and suspicious, for he refused to obey the summons. The pirates responded to this perceived insolence by running out their lower tier of guns. To a sixteen-gun merchantman the enormity of the *Fancy*'s firepower, now becoming apparent, must have been daunting indeed. Merchant ships carried guns to protect themselves from pirates and enemy privateers, but their crews were rarely trained for fighting, nor sufficiently motivated to protect somebody else's (usually insured) cargo.

As the gun ports of the *Fancy* creaked open and the heavy lower tier of guns trundled out through them, Bickford and his crew realised that the men aboard the unknown newcomer were serious. The pirates hardly needed to threaten to sink the *James and Thomas*, but when they did whatever courage remained aboard the merchantman dissipated.

Bickford and some of his men dutifully rowed across to the *Fancy* and stepped aboard. There they were joined by the masters of the other English vessels and some of their crews who had obeyed Every's summons. Every told the three captains that their entire crews were to be brought aboard the *Fancy*, and the boats were sent back to their respective ships to pick up the remaining men.

Once aboard the *Fancy* the frightened crewmen and their captains were herded under the quarter-deck, and into the steerage. The hold might have seemed a better place to secure prisoners, but there they could do inestimable damage to the precious stores if they had a mischievous inclination. In the steerage they could do little damage, and it would be easier for the pirates to keep an eye on them. Guards were set over the prisoners, and the pirates proceeded to go through the three little ships in search of the supplies they required. It is important to note, particularly in light of later circumstances, that all accounts agree that the pirates mostly only took necessary supplies. It may well have been that apart from the crews' own valued possession there was little of worth to be found on the small trading ships who were collecting a cargo of salt (which the pirates already had in abundance).

The rummaging took around twenty-four hours, after which time the prisoners in the *Fancy*'s steerage were released and sent back to their own ships. Nine men remained aboard the *Fancy*; whether these men, mostly from the West Country, were detained against their will or were willing volunteers is debateable. Certainly, at least two of them, Welshman David Evans and Cornishman Edward Carwitheris, later claimed that they had been forced to join the pirates, and were kept as prisoners until the *Fancy* sailed. It was very common for pirates to claim to have been forced when they were later apprehended by the authorities, so any such claims must be taken with a pinch of salt. In this particular case it seems unlikely that the men were forced; Every and the gang had allowed several of the *Fancy*'s original crew to leave unmolested after the mutiny, so to have later forced other men to join would have been somewhat out of character. Phillip Middleton deposed that 'James Grey, Thomas Somerton, John Reidy, Edward Kirkwood, William Down, and some others... entered aboard the said *Fancy*'. Middleton's wording, while certainly not conclusive, tends to imply that the nine men were volunteers.

The *Fancy* remained at the Isle of May for a further two or three days, during which time one of the quartermasters, probably Henry Adams, gave the masters of the three English ships 'bills' for the supplies that had been taken from them. What form these bills took is difficult to imagine, since the pirates can hardly have held funds at a bank, and there were no merchants prepared to fund the mutinous crew. Perhaps the bills were simply accounts of what had been taken, receipts which the masters could present to their merchant backers, or perhaps they were bills of payment, drawn on a fictitious bank. Later on we shall see how the pirates were quite happy to 'buy' supplies with forged bills. The possibility also remains that the bills were to be drawn on the finances of Sir James Houblon and his consortium, and had been left aboard the *Fancy* after the mutiny. Houblon would hardly have been prepared to honour such bills, and Bickford and the other captains must have known that when they were presented with them. The captains had little choice however. The supplies had been taken whether they liked it or not, and men on a 'piratical account' as Every and company claimed to be were under no obligation to pay for their plunder, so even if they suspected the bills were worthless the captains must have realised that it was the only chance they had, albeit a slim one, of regaining anything from the incident.

Among the non-essential supplies which the pirates took was some linen, probably brought along as a trade good by one of the ships. The pirates spent their days at the Isle of May bartering this linen, demanding twice its value which, in view of the heavily armed ship riding at anchor, the inhabitants paid. At least some of the linen was bartered for fresh supplies, including twenty bullocks, which the pirates shared with the merchantmen in part payment.[4] Like the confining of plunder to necessary supplies, the giving of bills and fresh food was significant in a way which will become apparent later.

From the Cape Verde Islands, the *Fancy* sailed to the African coast where Every got up to his old tricks. Somewhere on the Guinea coast the *Fancy* anchored, and hung out an English flag. To the natives on shore this was a common signal that the crew of the ship wanted to trade, and accordingly a dozen or so manned their canoes and paddled out to meet the pirates. No sooner were they aboard than Every ordered his men to seize them. The poor men were relieved of their gold dust, between 3 and 5lb, and bundled below decks and thence into slavery.[5]

Among the many European nations trying to exploit the gold and slave trades of Africa in the seventeenth century was Denmark. The Danes built a trading fort at Accra, now the capital of Ghana, but its existence was a precarious one. In 1693 a group of local natives entered the fort under the pretence of wanting to trade. While the fort's second in command was showing the natives the merchandise stored there for trading, one of them slipped out a concealed blade and stabbed the Dane in the back. The natives then scattered over the fort and captured and secured the small garrison. More natives waited outside, ready to join in the fight at a given signal.

The Danish governor or general, a twenty-six-year-old man, hearing the disturbance rushed from his chambers with his sword in hand, only to be confronted by two of the attackers. He fought with them and held his own, calling all the while for support from his officers and soldiers. The rest of the garrison, however, were engaged in their own fights, or had already been captured, so when more of the attackers joined his adversaries he ran and leapt from a window. He was received by the Dutch in their nearby fort, and had his wounds dressed while the natives took over his fort.

The new black masters of the Danish fort hoisted a white flag 'with a black man painted in the middle brandishing a scimitar', and began to trade with European interlopers. The fort was in a poor state of repair and the sixteen guns were cheaply cast, but the Danish general had no men or resources with which to retake it.

In mid-May 1694 two Danish ships★ arrived at Accra with orders to retake the fort. With the ships came the officers and soldiers of a new garrison, provisions, and trading merchandise. Despite the weak defences the Danes were ill prepared for a full-scale siege of the fort, and so first settled down to negotiate. The leader of the black natives, who had once been a servant of the English Royal African Co., set such a price on the return of the fort that the Danes at first balked. Eventually he agreed to hand the fort back in exchange for an undertaking that he and his followers would not be punished for taking the fort, that they would be allowed to keep the trade goods and money which had been in the fort at the time of the capture, and would be given further a sum of fifty gold marks in ransom.

Once the fort was resettled the two Danish ships sailed to Whydah (in modern-day Benin) to purchase slaves to sell in the West Indies to try and recoup some of the expenses of the expedition. From there they sailed to the island of Principe, a common place for ships to stop in search of water.[6]

Twenty-five years later British Royal Navy surgeon John Atkins visited Principe and its neighbouring island and described the almost idyllic life to be found there. The waters teemed with whales, threshers, and sword-fish, the skies above were filled with boobies, terns, and other birds. In the rolling hills and valleys grew an abundance of fruit trees, palms, coconuts, pineapples, bananas, and guavas. In between the trees lived monkeys, parrots, fowls, goats, pigs, ducks, turkeys and wild cows. Even the slaves who served the Portuguese masters of the island had a comparatively easy life: their work was mostly domestic or horticultural, their hardest task was ferrying their masters about in hammocks slung on poles, and they were well fed for their troubles. It was, in short, 'a pleasant and delightful spot... an improvement to country retirement, in that, this may be a happy and uninterrupted retreat from the whole world.'[7]

The Danes however would not have such a happy experience of the island, for while they were watering their vessels 'a ship of forty-six guns under English colours came in'. The *Fancy* had arrived.[8]

This is perhaps a good time to discuss the colours, or flags, flown by Every. Most books (and other media) which depict the flags flown by various pirates attribute to Every a skull and crossed bones, in which the skull faces to one side

---

The size and armament of the Danish ships is very difficult to ascertain as eye-witnesses who saw them give wildly varying accounts: Thomas Phillips of the *Hannibal* stated that each ship had twenty-six guns; John Sparks claimed that they were of thirty-six and twenty-two guns; David Evans deposed that there were five Danish ships but did not specify their armament; William Phillips gave the figures of twenty-six and twenty-four guns. Possibly the most reliable testimony is that of Peter Claus, a Danish seaman who joined the pirates, who said that his ship mounted sixteen guns, but gave no figure for the other ship.

and is sporting a bandanna and earring. There is no reference contemporary with Every which describes or depicts such a flag, and in fact the earliest depiction of this flag did not occur until the second half of the twentieth century. Grey, writing in 1933, shows several flags, but despite dedicating a considerable space in his book *Pirates of the Eastern Seas* to the activities of Every, does not mention the flag. The earliest record of this flag which I have found, along with its attribution to Henry Every, comes some decades later.

Neither is it a particularly likely flag for Every to have flown. The strong association between pirates and the famous skull and crossed bones post-dates Every's career by nearly two decades (though a 'jolly roger' type flag is recorded as having been used by pirate Emmanuel Wynne as early as 1700). Furthermore, the imagery of the bandanna and earring would not become associated particularly with pirates until the later nineteenth century, through the exciting but historically inaccurate work of American artist Howard Pyle and his followers. Although the ballad quoted in the previous chapter makes mention of a shield with four chevrons, similar to the arms of the Every baronets, this is most likely down to the imagination of the balladeer. The only flag which reliable records state as having been flown aboard the *Fancy* was the St George's cross of England.

The pirates on the *Fancy* hailed the Danes and promised that if they surrendered and sent across all of their money they would not be harmed. The two Danish ships, the *Golden Lion's Arms*, commanded by Jan Janson, and the *Christianus Burge*, commanded by Captain Mordrees, prepared to fight. None of the pirates who later described their adventures thought to include much detail about the fight between the *Fancy* and the Danes, which is a pity because the Danes must have fought bravely, and John Dann deposed that the pirates 'took [them] after some restrain'. The *Fancy* fought both ships simultaneously, and the fight lasted about an hour, during which one pirate and four or five Danes were killed.

Every claimed that England and Denmark were at war (which was entirely untrue), and that his attack of Danish vessels was thus justified. Whatever excuses he made there can have been little doubt among the vanquished Danes as to Every's real purpose.

The battle over and victory complete, the pirates settled down to plunder the two ships. The Danes had evidently done fairly well at their trade on the coast, for the pirates took a significant amount of elephant ivory and a large quantity of gold dust, estimated to be about 40lb in weight. During the fighting one of the Danish merchants had managed to slip ashore, carrying with him a chest of gold. When the pirates found out they sent a Dutchman to the shore with the message that if the merchant and his gold did not return aboard then the whole crews of the Danish ships would be hanged. Whether or not the pirates would have carried out their threat we shall never know, for the merchant hurried back to the ships, and carried his gold with him.

Also plundered from the Danes were a quantity of small arms, and several chests of linen and wool. For men who had waited so long to earn money at Corunna the gold taken from the captured blacks and from the Danish ships must have been like manna. However, the commodity which most of the pirates remembered taking from the Danes when later questioned was 700 or 800 cases of brandy.

Most of the Danes were put on shore at Principe, from where they watched the pirates set fire to the largest of their ships and sail away with the other and fourteen of their shipmates who had volunteered to join the *Fancy*. Seven of the blacks captured earlier were also given away as slaves, or more likely, exchanged for provisions which included rum and sugar. The young former general of Accra had been in some fear about his return to Denmark and the treatment he was expecting there, but he need not have worried – for he was killed during the battle.[9]

The pirates sailed then to Fernando Po (now Bioko), an island off the African coast named after its European discoverer who landed there in 1472. The island was a popular watering hole and meeting place amongst pirates and it is possible that Every, with his experience of the African coast, knew this and was hoping to meet other pirates there. In any case, after so many months at sea the *Fancy* was badly in need of graving. Over time a ship's hull becomes encrusted with barnacles and weed, and it is essential that these are occasionally cleaned and scraped off because they will eventually slow even the fastest ship down. For pirate ships, relying as they did on their speed when chasing their prey or running from pursuers, the importance of graving was clear. Nathaniel Butler, writing earlier in the seventeenth century, described the process:

> [Graving] is when a ship is brought on ground, of purpose to burn off the filth and foulness, that cleaveth to her sides without board, the which burning is done with reeds, broom, or the like; and being thus burned, she is then to be newly payed… [that is] when a little canvas, about a hand's breadth, is laid upon the seams of a ship newly caulked; and the canvas thus put upon the seams laid over with tar.[10]

At Fernando Po the pirates also took the time to make some structural alterations to the *Fancy* and their Danish prize. It was a very common practice for pirates to make such alterations to their ships, to make them more suited to their purposes. Often this meant the removal of any unnecessary internal bulkheads for ease of movement during action, and frequently the lofty upperworks common on ships of the time were removed. In the case of the *Fancy*, she was 'lowered', meaning probably that the upper decks were cut away, giving her a more flushed appearance, and improving her handling qualities. The reduced top-hamper would also have increased her speed. When a squadron of East India Co. ships later chased the *Fancy* they reported how effective the alterations had been: '[the *Fancy*] was too nimble for them by much, having taken down a great deal of his upper work and made her exceeding snug, which advantage being added to her well sailing before, causes her to sail so hard now that she fears not who follows her'.[11]

Having carried out these alterations and graved their ships the pirates were ready to make the journey towards the East Indies. Near Cape Lopez they captured a small Portuguese ship carrying slaves and other commodities. The pirates took some clothing and silks, and gave the Portuguese some provisions in exchange. They landed briefly at Cape Lopez and bought some wax and honey, but a short while later disagreement broke out. The cause and nature of the quarrel are not recorded, but the crew of the Danish ship-turned-consort became dissatisfied with their commander (who goes unnamed, but was possibly either Henry Adams or Joseph Dawson, quartermasters of the *Fancy*). The pirates on the Danish ship were recalled aboard the *Fancy*, a shot was fired through her hull below the waterline, and she was left to sink.

After a brief call at Annobon, one of Principe's neighbouring islands, where the pirates took on yet more provisions, paid for partly in cash and partly in small arms, they sailed for the Cape of Good Hope. Since the Dutch settlement at the Cape was one of the principal stopping places for ships travelling between the Atlantic and Indian Oceans, it would have been a dangerous place for the *Fancy* to call at, so they headed straight for Madagascar.[12]

Madagascar had been growing steadily as a rendezvous and stopping-off point over the previous decade. The island offered several sheltered harbours, far beyond the effective reach of any European authorities. It was also a centre of slave trading in the East Indies, and these considerations made it an ideal place for Every in the *Fancy* to stop off after the arduous twelve-week journey from Annobon and round the Cape.

Captain Johnson described Madagascar thus:

[It] is an island larger than Great Britain, most of it within the Tropic of Capricorn, and lies East from the eastern side of Africa. It abounds with provisions of all sorts, oxen, goats, sheep, poultry, fish, citrons, oranges, tamarinds, dates, coconuts, bananas, wax, honey, rice; or in short, cotton, indigo, or any other thing they will take pains to plant, and have understanding to manage. They have likewise ebony, a hard wood like brazil, of which they make their lances; and gum of several sorts, benzin, dragon's blood, aloes etc. What is most incommodious, are the numerous swarms of locusts on the land, and crocodiles or alligators in the rivers. Hither, in

St Augustine's Bay, the ships sometimes touch for water, when they take the inner passage for India, and do not design to stop at Johanna [now Anjouan]…

Since the discovery of this island by the Portuguese, A.D. 1506, the Europeans, and particularly pirates, have increased a dark mulatto race there, though still few in comparison with the natives, who are negroes, with curled short hair, active, and formerly represented malicious and revengeful, now tractable and communicable, perhaps owing to the favours and generosity, in clothing and liquors, they have from time to time received from these fellows, who live in all possible friendship, and can, any single man of them, command a guard of 2 or 300 at a minute's warning. This is farther the natives' interest to cultivate with them, because the island being divided into petty governments and commands, the pirates settled here, who are now [writing in the 1720s] a considerable number, and have little castles of their own, can preponderate wherever they think fit to side.[13]

St Augustine's Bay lies at the south-western corner of Madagascar, a large natural harbour which was used as a meeting place in the late 1680s by buccaneers raiding in the Pacific Ocean. The most important thing perhaps about the bay was that it was the first good spot available to a ship rounding the Cape of Good Hope to re-supply and refit, and in this capacity full use was made of it by East Indiamen of several nations. In 1645 the English attempted to establish a permanent settlement at the bay, but a poor harvest and poor relations with the local Malagasy resulted in the colony's failure after the first year.

A French colony on the south-eastern side of the island was established at about the same time, and named Fort Dauphin. They had more luck than the English settlers, but after a troubled history the colony was abandoned after about thirty years. Although a settlement was later built at the deserted colony by shipwrecked pirates led by Abraham Samuel, in Every's day the area was devoid of Europeans.

To the north-east of Madagascar lies St Mary's Island, which in time would become famous as a safe-haven for pirates. Although Johnson wrote of the great population of pirates three decades after Every's visit to Madagascar, the seeds of settlement were sown in Every's own day. A fort was built there in 1690 by entrepreneur Adam Baldridge, a former pirate with an eye for a good market. Pirate ships could anchor in the harbour, protected by the narrow entrance and Baldridge's guns while they refitted between voyages. From time to time a New York merchant ship sent out by Baldridge's master, Frederick Phillipse, would arrive with supplies of food, clothing, rum and wine, as well as tools, nails, and other necessaries for the repair of ships and shore settlements. These supplies were sold to the pirates by Baldridge, who sent home money and Eastern luxury goods on Phillipse's ships.[14]

Where exactly on Madagascar the *Fancy* touched is uncertain. One historian, writing a history of the pirate settlement at St Mary's, states that Every visited there in 1695, but the evidence is lacking. In fact it is unlikely that the *Fancy* called at St Mary's, since Baldridge's account of the ships stopping at the settlement between 1690 and 1697 makes no mention of the *Fancy* or of Henry Every. If Every had stopped at St Mary's he could hardly have escaped the notice of Baldridge.[15] Far more likely is that the *Fancy* broke her long voyage around the Cape at St Augustine's Bay. Considering the direction the pirates had come from, and the direction they headed next, this would be the most logical place for them to have landed. Wherever they landed on the Madagascan coast, the pirates 'watered their ship, and got provisions, and cows to salt up'. They also 'cleared the ship'.[16]

A month later, fully provisioned with 100 freshly salted bullocks (paid for in powder and arms) and with a ship ready for action, the pirates made next for the Comoros Islands, a chain of islands between Madagascar's northern tip and the African mainland. When they reached Johanna they came up with a small Arab trading vessel of a type called a 'grab', which they quickly took. In the brief fight one of the pirates was killed, but the small prize yielded up a cargo of cotton, and about forty pieces of eight. Perhaps because of the death of one of their fellows, the pirates ran the grab ashore.

Shortly afterwards the *Fancy* came to anchor and some of the pirates went ashore. One of them, William May, had been sick for some time and by the time they reached Johanna had 'lost the use of his limbs'. He was put ashore and remained there while his companions spent a day or so filling their barrels with fresh water and transporting it out to their ship. The following day, while May and others were recovering ashore from their sickness, there appeared on the horizon three large English merchantmen, well-armed East Indiamen.

Heavily outnumbered and not wishing to be caught at anchor by the English ships Every ordered his men to come aboard the *Fancy* immediately. Backs bent against the capstan, the pirates got the ship under way and stood out to sea, escaping the English ships, but leaving William May behind.[17]

The pirates then sailed to the north, but having been disturbed by the East Indiamen while they were refilling their casks found themselves very short of water. Somewhere near the equator, having met with no ships to plunder, they turned south again in search of water. At Comoro, the largest of the Comoros Islands, they came across a French trading vessel, from which they took a quantity of rice and two French volunteers. Every and his crew then landed briefly at the island and took in further supplies.

From Comoro the pirates made their way back towards Johanna and on the way captured another small Arab grab which they plundered of her cargo of rice before sinking her. The French ship which the pirates captured at Comoro was not the only vessel of that nation in those waters. A short while before a French pirate ship had been enjoying a successful cruise 'under English colours' before being wrecked on Molila (now Mwali), an island between Comoro and Johanna. Twelve or thirteen of the Frenchmen had managed to reach Johanna, where they were picked up by Every – and like their fellow countrymen before volunteered to join the crew of the *Fancy*. Somewhere on the coast of Johanna the *Fancy* met with another French ship, this time a pirate. The size of the vessel goes unrecorded, but aboard her were only forty or so pirates who surrendered to the *Fancy* and also joined her crew. These pirates had had some success, and the 'good booty [they had] with them' was also transferred into the hold of the *Fancy*. By now Every's crew numbered some '170 in all, of whom 104 were English, fifty-two French, and fourteen Danes'.[18]

The round trip from Johanna and back again had taken about eight weeks, and during this time William May had been having adventures of his own. Left ashore when the *Fancy* sailed from the three English ships he had been effectively at the mercy of the newcomers. One of the ships was the *Mocha*, commanded by Captain Leonard Edgecomb, and if there were ever a merchant captain the pirates left on Johanna should have feared meeting it was he. Edgecomb was a notorious bully. Many authors have written at great length of the abuses suffered by seamen in the Royal Navy and merchant services at the hands of a tyrannical captain, and in many cases, either deliberately or unwittingly, they have exaggerated the truth. However, in the case of Leonard Edgecomb it would be difficult to overstate the cruelty and arbitrariness of his manner towards his crew. Even his officers were not safe.

A letter written by John Leckie, surgeon of the *Mocha*, gives an insight into the behaviour of this sea monster. Edgecomb suffered paranoid delusions that the surgeon was trying to poison him, and as well as taking precautions that neither the surgeon nor any of his staff should be allowed in the cook's room, he also meted out punishments for the imagined offence. Shortly after leaving Johanna Leckie was beaten with a cutlass by Edgecomb; a couple of months later he was beaten again, and this time received some wound, while on the same day Leckie's servant and the ship's barber were also beaten 'without any crime'.

Two days later Leckie was tied up preparatory to being keelhauled (the worst naval punishment after death, in which the victim was dragged by ropes beneath the ship's hull – if he did not drown he would be cut to shreds by the barnacles and probably have his arms and legs dislocated). The officers and crew of the *Mocha* refused to carry out this illegal punishment on a man who had not received a proper trial, and was probably innocent of the charges against him anyway. Edgecomb threatened them in turn with his cutlass, but was finally forced to relent. Leckie's private stores were kept from him, and his letter makes it clear that he was not the only member of the crew to receive abuse from Edgecomb.[19]

This, then, was the man to whom William May had no choice but to entrust his safety. When Captain Edgecomb went ashore he found May out, and must have had an idea of how he came to be there, particularly in light of the suspicious ship – the *Fancy* – which had fled at his arrival. May later maintained that he begged Edgecomb to allow him to serve the East India Co. and join the crew of the *Mocha*. Edgecomb berated him with 'scurrilous language', and said that far from being allowed to join the crew May would be taken to Bombay for trial and execution. Given the alternative of being left alone with the native inhabitants of Johanna, May agreed to be tried 'according to the law of the nation'.

Several of the *Mocha*'s crew took pity on May and did what they could to see that he was comfortable until the time came to depart. Surgeon Leckie was one of those sent to tell May that a boat was being sent for him, and May prepared himself to leave: however, at about 2 a.m. Edgecomb and the *Mocha* set sail, leaving him behind. Perhaps Edgecomb's cruel streak had noted May's fear of being left to the mercy of the natives, and thought that it would be a fitting punishment.

May was left alone in the world, surrounded by black faces with whom he could not communicate, but fate smiled kindly on him and sent a guardian angel to watch over him. One of the blacks then living at Johanna was not a native of the island at all, but had lived for some time in Bethnal Green, England. He had shipped aboard the *Rochester*, and after some adventures of his own had ended up at Johanna where, hearing that an Englishman was stranded alone on the island, he found May and nursed him and fed him until Every's return.[20]

Knowing that Johanna was a popular port of call for English ships, on 28 February 1695 Every wrote the following curious letter and left it with the natives of the island with instructions to give it to the first English ship which called there after his departure:

> To all English commanders, let this satisfy, that I was riding here at this instant in the ship *Fancy* man-of-war, formerly the *Charles* of the Spanish Expedition who departed from Corunna the 7th of May 1694 being (and am now) in a ship of 46 guns, 150 men, and bound to seek our fortunes. I have never yet wronged any English or Dutch, nor ever intend to whilst I am commander. Wherefore as I commonly speak with all ships, I desire whoever comes to the perusal of this to take this signal, that if you, or any whom you may inform, are desirous to know what we are at a distance, then make your ancient [i.e. ensign] up in a ball or bundle and hoist him at the mizzen peak, the mizzen [sail] being furled. I shall answer

with the same and never molest you, for my men are hungry, stout, and resolute, and should they exceed my desire I cannot help myself.

> As yet an Englishman's friend,
> Henry Every.[21]

Every's motives for writing this letter have long been argued. It has often been pointed out that his claim never to have 'wronged any English' was a lie, for he had attacked three English ships at the Isle of May. In fact, in Every's own mind it is quite conceivable that he believed he had done the ships no harm. He had taken supplies from them, but had given them payment in the form of bills and fresh supplies. The trade goods he had taken from them were sold for several times their value, and part of the proceeds – perhaps enough to recompense entirely for the goods – had been given to the merchants. Some men had left the merchantmen, but if they had all been volunteers then Every had not done any wrong on that score.

So, assuming Every's intentions with the letter were honest, it appears that he genuinely did not want to attack English or Dutch shipping. This was probably more than national pride or patriotism, for there was a wide belief among pirates that it was perfectly acceptable to attack 'heathen' shipping. However, the letter had another effect. It was a clear statement of piratical intentions.

A short while later the letter was given to the captain of an East India Co. ship, who carried it to Bombay and presented it to the Company officials there. They received and read Every's words at the end of May, before the raid that would make his name, and he was instantly branded a pirate. Meanwhile, Every in the *Fancy* sailed north towards the great pirate hunting-grounds in the Red Sea.

En route the *Fancy* called at the town of Maydh in modern Somalia for provisions. The natives there refused to trade with the pirates so a party of men went ashore and burned the town. In search of supplies the pirates then sailed on to Aden.[22]

CHAPTER FOUR

Gang-i-Sawai

A bove the Gulf of Aden lies the Red Sea which separates the Arabian
Peninsula from Africa: in the seventeenth century it was crossed by ships
carrying some of the richest cargoes in the world. Spices, silks, slaves, jewels
and specie were ferried through the Red Sea. Of the many ports on the Red
Sea the most important in Every's day was that of the city of Jeddah, the place
at which pilgrims to Mecca arrived in Arabia if they had come by sea, and
from whence they departed to return home. Separating the Red Sea from the
Gulf of Aden is a narrow strait known as Bab-el-Mandab, literally 'Gate of
Tears', said to be so named because the fast currents which run through the
straits are treacherous and have caused countless lives and fortunes to be lost.
To the pirates the strait was more usually known as the Babs (which name
will be used hereafter).

When European pirates realised the value of the ships involved in the Red
Sea trade a new danger was added to the currents. At only twenty miles wide,
the straits could be easily patrolled by the pirates, and with no alternative route
out of the Red Sea ships could not avoid making the passage, running the
gauntlet of marauders. Liparan or Bob's Key (now Perim) is a small island which
further divides the narrow straits in two, leaving a narrow passage only two
miles wide on the Arabian side, and a sixteen-mile-wide passage between the
island and Africa. The wider passage also contains several smaller islands known
as the Seven Brothers or Sawabi Islands, whose treacherous shoals force ships to
give them a wider berth. Thus any ship or fleet coming down the Red Sea and
through the Babs must steer well within sight and even within easy range of
any ship waiting for them off Bob's Key.

English pirates had been cruising off the Babs since at least 1635, in April of which year the *Roebuck* arrived. The *Roebuck* was a ten-gun privateer commanded by William Cobb, sponsored by a pair of notable London merchants, and carrying a letter of marque issued by Charles I himself, who also authorised Cobb to fly naval colours. The *Roebuck* had followed a similar route to the Fancy from the Cape to the Babs, calling at St Augustine's Bay and Johanna on the way.

Cobb anchored off the Babs, probably near Bob's Key, and waited for merchant vessels to pass. In a few days the privateers became pirates by capturing first the *Taufiqui*, a native vessel under the protection of the English East India Co., and then the *Mahmudi*, another native vessel, this time in the employ of the Portuguese East India Co. Portugal was, at that time, allied to England so Cobb's capture of both ships went against the terms of his privateering commission.

The passengers and crew of both vessels were put ashore while parties of pirates tore the ships apart searching for hidden valuables. When little was found they turned to torturing the officers and merchants to make them reveal the whereabouts of their wealth in an episode which was to set a sad precedent for piracy in eastern waters.

The *Roebuck* was eventually captured by the East India Co. ship *Swan* off Mohilla, but after a brief armed standoff was allowed to continue home after handing over the plunder. Once the *Swan* was out of sight Cobb continued his voyage and returned to the Red Sea where he took several more ships, before finally sailing for England. Cobb and others were arrested but released on bail. In 1639 the East India Co. ship *Discovery* captured the French pirate Gilles de Regimont, captain of the *Eendracht*, in the straits, and by the end of the century the area was known as a good hunting ground. In 1697 the infamous Captain Kidd cruised off the straits for a while, but failed to make any captures.[1]

But before Kidd's failed attempt at the Babs, Every and his company sailed there in expectation of meeting Indian or Arab vessels carrying the precious cargo that might make the pirates' fortunes. Every, however, was not alone in his thinking. Somewhere in the Gulf of Aden a lookout spied a small vessel under English colours. True to his word, Every made no attempt to attack them, and when the ships came near it was discovered that the stranger was a privateer fitted out in America. The two ships lay side by side, exchanging news, and as the evening wore on a third vessel arrived and likewise joined them.[2]

The first of these ships was the *Dolphin*, formerly a Spanish vessel of six guns and about sixty men led by Captain Richard Want. The *Dolphin* had been fitted out for privateering in Delaware in early 1694, and had spent some time hunting French ships off the Canadian coast before heading into the eastern seas. Want himself was from Carolina and was well known in those parts. In 1693 he had returned to America after a successful voyage as mate of the privateer *Amity* under the command of the famous Thomas Tew. Tew's share in the profits from that voyage, as captain and part-owner, had been estimated at around £8,000, and many of the men, it was rumoured, had earned £1,000. Want had spent a great deal of money in Carolina and Pennsylvania, and perhaps it had run out, or perhaps he was just greedy, for he was soon at sea again. Unlike many privateer ships, which were owned by consortia of merchants, the *Dolphin* was owned by Want himself, presumably paid for out of the profits of the *Amity's* cruise.

The second ship was the *Portsmouth Adventure*, a six-gun vessel outfitted at Rhode Island, and sent out with a privateering commission similar to the *Dolphin's*. The letter of marque was given to Captain John Banks, but at the last minute Joseph Farrell was placed in command, with Dutchman Dirk Chivers as mate.[3]

Almost from the beginning of English colonisation in America the colonies had been setting forth privateers, at first limited to the protection of the colonies and raiding the commerce of neighbouring foreign colonies, but in later years extending to protracted overseas voyages with profit in mind rather than defence. Thomas Hawkins of Boston was given a privateer commission in 1644, and Thomas Cromwell of the same city was given a commission the following year. Captain Edward Hull was given a commission in 1653 and enjoyed some success preying on French and Dutch shipping, but exceeded his commission by a land attack on Block Island in the English colony of Rhode Island.

By the later part of the seventeenth century the quest for profit had overcome integrity in many colonial officials, and several of the men who had enjoyed success as buccaneers in the Caribbean began to base themselves in the English colonies of North America. The many ships and crews who were given commissions by the colonial governors and councils are well illustrated by the story of one gang who arrived in New York aboard the *Blessed William* in May 1690.

The *Blessed William* is noteworthy because she had once been under the command of Captain William Kidd, until the crew, led by William Mason, Samuel Burgess and Robert Culliver stole the ship while Kidd was ashore on Antigua. Now under Mason's command, the *Blessed William* captured two Spanish ships and the pirates made an attack on a Spanish settlement. Seeking a place to refit they then sailed for New York.

News of James II's flight from England and the accession of William of Orange to the throne in 1688 had reached America early in 1689 and thrown the governments of the colonies into disarray. In New York a popular movement led by wealthy merchant and militia officer Jacob Leisler took control of one of the city's forts and a rebellion began. In June 1689 Leisler was formally elected commander of the rebellion and in December assumed the title of lieutenant-governor. In May 1690 he summoned an Inter-Colonial Congress which planned a campaign against the French. Within a few weeks the *Blessed William* arrived, seeking a privateering commission.

Mason and the crew, armed with some measure of legitimacy, sailed north to raid French shipping in the Gulf of St Lawrence. They captured six ships and made havoc plundering Port Royal (now Annapolis Royal). On their return to New York Mason and the crew transferred themselves to one of their prizes, *L'Union*, which they renamed the *Jacob*. In December 1690 the *Jacob* set sail on a course for the Indian Ocean.

The cruise was not immediately profitable and at the Nicobar Islands the crew broke up and Captain Mason, with others including Culliver, left the ship. After re-supplying at Madagascar the *Jacob*, now commanded by Captain Coates, sailed into the Red Sea and made enough captures for each man to be given a share of £800. Having made a small fortune Coates then sailed the *Jacob* back to New York. They arrived in 1693, by which time Leisler's rebellion had been defeated and his authority to grant privateering commissions had been called into question. Such was the power of hard currency in the colonies at that time that for a fee of £100 paid to the new governor each man of the crew was guaranteed protection.[4]

This, then, was the shady world of outward legality and inward unscrupulousness in which the *Dolphin* and the *Portsmouth Adventure* sailed. Farrell and Want were ordered aboard the *Fancy*. When they went aboard they took with them a gift of two barrels of flour and a proposition. They suggested that they should all three sail together, and go 'share and share' with one another. They also brought news of two more American ships at Madagascar planning to prowl the Red Sea for prizes. Every agreed to the union and the three ships set course together for Bob's Key.

For Every the company of two smaller vessels would be advantageous, for their shallower draught enabled them to sail in inshore waters which might prove dangerous for a ship of the *Fancy*'s size. For Want and Farrell the choice was perhaps made easier by the vast difference in armament between their ships, even combined, and the *Fancy*. Though there is no evidence that they were unwilling partners of Every, they could not compete with him – their only choice was to join with him or abandon their hopes of raiding ships passing through the Babs.

That very night a storm blew up and the three ships were separated. The storm was fierce, and despite all the care which had been lavished on the *Fancy* throughout the voyage her fore-top mast was lost.

When the *Fancy* arrived at Bob's Key, sometime in June 1695, Every found the *Portsmouth Adventure* had already arrived. Farrell was afraid that the *Dolphin* was such a poor vessel for speed that she would not catch them up. However, as the *Fancy*'s crew set to work rigging and setting up a new top mast the *Dolphin* arrived. She was late because on the way she had captured a small French pirate ship. The Frenchmen had run low on provisions and were half starved when the *Dolphin* came across them, so they readily agreed to join Want, and were now transferred to the larger *Fancy*. With three ships, a combined firepower of fifty-eight guns, and crews consisting of nearly 300 armed men, the pirate squadron was formidable enough to take on all but the most heavily armed and determined merchantmen.[5]

Three days after the *Fancy*'s arrival three ships were spotted, but they were not potential targets for they were sailing up from the Gulf of Aden (not down from the Red Sea) — and more importantly they were flying English colours. These ships turned out to be the *Susanna* of ten guns, commanded by Thomas Wake, the *Pearl* of six guns, commanded by William Mace,★ and the *Amity* of eight guns, commanded by Richard Want's former captain, the famous privateer Thomas Tew. All three ships had left America with privateering commissions, but now arrived at the Babs with piracy in mind.[6]

Like Tew, Thomas Wake was an old pirate, a New Yorker who had received a pardon during the reign of James II. Wake was commissioned by the governor of Rhode Island to attack the French, and set sail from Boston towards the end of 1694. Once at sea Wake changed course, and instead of sailing to the African coast, made for Madagascar. At that island the crew of the *Susanna* took on water, wood and provisions, then sailed for the Red Sea. Aboard the *Susanna* was one James Brown, who knew Every personally, having sailed with him aboard HMS *Rupert*.[7]

William Mace was also a New Yorker who had been granted a privateering commission in 1693 by Governor Fletcher. The *Pearl* arrived at Madagascar near the end of that year and set sail again in January 1694. Mace spent most of that year cruising, but no record remains of how successful he was. Following his association with Every he would go on to have a long career as a pirate in the eastern seas.[8]

Little is known of Thomas Tew's early life, but he was from Rhode Island and was probably a grandson of Richard Tew, an eminent citizen who had arrived in America from England in 1640. Various records suggest that he may have been a pirate operating in the Caribbean in the last quarter of the seventeenth century, and he was certainly at Bermuda in 1682.[9]

In 1692 Tew was at Bermuda again, and involved himself with a group of merchants fitting out the *Amity* for privateering. Tew was given command and in company with another ship sailed off to attack the French in Africa. Tew's

---

William Mace's name is variously given as Mues, May, Mason, Meese, and Maze. Similarly, William Mason of the *Blessed William* is sometimes called May. To avoid any confusion I have referred to each man by a different name throughout: 'William May', the *Fancy*'s crewman left on Johanna; 'William Mason', mutineer and captain of the *Blessed William* and *Jacob*; and 'William Mace', captain of the *Pearl*.

consort ship suffered damage to her mast during the voyage and was forced to turn back to Bermuda, leaving the *Amity* to continue alone.

Instead of sailing for Africa, Tew, like so many to follow, abandoned his original commission and sailed for the Red Sea. Accounts of what happened there are fragmentary, making it difficult to ascertain the truth. Captain Johnson wrote that after passing the Babs:

> …they came up with a tall ship bound from the Indies to Arabia; she was richly loaden, and as she was to clear the coasts of rovers [i.e. pirates], five more, extremely rich (one especially in gold), being to follow her, she had 300 soldiers on board, besides her seamen.
>
> Tew, on making this ship, told his men she carried their fortunes, which they would find no difficulty to take possession of; for though he was satisfied she was full of men, and was mounted with a great number of guns, they wanted the two things necessary, skill and courage; and, indeed, so it proved, for he boarded and carried her without loss, everyone taking more care to run from the danger, than to exert himself in the defence of his goods.[10]

Much of Johnson's chapter on Tew is unreliable, indeed demonstrably fictional, so it is difficult to know how much trust to place in his account of this incident. However, what is clear from numerous other sources is that Tew and his men did indeed take a rich vessel. Adam Baldridge wrote that the *Amity* arrived at St Mary's in October 1693, 'having taken a ship in the Red Sea that did belong to the Moors', and that each man expected a share worth £1,200. Tew's own share was estimated at £8,000.[11] After refitting and taking on supplies at St Mary's the *Amity* sailed for America and arrived at Boston where many of the crew openly paraded about the streets, but where Tew could not get the political protection he so desired. In search of a new privateering commission Tew made for Rhode Island where he was welcomed but told that a new commission would cost him £500. Thinking this too high a price to pay Tew then tried his luck at New York where he was received courteously by Governor Fletcher, the same man who had been so enthusiastic at the return of the *Jacob*.

Thanks to the charges of colluding with pirates which were later laid against Fletcher we have a wonderful description of Tew. Fletcher wrote:

> Tew appeared to me not only a man of courage and activity, but of the greatest sense and remembrance of what he had seen of any seaman that I had previously met with. He was also what is called a very pleasant man, so that sometimes after the day's labour was done, it was a divertissement as well as information to me to hear him talk. I wished in my mind to make him a sober man, and in particular

to cure him of a vile habit of swearing. I gave him a book for that purpose, and to gain the more upon him I gave him a gun of some value. In return he made me a present which was a curiosity, though in value not much.[12]

Aside from this evident high opinion of him the relationship between Fletcher and Tew is clouded in controversy. Fletcher granted Tew the privateering commission he sought, and it was later alleged that Tew paid him £300 for it. It was also said that Fletcher told Tew that if he didn't come back wealthy he shouldn't come back at all. As was typical, Tew had to give a bond to ensure his sticking to the terms of his commission, and this bond was signed by Edward Coates, the former captain of the *Jacob*.

Tew's commission was, like so many others, to cruise against the French. Around town it was put about that the real purpose of the voyage was to trade for slaves at Madagascar. However, on the quays and wharfs of Rhode Island, where the *Amity* was fitting out, it was common knowledge that Tew was bound for the Red Sea. Tew himself openly told passing acquaintances of his previous success and his intention to return to piracy.[13]

The three newcomers anchored off Bob's Key and the captains of all six vessels there met for a consultation. They decided to act in consort: Every was elected Admiral of the pirate squadron in view of the fact that he commanded by far the most powerful ship, and articles were drawn up and signed agreeing to 'share and share alike'. Every now had a total of six ships, around 400 men, and eighty-two guns at his command. With such a force he was powerful enough to attack the famous pilgrim fleet that sailed through the Babs on its way from Jeddah to India.

Since the time of Muhammad himself, all able-bodied Muslims with the wherewithal to do so have been required to make a pilgrimage to Mecca, the holiest of cities, at least once in their life. From Cairo and other great cities vast parties of pilgrims have set forth annually on the Hajj, as the journey is called. In AD 647 the third caliph, Uthman Ibn Affan, declared Jeddah on the Red Sea to be the meeting point for pilgrims travelling by sea. Thus, every year a great fleet of merchantmen carrying pilgrims and merchants sailed through the Babs twice, first on the way to Jeddah, and later on their return journey.

In any place that pirates and other sea raiders have become common it has rarely taken merchants long to realise the safety to be found in numbers. Thus, as well as devout pilgrims the fleet also carried large numbers of merchants and agents whose ships not only helped to protect the fleet, but were in turn protected by it. Because of the importance of Mocha as a mercantile centre, and thanks to the influence of the merchants, the pilgrim fleets frequently called at that port on their outward and homeward journeys. The pilgrim fleet was often known for this reason as the Mocha fleet.

Because of the important nature of the pilgrim fleet, both spiritually and financially, many important people of the day were involved in one way or another. Most important of all was the Grand Moghul, ruler of the Moghul Empire which spread over most of the Indian sub-continent.

The Moghul Empire is generally reckoned to have been founded by Babur in 1504 when he took control of Kabul, but it was Babur's son, Akbar, who properly established the Empire. As the Moghuls swept through India they carried with them the Muslim faith. The Muslim Moghuls however never outnumbered the predominantly Hindu natives of the lands they conquered, and the religious dissension which came about as a result of this was always a problem for the Moghul rulers. Akbar was well known as a tolerant ruler: he abolished taxes for non-Muslims, and tried to implement a state religion which was a mixture of Islam and Hinduism, with elements of other religions thrown in.

Akbar also interested himself in secular affairs, and some of the policies he formulated and personally oversaw the implementation of remained in use until the end of Moghul rule. Taxes were finely balanced to provide for the Empire's needs without robbing the peasants of more than they could spare, and Akbar built up an impressive imperial library. He was also a great builder, and among the many edifices which he ordered the famous fort at Agra is perhaps the most impressive. Akbar died in 1605, sparking a civil war, from which his son Salim emerged victorious to claim the throne.

Salim adopted the title Jahangir ('Seizer of the World'), and his reign, marked by corruption, was followed by that of Prince Khurram, who took as his imperial title Shah Jahan. Shah Jahan was more in the mould of Akbar than his father had been. The empire was expanded through military force, and it was on Shah Jahan's orders that India's greatest monument to love, the Taj Mahal, was built. Shah Jahan was also the first owner of the fabled 'Peacock Throne', a jewel-studded throne covered by a jewel-studded canopy, but his reputation was marred by rumours of an incestuous relationship with his daughter.

In 1657 Shah Jahan fell ill and rumours of his death led to more civil war to decide the succession. Four of Shah Jahan's sons raised armies to support their claim and a series of bloody battles followed. In fact Shah Jahan was not dead, and so the imperial armies supported his chosen heir, Dara Shikoh. A shaky alliance between Aurangzeb and Murad led to the defeat of Dara and the surrender of Shah Jahan, whose armies had already defeated the fourth son, Shuja. Aurangzeb turned on Murad and had him executed. Shuja made a tentative peace with Aurangzeb, but continued to fight against him and was banished. When Dara, who had fled north after his defeat, was finally captured he, too, was executed, leaving no opposition against Aurangzeb.

In 1659 Aurangzeb was crowned as Emperor, and so began a reign that was to last until his death in 1707. Aurangzeb is sometimes remembered as the greatest of the Moghuls because it was in his reign that the empire reached its geographical zenith. Aurangzeb's detractors, on the other hand, will point out his rule as possibly the worst of all the Moghul Emperors.

The religious toleration begun by Akbar and for the most part continued by his successors was abandoned under Aurangzeb's rule. The tax on non-Muslims which had been abolished by Akbar was replaced; temples were destroyed along with religious schools that were not Muslim. Intolerant as they were, Aurangzeb's actions speak of the fierce conviction of his own orthodox Muslim faith. He called a halt to the production of representational art, and allowed the destruction of such art in public places.

These moves led to a number of religious rebellions against his rule, by both Hindus and Sikhs. The rebellions were put down mercilessly, though such was the popular mood against Aurangzeb that some of the rebellions continued for years before they were crushed. In the west of India the revolt of the Marathas, a Hindu sect, lasted for most of Aurangzeb's reign; in the north the Pashtun Rebellion which broke out in 1672 cut off several trade routes for nearly two years.

Aurangzeb's constant wars put a huge strain on the economy of the empire, a strain which was exacerbated by the corruption of many of his officials. His religious intolerance similarly put a strain on the empire and created rifts which could never be healed, only pounded closed by violence and bloodshed. Furthermore, the sheer size of the empire meant that it was difficult to control the extremities, and one after another provincial rulers declared their independence. Thus, the rule of Aurangzeb saw the beginning of the disintegration of the Moghul Empire, which would finally be ended by British rule in later years. Despite all this, however, Aurangzeb was still one of the most powerful rulers in the world when Every and his pirate band waited off the Babs for the pilgrim fleet to pass.

And they waited there. And waited. The days rolled into weeks, and the weeks into a month. For six or seven weeks the pirate fleet waited off Bob's Key.[14] Sadly, it is not recorded how the pirates spent their time idling under the tropical sun. Knowing there was likely to be a fight ahead they doubtless sharpened their cutlasses and axes, oiled their gun locks, and prepared themselves for the task ahead. Perhaps they even practised loading and firing their cannon. Some of Tew's and Want's men had been here before, and probably spent some time telling their comrades that the crews of the Indian ships were unlikely to put up much of a fight, but none of the experienced captains would have wanted to let their men grow too bored or idle, for inactivity is seldom conducive to good morale.

The ships might have set off singly or in groups to patrol in the Gulf of Aden, but with such a rich collection of prizes expected to pass through the Babs any day they would not have wanted to stray far from their post. Minor repairs and maintenance were probably carried out to the rigging, sails and decks of the pirate vessels, ensuring they were in the best of shape. But every day idling in the water meant more and more weed and barnacles accumulating on the hulls beneath the waterline. The pirates could not afford to careen their vessels: they must be ready for the chase when the pilgrim fleet appeared. Every day the ships got a little slower, imperceptibly at first, but over six or seven weeks probably quite significantly – as later events bear out. Each day the stock of food and drink got a little smaller as 400 men ate their rations.

Surely not all the time at Bob's Key was spent at work and preparation. In the forecastles the men probably exchanged tall stories of past adventures and riches. Cards and dice would be found and the men would gamble away whatever they had, or hoped to get. On deck more vigorous games were perhaps played when the heat of the sun allowed them: football, skittles, and perhaps cricket. Proud seamen might even have challenged the men from other ships to rowing races.

But after a month and a half of waiting a panic began to spread around the little fleet. What if the pilgrim fleet wasn't coming? What if news of the pirates' presence at the Babs had reached Mocha and the merchant captains had decided to wait in harbour? Worst of all, what if the pirates had already missed the pilgrims' fleet? They could not wait indefinitely at the Babs for a fleet which might never turn up.

The pirates decided that they needed intelligence, and so fitted out a pinnace to sail up to Mocha, thirty-five miles to the north west. At the same time the pirate fleet stood out to sea to await the return of the boat. The men in the pinnace managed to capture two trading vessels, and brought two prisoners back to the fleet. The prisoners told the pirates that a fleet of twenty-five ships was preparing to sail from Mocha. At this news the pirates sailed back to Bob's Key, eager for the coming attack.[15]

For a further five or six days the pirates waited at Bob's Key, until one Sunday they spied a sail coming through the passage. The ship was an Arab coastal-trading vessel, and was probably unarmed, but in any case could not have withstood an attack from such a powerful fleet as the pirates had.

The pirates had no great desire to plunder the Arab ship: they had their sights set on bigger targets and could not afford to be busy rummaging when the pilgrim fleet hove in to view. What they needed desperately was fresh information: was the pilgrim fleet yet ready to sail from Mocha?

The captain of the prize carried the worst news the pirates could wish for – the pilgrim fleet had already sailed. After nearly two months of waiting, the great prize the pirates had been expecting had sailed past them in the night.

Merchant ships were rarely built for speed, giving pirates and privateers a distinct advantage in a chase. Furthermore, ships sailing in convoy can only sail as fast as the slowest of their number, so the pirates had a good chance to catch them still. If there were any dissension between the pirate crews at this disastrous news none of the pirates later captured and interrogated thought fit to mention it. That a harmonious partnership still more or less existed is borne out by the fact that none of the vessels set sail immediately in pursuit leaving their fellows behind. A council was called and the captains and officers met to discuss whether it would be better to remain off the Babs in the reasonable expectation of capturing some lesser merchantmen, or to set sail and give chase to the pilgrim fleet. The following day, Monday, all six pirate ships set off together in pursuit.[16]

What was true of merchantmen sailing in convoy was also true of pirate ships; the fleet could only sail as fast as the slowest ship. In this case the slowest ship was the *Dolphin*, commanded by Tew's old mate Captain Want. Unwilling to wait for the *Dolphin* to keep up, but equally unwilling to leave men behind, it was decided to burn the *Dolphin* and bring her men aboard the *Fancy*. The *Fancy* would have begun to get crowded with the extra men aboard, but with a crew of over 200 she was formidably strong.

With such a chase in hand it is not surprising that before too long the pirates should grow afraid that the next slowest ship would be the cause of their undoing. Not long after the *Dolphin* was burned the *Pearl* began to lag behind. There was no room aboard the *Fancy* for another full crew, so the *Pearl* was taken in tow by the *Fancy*.

Captain Wake in the *Susanna* was having difficulty keeping up, even with the *Fancy* slowed somewhat by her tow. Eventually he, too, fell too far astern to catch up, but he did keep course with the other three vessels. In the *Amity* Thomas Tew was also unable to keep up.[17]

It is impossible to say how the pilgrim fleet managed to slip past the pirates at the Babs. The passage they took was the narrower one, and two miles of sea would have been easy for a pirate fleet of six ships to keep watch over, though some reports suggest there may have been a fog.[18] To have tried to find the narrow passage through the Babs in the dark and fog would have been a terrible risk for the pilgrim fleet, but to be found in the morning waiting for the visibility to improve would have been a greater one with a nest of pirates lurking at the other end of the passage. Whether it was incompetence on the part of the pirates or a spell of good luck on the part of the pilgrim fleet, the incident was crucial. Every now had at his command only half the number of ships he had had before, and a significantly reduced firepower.

He knew that the pilgrim fleet would be making for the harbour of Surat. Situated fourteen miles up the Tapi River in the north-west corner of India, Surat had risen under the Moghul regime to become the principal trading port of India. A substantial fort protected the walled city, though it had suffered at the hands of Maratha rebels during the uprisings earlier in Aurangzeb's reign. Following in their wake Every turned his squadron towards Surat and on 3 September, twenty or thirty leagues off the Highlands of St John (Daman today), and four or five days' sailing from the Babs, they spotted a ship.

This ship was the *Fateh Muhammad*, a merchantman of six guns and 200 or 300 tons. To a fleet such as Every's the *Fateh Muhammad* should have been easy pickings. The pirates far outnumbered the Indian crew, and the merchantman's half-dozen guns were no match for the firepower commanded by Every's three ships.[19]

The *Fateh Muhammad* was owned by an Indian Mullah, Abdul Ghafur, who was one of the wealthiest and most influential merchants of the day. Alexander Hamilton, who knew Ghafur personally, wrote that the merchant 'drove a trade equal to the English East India Co., for I have known him fit out in a year, above twenty sail of ships, between 300 and 800 tons.'[20]

Ghafur already had a distaste for pirates, and for the English. In 1691 one of his ships had been captured by pirates who, it was assumed in India, were English. In fact the pirates were Danish, but so powerful was the assumption that all pirates were English that the East India Co. factory at Surat was forcibly closed down and its workers confined within. Ghafur demanded recompense of £100,000 – which the Company refused to pay. To have paid would have been an acknowledgement that the pirates were English, as well as being a crippling sum. Evidence surfaced that the pirates were not, after all, English, and the factory at Surat was allowed to continue operations, but only after its inhabitants had spent five months cooped up, imprisoned within its walls. The following year Ghafur again had the English at Surat confined in their factory for a brief time.[21]

As the pirate ships drew closer to the *Fateh Muhammad* one or more of them probably fired a shot, signalling to the merchantman to heave to. As the pirates crowded the gunwales of their ships, brandishing cutlasses and pistols, muskets and hatchets, and screaming foul obscenities and threats, they must have presented a fearsome sight. From the deck of the *Fateh Muhammad* the captain would first have seen a puff of smoke issue from one of his pursuers' gun ports. Next would come a faraway report of the cannon firing. Finally would come the splash of a cannonball in the sea nearby if he was lucky, or the crash of breaking and straining timber as the cannonball hit his vessel if he was not.

Pirates and privateers, on the whole, preferred to scare their victims into submission. A show of force, shouted threats, and perhaps one or two shots to prove their earnestness, and the pirates could hope for a quick surrender. It was better not to risk damaging a prize by shooting at it more than necessary, and though many of the former privateers were skilled and experienced in hand-to-hand combat, it was to be avoided if possible. Only very rarely did a prize put up much resistance, and even then it was often only a token show of defence. But Ghafur clearly commanded a great deal of loyalty: the *Fateh Muhammad* fired back at the pirates.

It appears that the *Fateh Muhammad* fired three shots. It may well be that the crew were not in a position to reload their guns for one reason or another – a not-uncommon state on merchantmen – and the three shots may represent a broadside from the six-gun ship. In response the pirates fired a broadside from the *Fancy*. The movement of the ship from the recoil would have been felt beneath the pirates' feet. The captain of the *Fateh Muhammad* would have watched as the *Fancy* was momentarily hidden from view behind a bank of smoke, and again he would have heard the ripple of gunfire – not a single shot this time, but twenty or more guns firing almost simultaneously. And then he would have waited perhaps a second or two for the inevitable sounds of timber being pummelled by iron, and torn apart, mixed in the cries of the fearful and the screams of the injured.

Then, as the ships drew closer, individual men on the decks of the pirate ships would become distinguishable. Slowly, inexorably, the pirate ships would come within small-arms range, and the pirates on the deck start to fire ragged volleys of muskets and pistols at the men left standing on the deck of the *Fateh Muhammad*. Compared to the cannon fire the muskets crackled quietly, but nonetheless destructively. Former buccaneers from the Caribbean might recall their old tactic of using long-barrelled hunting muskets to pick off prominent targets.[22]

The pirates manoeuvred their ships alongside the *Fateh Muhammad*, threw grappling irons across and pulled the ships together. The armed men rushed across, onto their prize. The fight lasted between one and two hours in total, casualties were low, and at the end the pirates found themselves in possession of a very rich prize.

Rummaging in the cabins and hold the pirates recovered pieces of eight and chaquins (Arabic gold coins) to the value of £50-60,000. Here, at last, was the kind of prize the pirates on the *Fancy* had been dreaming of for the past sixteen months. As the gold and silver coins were transferred aboard their own ships the pirates finally realised that their mutiny and the hardships they had suffered since were worthwhile. They had no use for the slow lumbering merchantman or her puny armament, so the ship was returned to her captain and crew. Neither did the pirates waste time searching her. A small prize crew was put aboard to search for hidden valuables while the pirate squadron sailed off in search of further prizes. The *Fateh Muhammad* and her prize crew kept company with the rest of the squadron, lest she sail off and warn other shipping of the *Fancy*'s presence.[23]

During the chase across miles of open sea the pirates had actually overtaken the pilgrim fleet, so now lay between the merchantmen and safety. However, warned of the pirates' presence at the Babs the captains of the merchantmen had thought it wise to change their course, in case they should meet the pirates later. The captain of the *Fateh Muhammad* told the pirates that the bulk of the pilgrim fleet had reached port safely, and the only vessel they could hope to meet was the heavily armed flagship. Nevertheless, the pirates knew that the flagship, as the strongest and most secure vessel in the fleet, would also be heavily laden with treasure, and so they decided to lie in wait for her.

Within sight of land the *Fancy* anchored off the Highlands of St John. They had not so long to wait here as they had waited at the Babs, for on the same day they dropped their anchors, 5 September, they spied a large ship sailing in for Surat. Anchors were weighed and the pirates stood out to sea to intercept her. In the far distance another ship could be seen, smaller, but racing towards them. From a distance she looked like the *Susanna*.

The larger ship proved to be a much bigger prize even than the *Fateh Muhammad*. At 700 tons or more she dwarfed even the *Fancy*, and from her gun ports poked sixty or more muzzles. Her crew of 200 men was more or less equal to that of the *Fancy*, but she also carried 600 passengers and a massive guard of 400 or 500 soldiers. In her hold was a vast treasure of gold and silver, cargoes of rich silks and other luxurious commodities, and the personal wealth of the passengers must have been worth a small fortune by itself. She was called the *Gang-i-Sawai*, and she was not owned by a wealthy merchant like Abdul Ghafur: she was the pride of the fleet of Grand Moghul Aurangzeb himself. Aboard the great ship were the most important of the pilgrims who had sailed to Mecca that year: noblemen, wealthy merchants, and members of Aurangzeb's court, perhaps even his relations.[24]

Captain Johnson related the battle which followed:

> When [the pirates] fired at her to bring to, she hoisted the Moghul's colours, and seemed to stand upon her defence; Every only cannonaded at a distance, and some of his men began to suspect that he was not the hero they took him for: however, the sloops made use of their time, and coming one on the bow and the other on the quarter of the ship, clapped her on board, and entered her, upon which she immediately struck her colours and yielded.[25]

While Johnson's version of the battle has long been believed without question it is not entirely accurate. The *Fancy* probably did fire a warning shot to signal the *Gang-i-Sawai* to heave to, and at that point she probably did hoist the flag of the Grand Moghul, but what followed afterwards was a testament to the courage and determination of not only the Indian crew, but that of the pirates as well.

As the *Fancy* gained ground on the *Gang-i-Sawai*, and the ships edged into cannon range of one another, the Moghul's ship fired two 18-pounder chase guns (guns facing aft from the ship's stern) at the pirates. For the men now standing on the deck of the *Fancy* the tables were turned; they would have seen the bank of smoke issuing from the muzzles of the Indian guns, heard the rippling volley, and witnessed close at hand the devastation wrought by heavy iron balls smashing into their ship. One of the shots hit the *Fancy*'s mizzen mast, but did little damage. When the confusion on the *Fancy* died down they would have cleared away whatever wreckage cluttered the decks and braced themselves for the next shots.

The *Fancy* did not yet fire back. Although the pirate captains had previously agreed that the *Fancy* should bombard the *Gang-i-Sawai* from a distance while the smaller vessels closed to board her, Mace and Farrell had been dismayed by the size and strength of the prize. So the *Fancy* crept closer to the *Gang-i-Sawai*, her guns eerily silent. As the two larger ships came side by side the *Gang-i-Sawai* began to fire broadsides at the *Fancy*. Because the main armament of the Indian ship was so much higher than the pirate ship the first broadside, fired at a close range, was too high and the shot splashed into the water on the far side of the *Fancy*.

The *Fancy*'s gunners, more experienced than the Indians, perhaps had better luck, and with a roar of flame and smoke the pirates' own guns at last opened up. The key to successful naval gunnery was being able to anticipate the exact moment of the ship's roll at which to fire the guns. If the guns were aimed too high the shots might pass harmlessly over the top of the target to splash into the sea on its far side. Fired too low, the cannonballs would fall short of the target. As the ships got closer to one another the aim changed from trying to hit the enemy at all to trying to hit the enemy in the right place. The pirates had no wish to sink their prize before they could board her, and so aimed high, firing into the sails and rigging in the hope of disabling her.

Suddenly, the firing from the *Gang-i-Sawai* ceased. The pirates could not have known what caused the lull, but they could see the confusion which reigned on the deck of the enemy. In fact, one of the *Gang-i-Sawai*'s great guns had exploded, sending a shower of hot, jagged iron fragments across the deck. Only three or four men were killed in the accident, but more were doubtless wounded, and many more numbed by the unexpected shock.

A lucky shot from the *Fancy*'s next broadside, one of eleven she fired that day, felled the *Gang-i-Sawai*'s main mast. Each mast on a sailing ship is connected to the other masts by a system of stays, so the loss of one mast, particularly the main mast, weakens the other masts and makes the ship difficult to handle. Added to this was the more tangible problem of falling ropes and spars, the largest of which weighed tons. Anyone caught beneath the falling mast would have only moments to dive for shelter to avoid being crushed. The sailors up the mast, working the sails, were pitched into the sea. The debris from the fallen mast littered the deck, making an obstacle course for anyone trying to move from one end to the other, and the mast itself, dangling in the sea but still attached by its rigging, would act as a giant sea-anchor, dragging the ship over to one side and making steering impossible.

The loss of the main mast, added to the confusion of the exploding gun, threw the Indian seamen and soldiers into a panic. The pirates, seeing the panic spread through the *Gang-i-Sawai*, knew that their best opportunity to board her and win the day had arrived.[26]

Seeing the *Fancy* and the *Pearl* bearing down on them, fear gripped the Indians. What passengers had remained on deck to see the *Gang-i-Sawai*'s victory now scurried below and sought out hiding places for their valuables and their families. It is in times of panic and distress such as this that the bold actions of a steadfast and resolute officer can inspire scared men and turn the tide of battle. Despite the damage to the ship and the losses to the crew, the *Gang-i-Sawai* was still considerably more powerful than the *Fancy* and the *Pearl*, and a strong leadership could still save the day. Ibrahim Khan, captain of the *Gang-i-Sawai*, had no such qualities however, and in this crucial moment fled below decks, leaving the fighters on deck leaderless. As the *Fancy* and *Gang-i-Sawai* came together the pirates continued firing their cannons while the Indians responded by throwing incendiary bombs onto the deck of the pirate ship.

Every had other problems, too. His men were inspired by the damage they had caused and the disorganisation they could see on their prize, but he knew she was still a formidable adversary, and to make matters worse the *Portsmouth Adventure* under Captain Farrell had not yet joined in the fight. Farrell's ship was only small, tiny compared to the *Gang-i-Sawai*, but the extra firepower she could have provided, and the extra men in the boarding party, might yet prove to be crucial.

Unaware of the true state of affairs onboard the *Gang-i-Sawai* Every was taking a grave risk trying to board her, but he had come this far and was not going to be thwarted at the last moment by the cowardice of his colleague. The *Fancy* and *Pearl* came alongside the *Gang-i-Sawai*, and their crews scrambled up the sides of the larger ship and dropped onto the deck. Cutlasses swung through the air, pistols were fired, and men were clubbed to death with musket butts. The fighting was fierce and casualties were high. Of the 290 or so men who had chased the pilgrim fleet across the sea in the *Fancy* and *Pearl*, only 180 survived to collect a share of the plunder. Some of the losses may have occurred during the fight with the *Fateh Muhammad*, and some had perhaps died of natural causes during the voyage, but at least one of the pirates later deposed that many of the attackers had been killed during the battle.

Below decks Ibrahim Khan kept a number of Arab girls he had purchased to be his concubines, and these he exhorted to go and join in the fight. Turbans were placed on their heads and they were given weapons, but by the time they reached the deck the fighting was all but over. After a fight lasting two hours from start to finish, Henry Every and his men were masters of one of the greatest prizes ever captured by pirates.[27]

The events which followed the capture of the *Gang-i-Sawai*, or 'Gunsway', as the pirates often referred to her, have become infamous. In their later depositions and testimony most of the pirates glossed over the few days following the capture of the *Gang-i-Sawai*, saying only that they had 'plundered her', but in a pamphlet titled *The Last Dying Words and Confession of John Sparks, of the Fancy* (which may or may not be an accurate rendition of Sparks' last thoughts), we read, 'This villain expressed his contrition for the horrid barbarities he had committed, though only on the bodies of heathens. The inhuman treatment and merciless tortures inflicted on the poor Indians and their women still afflicted his soul.'[28]

Phillip Middleton, who was just a boy and had perhaps taken no active part in the atrocities, admitted that the pirates had tortured several of the passengers for information as to the whereabouts of their hidden treasures. Steadfastly the passengers refused to speak, and so the pirates took a leisurely few days to plunder the ship from deck to keel, hunting out coins, jewels – and a ruby-studded saddle bound for the stables of Aurangzeb himself.[29]

Once the search for plunder had been completed the pirates turned their minds to other pursuits, and began to hunt out the women aboard the *Gang-i-Sawai*. Ibrahim Khan's Arab girls had already fallen into the pirates' hands when they appeared on deck at the end of the battle. No doubt they were passed from man to man, but there were not enough to go round and so the pirates turned to the prisoners. 'Several of the Indian women on board were, by their habits and jewels, of better quality than the rest', said Middleton, but in the semi-egalitarian world of the pirate crew social class, especially of 'moors', meant little. Neither, it seems, were women spared because of their youth or advanced age. Middleton only went as far as to say that, 'The men lay with the women aboard', but reports soon reached India of just how ruthless the pirates had been.

Khufi Khan wrote that the pirates, 'busied themselves stripping the men and dishonouring the women, both young and old'. The Indian historian was no friend to the English pirates, so his words might be taken with a pinch of salt had the East India Co. officials at Bombay not written to the Privy Council:

> it is certain that the pirates… did do very barbarously by the people of the Gunsway and Abdul Ghafur's ship, to make them confess where their money was, and there happened to be a great Umbraw's wife (as we hear) related to the King [Aurangzeb], returning from her pilgrimage to Mecca, in her old age. She they

abused very much, and forced several other women, which caused one person of quality, [and] his wife and nurse, to kill themselves to prevent the husband's seeing them (and their being) ravished.[30]

Other women, it was reported, threw themselves overboard to escape the orgy of rape, or stabbed themselves with knives and swords belonging to the pirates.[31]

When the pirates had exhausted themselves with the women of the *Gang-i-Sawai*, and taken all the gold, silver, and provisions they could find, the half-crippled ship was given back to her crew, as was the *Fateh Muhammad*. The pirates sailed off to share out their gold, having kept some of the women aboard their ships, while the two Indian ships limped home to Surat.

A 1732 woodcut illustration of Henry Every.

A

COPY of VERSES,

COMPOSED BY

Captain Henry Every,

LATELY

Gone to SEA to seek his FORTUNE.

To the Tune of, *The two English Travellers.*

Licens'd according to Order.

COme all you brave Boys, whose Courage is bold,
Will you venture with me, I'll glut you with Gold?
Make haste unto *Corona*, a Ship you will find,
That's called the *Fancy*, will pleafure your mind.

Captain *Every* is in her, and calls her his own ;
He will box her about, Boys, before he has done :
French, Spani ard and *Portuguese*, the *Heathen* likewife,
He has made a War with them until that he dies.

Her Model's like Wax, and fhe fails like the Wind,
She is rigged and fitted and curioufly trimm'd,
And all things convenient has for his defign ;
God blefs his poor *Fancy*, fhe's bound for the *Mine*.

Farewel, fair *Plimouth*, and *Cat-down* be damn'd,
I once was Part-owner of moft of that Land ;
But as I am difown'd, fo I'll abdicate
My Perfon from *England* to attend on my Fate.

Then away from this Climate and temperate Zone,
To one that's more torrid, you'll hear I am gone,
With an hundred and fifty brave Sparks of this Age,
Who are fully refolved their Foes to engage.

Thefe Northern Parts are not thrifty for me,
I'll rife the Anterhife, that fome Men fhall fee
I am not afraid to let the World know,
That to the *South-Seas* and to *Perfia* I'll go.

Our Names fhall be blazed and fpread in the Sky,
And many brave Places I hope to defcry,
Where never a *French man* der yet has been,
Nor any proud *Dutch man* can fay he has feen.

My Commiffion is large, and I made it my felf,
And the Capfton fhall ftretch it full larger by half ;
It was dated in *Corona*, believe It, my Friend,
From the Year Ninety three, unto the World's end.

I Honour St. *George*, and his Colours I wear,
Good Quarters I give, but no Nation I fpare,
The World muft affift me with what I do want,
I'll give them my Bill, when my Money is fcant.

Now this I do fay and folemnly fwear,
He that ftrikes to St. *George* the better fhall fare ;
But he that refufes, fhall fudenly fpy
Strange Colours abroad of my *Fancy* to fly.

Four Chiviliges of Gold in a bloody Field,
Environ'd with green, now this is my Shield ;
Yet call out for Quarter, before you do fee
A bloody Flag out, which is our Decree,

No Quarters to give, no Quarters to take,
We fave nothing living, alas 'tis too late ;
For we are now fworn by the Bread and the Wine,
More ferious we are than any Divine.

Now this is the Courfe I intend for to fteer ;
My falfe-hearted Nation, to you I declare,
I have done thee no wrong, thou muft me forgive,
The Sword fhall maintain me as long as I live.

London : Printed for *Theophilus Lewis.*

384

Printed version of Henry Every's 'declaration', supposedly left at Corunna in 1694. (Courtesy of Joel H. Baer)

The Grand-Moghul, Aurangzeb. (Courtesy of Joel H. Baer)

The façade of East India House, the East India Co.'s headquarters in Leadenhall Street. (Courtesy of Joel H. Baer)

A 1734 engraving of Henry Every. In the background, the battle between the *Fancy* and *Gang-i-Sawai* rages.

Newgate Prison, London, where some of the *Fancy*'s crew were detained.

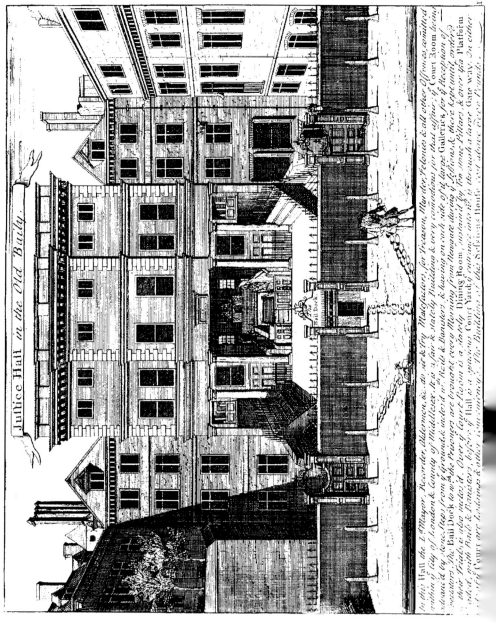

Above: The Old Bailey, London, where the trial of May, Sparks, Bishop, Lewis and Forseith was held. (Courtesy of Joel H. Baer)

Opposite: 'Villainy Rewarded'. A broadside ballad which circulated at the time of the trial and execution of May and co. (Courtesy of Joel H. Baer)

+ Villany Rewarded;
OR, THE
PIRATES Last Farewel

To the World:

Who was Executed at Execution Dock, on *Wednesday* the 25th. of *November*, 1696. Together with their free Confession of their most Horrid Crimes.

To the Tune of, *Russels Farewel*.

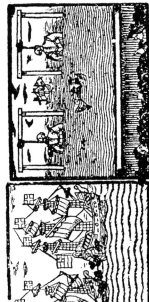

WEll may our fall'n adventurous crew,
for their hard Deaths must dye,
For which, alas! we now must dye,
Don't look us in the face,
Which is no more than what's our due,
Since we so wicked were,
As here that we return'd to you,
let Pyrates then take care.

The Hills our Treasures, not put to run,
together his aged;
And took a Ship out from the Groyne,
is known upon the Sea:
With which we Robb'd, and Plunder'd too,
no Ship that was in sight,
. . .

These many a one we did undoe,
let Pyrates then take care.
Our Ship being well provided then
for this our Enterprise,
The Sundry and Eighty Men
there was in her likewise :
The Killing Do all we could come nigh,
no Nation was our spare,
For which a Shameful death we dye,
let Pyrates then take care.

Mr. Robb's a Ship upon the Seas,
the Gun-way call'd by name,
Which we met near the East-Indias,
and Kill'd the same ;

In it was Gold and Silver store,
of which all had a share,
Each man 600 pounds and more,
let Pyrates then take care.
Thus for some time we liv'd, and Reign'd
as masters of the Sea,
Every Merchant we detain'd,
and us'd most cruelly :
The Treasures took, we funk the Ship,
with those that in it were,
That would not unto us submit,
let Pyrates then take care.
Thus Wickedly we every day
liv'd upon others good,
Ore which, alas! we would repay
now with our dearest blood,
For we as no one mercy had,
nor any to us spare,

How can we then for mercy look,
let Pirates then take care.
We thus did live most cruelly,
and of no danger thought,
But were led, as you may see,
for all our ill we bought,
For, Thro' fear of *England*,
at lest the Guilt was,
And now we very day must dye,
let Pirates then take care.
Now farewel to this wicked World,
and our Companions too,
From whence we quickly shall be hurl'd
to clear the way for you,
For certainly if we pursue
to Justices we are,
We here do rest till be your doom,
then Pirates all take care.

LONDON: Printed for Charles Barnet, 1696.

CHAPTER FIVE

The Aftermath

The East India Co., or to give the Company its full title, 'The Company of Merchants of London Trading into the East Indies', was awarded its first charter by Elizabeth I in 1600. By 1610 the Company had built its first factory, as their trading posts were known, at Surat, one of the busiest ports on India's west coast. Over the following years the English factory at Surat grew increasingly wealthy so that in 1638 the traveller Albert de Mandelslo was able to write:

> At the entrance to the house I met the President [of the English factory], with his second… The President, who spoke Dutch very well, told me I was very welcome; that in the country where we then were, all Christians were obliged to assist one another… He thereupon brought me to his chamber, where there was a collation ready. It consisted of fruits and preserves according to the custom of the country. As soon as we were set, he asked me what my design was, and understanding that I intended to return to Germany within twelve months, he told me I was come too late to get away that year, by reason no more ships would come that way, but that if I would stay with him five or six months, till there was a convenience of passage, he would take it kindly… This obliging discourse soon prevailed with me to accept of these proffers, so that he showed me all the house that I might make choice of a convenient lodging, which I took near his Second's chamber. In the evening, some merchants and others belonging to the President, came and brought me from my chamber to supper into a great hall, where was the Minister with about a dozen merchants, who kept me company, but the President and his Second supped not, as being accustomed to that manner of life, out of a

fear of overcharging their stomachs, digestion being slowly performed, by reason of the great heats which are as troublesome there in the night time as in the day. After supper the Minister carried me into a great open gallery, where I found the President and his Second taking the coolness of the sea-air. This was the place of our ordinary rendezvous, where we met every night; to whit, the President, his Second, the principal merchant, the Minister and myself; but the other merchants came not but when they were invited by the President. At dinner he kept a great table of about fifteen or sixteen dishes of meat, besides the desert.

The respect and deference which the other merchants have for the President was very remarkable, as also the order which there was observed in all things, especially at Divine Service, which was said twice a day, in the morning at six, and at eight at night, and on Sundays thrice. No person in the house had but his particular function, and their certain hours assigned them as well for work as recreation. Our divertissement was this ordered. On Fridays after prayers, there was a particular assembly, at which met with us three other merchants, who were kin to the President, and had left as well as he their wives in England, which day being that of their departure from England, they had appointed it for to make commemoration thereof, and drink their wives' healths... every man was at liberty to drink what he pleased.[1]

Dr Fryer, a Company surgeon, was stationed at Surat later in the century and left an excellent description of the fabric of the English factory in 1674:

The House the English live in at Surat is partly the King's gift, partly hired; built of stone and excellent timber, with good carving, without representations; very strong, for that each floor is half a yard thick at least, of the best plastered cement, which is very weighty. It is contrived after the Moor's buildings, with upper and lower galleries, or terrace-walks; a neat oratory, a convenient open place for meals. The President has spacious lodgings, noble rooms for counsel and entertainment, pleasant tanks, yards, and an hummum to wash in; but no gardens in the city, or very few, though without the city they have many, like wildernesses, overspread with trees... It is known, as the other factories are, by their several flags flying.[2]

In 1661 Charles II married Catherine of Braganza, and included in her dowry were a number of Portuguese colonies whose ownership now passed to England. In India the Company found themselves with a new factory at Bombay. For the while Bombay remained subordinate to Surat, but because of its superior size slowly grew in importance. The Portuguese had colonised the island of Bombay years earlier, and by the time it passed to the Company it had several splendid churches and adequate housing. It was, however, a pestilential place, and Dr Fryer listed a number of common diseases which were prevalent there, including, 'fluxes, dropsy, scurvy… gouts, stones, [and] malignant and putrid fevers'.

Nonetheless, the Company determined to make full use of the new colony, and began to ship women out so that the island might become a permanent colony rather than a mere trading post. The unwholesome, fever-ridden climate was not conducive to child rearing, and it was reckoned that the only healthy children were those born of a European father and Indian mother. Despite these difficulties the colony grew, and by the time Every arrived in the region it was strong enough to be made the seat of Company government in western India. Between 1661 and 1695 the colony at Bombay suffered several attacks at the hands of the Indians, and even a rebellion led by the Company's own soldiers, so the factory at Surat remained vital to the Company's trade in western India wherever the council sat.

The first of Every's victims to reach Surat, on 11 September 1695, was the *Fateh Muhammad*, presumably because she had suffered less damage at the pirates' hands than the *Gang-i-Sawai*. Rumours had already filtered back to Surat of the depredations of the pirates, but the crew of the *Fateh Muhammad* added their first-hand accounts of their suffering to the melting pot, and the damaged state of the ship spoke for itself. True to form Abdul Ghafur placed the blame for the outrages firmly at the door of the East India Co., whose employees in Surat were naturally the chosen victims of his fury.[3]

The president of the East India Co.'s factory at Surat at that time was an able and efficient man, Samuel Annesley. Annesley had arrived in India in 1678, working for the East India Co. at Bombay, and was shortly afterwards transferred to Surat. At Surat his steady and reliable services led him from a junior role to a place on the factory's council. When President Harris, Annesley's superior, died in May 1694 Annesley was elevated to the senior position at Surat.[4]

Annesley, too, had heard the rumours about the depredations of English pirates in the region and had the good sense to recall all his employees to the East India Co. compound. In fact, Annesley and his superiors in Bombay had anticipated some form of revenge against them from the Indians since they had first heard of Every's presence at Johanna, so the present crisis was no surprise to them. Although the Company did not possess great stocks of arms and ammunition, nor stockpiled provisions at Surat, the walls of the factory were tall and the gates strong. The angry mob outside the walls was doubtless frightening, but there was little they could do to jeopardise the safety of the English within.

Within a few hours the Indian military commander of the city, Ushor Beg, arrived at the factory with a troop of cavalry and demanded to be allowed entry. Seeing little advantage to be gained by offending the city officials at this tender time the Indian soldiers were allowed into the compound where, they announced, they would remain to protect the English from the mob outside.

Deprived of any hope of storming the compound the mob outside soon receded, but the soldiers remained within the compound walls as an assurance against the mob rallying. That evening several of the prominent merchants and religious and political men of the city went to the palace of the Governor, Ahmanat Khan, demanding reparations. The governor, though he must have been weary of hearing tales of English pirates and their atrocities, was well aware that the East India Co. had no direct involvement with the crime and refused to take any action beyond referring the case to his superiors at Aurangzeb's court.

Two days later however, on 13 September, the battered *Gang-i-Sawai* limped into port, and the whole situation changed. The Grand Moghul's ship was a holy vessel, sacred and sacrosanct, and the heathen English 'hatmen', as Europeans in India were often called, had violated that. The ship had been looted from keel to deck and the pilgrims aboard had been abused. Worse, many of the victims were female pilgrims who had had their honour befouled. The sack of the *Fateh Muhammad* had been bad, but the fate of the *Gang-i-Sawai* was unforgivable. The clamouring of the crowd on the Indian summer morning raised a din that nobody could ignore.[5]

That the villains were English there was no doubt, 'The [captain] and merchants, with one voice, proclaiming that they were robbed by four English ships.'[6] (The fourth English ship, if it was not an invention of the aggrieved merchants, was presumably the *Fateh Muhammad*, which, though it apparently played no part in the fighting, had been present and was manned by an English prize crew).

Even without the clamouring of the *Gang-i-Sawai*'s crew the blame would surely have been laid at the door of the English anyway. Pirates of all nations cruising in the eastern seas habitually flew English colours, and over the course of the preceding decades this practice had given the English a reputation for piracy which was perhaps only partly deserved. Occasionally foreign pirates were captured and shown not to be English, but that had little effect on the Indian people's automatic association of piracy with the English.

Naturally the East India Co.s of other European nations were quite happy to encourage the notion that all pirates were English, for a fall in the standing of the English often meant greater opportunity for themselves. Only very rarely by this time had ships of the English East India Co. fallen foul of pirates, mostly due to their superior size and firepower, but this too was seen as evidence of collusion at least, if not downright alliance between the Company and the pirates. However hard the English protested their innocence a mass of circumstantial evidence (not to mention the fact that many of the pirates in the area were English) weighed against them.

It rarely took long for news to travel around India in the late seventeenth century, and it was often difficult for Company officials to keep their workings secret. There is no record that news of the letter Every had left at Johanna ever leaked out, but it would not be surprising to find that its contents were known. If that were the case then there was distinct evidence that the East India Co. was in league with the pirates, for why else would Every have promised not to harm English shipping, even to the extent of arranging a signal to be made by 'friendly' ships?

The East India Co. men, both at Surat and Bombay, protested their innocence, of course. They argued that not all pirates were English; Sir John Gayer, the Company's president at Bombay, wrote:

> How often have we been falsely charged, nay, how often hath it been proved so, and yet upon every fresh alarm of a pirate on the coast all is still laid upon the English… Hath it not been sufficiently proved that that rogue that did so much mischief for two years together (all which was falsely charged on the English) was done by people of another nation and not the English.[7]

Whatever the nationality of the pirates mentioned by Gayer (he was perhaps referring to a Danish privateer squadron active off the Indian coast 1686-88, or to the string of piracies which had led to the imprisonment of the English at Surat in the early 1690s mentioned in the last chapter), this argument fell on deaf ears. Time and again it had been proven that when it came to piracy against Indian ships the English would bear the blame, whether they deserved it or not. In the case of the *Fateh Muhammad* and the *Gang-i-Sawai* there was no doubt that the pirates really were English, so Gayer tried a different line of reasoning:

> …and we further say, suppose it should be proved there is English pirates in the seas as well as other nations, is the English East India Company to be charged with their crimes? How unreasonable a thing would that be. Has not the great King of Hindustan [Aurangzeb] many pirates on his own coast of his own subjects that robs and plunders the vessels of his own as well as the subjects of others, notwithstanding all the care he takes to prevent it?

Even if the pirates were English, why should the East India Co. take the blame for their depredations? And Gayer could prove that the Company had nothing to do with Every and his band:

> …can it be imagined, if we were guilty of such horrible crimes as is laid to our charge by vile and unreasonable men as to rob the King's ships and bring their money so robbed to Bombay, that we should at the same time send a ship of so considerable cargo to be landed at the King's port [Surat] and supply his subjects with so large a quantity of guns?[9]

Unfortunately, Gayer's arguments of logic had little sway against the apparent proof of the East India Co.'s involvement in Every's piracy. Several of the *Gang-i-Sawai*'s crew were prepared to testify that they had recognised some of the pirates as men they had last known in the service of the English East India Co. at Bombay. The captain was even saying so in public.[10]

Whether this was true or not is difficult to ascertain. Certainly there is no evidence that Every added any Englishmen to the crew of the *Fancy* in the Indian Ocean or Red Sea, but the movements of the *Pearl*, *Dolphin* and *Portsmouth Adventure* prior to their meeting Every at the Babs are obscure. It is thus possible that some disaffected Company men joined one of the smaller vessels at Madagascar, Johanna, or some other port of call. It may also have been that some of Every's men had been in the service of the East India Co. much earlier in their careers, for there were certainly men aboard the *Fancy* who knew the eastern seas, but if that were the case it must be questioned whether anyone amongst the crew of the *Gang-i-Sawai* would have recognised them after the intervening years.

So it was that in Surat there was no question but that the English, personified by the East India Co., were responsible for the shocking crimes which were being reported about the city. The mob raised their voices and banged at the gates of the factory, and there must have been some doubt amongst the English within and their Indian guards whether they could hold off a determined attack by the enraged masses.

No longer could Ahmanat Khan afford to rest and wait for the advice of his masters. He dispatched a strong force to hold the English factory and sent his soldiers about the city to round up every Englishman, whether they were servants of the Company or not. At the port the East India Co. ship *Benjamin* (coincidentally the same vessel which had carried Every's letter from Johanna to Bombay) was unloading her cargo. Most of the crew were aboard the ship, but some of the men and several officers, including Captain Brown, her commander, were at that moment on shore. They were swept up with the rest and taken to the compound. The crew left aboard watched helplessly as their captain and comrades were carried away, but had little idea why. They sent one of their number ashore to the caravanserai, or market, to see what news he could find, but he too was gathered up by the governor's men and sent to the compound.[11]

Also in the city were a number of English interlopers, traders who did not operate under the auspices of the East India Co., including at least two, Messrs Vaux and Uphill, who had previously been in the employ of the Company but had left to go into business for themselves. Thus, within the walls of the compound was a very mixed bag of some fifty or sixty men, merchants, bureaucrats, accountants, seamen, and hated interlopers who could not be considered friends of the East India Co.

No longer were the soldiers in the compound there to protect the Englishmen from the native mob; the English were now prisoners and the soldiers their guards. The English were all placed in chains, their writing materials were confiscated, and planks were hammered over the windows. Extra guards were also sent to the factory so that the prisoners had a constant watch over them, with approximately four or five guards for each prisoner.

On the *Benjamin* the crew left aboard finally found out by some means the cause and nature of the uproar, and the remaining officers concluded that the best service they could render their captain and shipmates (and indeed themselves) was to sail at once for Bombay and report the day's events at the Company headquarters there. Unfortunately, because they had been in the middle of unloading their cargo they had not yet taken on any fresh supplies, and could not hope to make the voyage without them. Two Dutch ships in the harbour had so far escaped the wrath of the mob, but their captains were too afraid to offer the Englishmen any supplies in front of Indian eyes. One of the ships was, however, ready to sail for Batavia (now Jakarta), and offered to supply the *Benjamin* with enough supplies to reach Bombay once they were out at sea, so the two ships sailed out of Surat together. True to their promise the Dutch handed over some of their supplies and the *Benjamin* reached Bombay a short while later.[12]

Over the following days Ahmanat Khan showed the diplomatic skill which had qualified him for his job as governor. Even Samuel Annesley commented that the governor's actions were completely fair under the circumstances. Faced with a city in uproar he could do nothing less than imprison the English, but all along he refused to accede to the mob's demands for summary revenge. As a result of his fair-handedness the governor himself became the victim of accusations of collusion with the pirates, and it was even rumoured that he had received a share of the plunder. Nonetheless, he stuck to his guns (literally). On 16 September a meeting of Surat's council was due to be held, but the proceedings were dominated by the presence of some of the victims from the *Fateh Muhammad* and *Gang-i-Sawai*, including some of the women who had been violated. The victims shouted out accounts of the abuses they had suffered, the fortunes they had lost, and their relations who had been killed, so Ahmanat Khan called the meeting to a close and had his soldiers inform the mob that the English were in chains and that a report had been sent to Aurangzeb himself for consideration. He would do nothing until he heard back from the Grand Moghul.

Four days later another meeting was called, but again the multitude filled the council chambers, demanding that the English were brought forth immediately to be executed, or at the very least for some form of corporal punishment. With great presence of mind the governor asked one of the kazis (an Indian judge) present whether it was legal under Muslim law for such a summary punishment to be inflicted. The kazi responded that unless positive proof of the prisoners' involvement with the pirates was brought forth no such punishment could legally take place. The mob remained unsatisfied and one man threatened the governor himself, so the soldiers present were ordered to physically eject the crowd while the governor retired to his home. Such was the fury on the streets that even the military commander, Ushor Beg, did not dare show himself in public.[13]

Annesley managed to find some writing materials from somewhere and was permitted to open a correspondence with Ahmanat Khan. He stressed the innocence of the East India Co., and put forward several good indications of their lack of complicity:

> If we were [pirates] would we live amongst [the Indians] and bring so many 100,000 rupees' worth of goods to the city? ... Were we pirates would we rob under our own colours and tell everybody who we were? No, rather if we had plundered the ship we should have sunk her, that 100 years after none should know what had become of her... Is their King answerable for any of his runagate subjects that may do mischief abroad? No more is our prince or we for those of his that have shook subjection to the laws and pirate it up and down.[14]

He concluded with a request that he should be allowed to write to his superiors in Bombay, informing them in detail of events. Annesley's arguments evidently had some effect on the governor, for he was granted permission to write to Bombay, but the innocence of the English prisoners was still in some doubt as a result of the *Gang-i-Sawai*'s crew's assertions that several East India Co. servants had been amongst the pirates. Any further concessions would have to come from Aurangzeb himself.

Meanwhile in Bombay the news brought by the *Benjamin*, and later the missives from Annesley, had resulted in a flurry of letters being sent by Gayer all across India. He had written to Ahmanat Khan, to all of the local courtiers and officials – probably including Kazim Khan, an Admiral who commanded a large Army not far from Bombay – and to an Armenian merchant at Aurangzeb's court by the name of Issa Cooley, who he hoped would represent the East India Co.'s case to the Grand Moghul.[15]

Of course, since Gayer had been unable to get any reliable details of what was going on at Surat until Annesley was permitted to write to him, the Grand Moghul had already heard much of the events before any letter from Bombay reached his court. As well as the personal affront suffered as the owner of the *Gang-i-Sawai*, Aurangzeb was also a devout Muslim who viewed the atrocities meted out by the pirates with as much righteous horror as did his subjects at Surat.

Orders were immediately sent to seize the assets and employees of the East India Co. and, most ominously of all, Kazim Khan was ordered to take his army and capture Bombay. The English were to be entirely ejected from India.

Sir John Gayer's letters though had had some effects. In the event it was not the Armenian Issa Cooley who intervened with Aurangzeb on behalf of the English, but the Prime Minister, Assat Khan, who had been paid 30,000 rupees for his troubles. He soothed Aurangzeb's anger, pointing out the great loss to trade which would result from the expulsion of the English, and he echoed the arguments that Annesley and Gayer had put forth earlier that the East India Co. could not be held responsible for the actions of individuals, whatever their nationality, over whom they had no control.

Gayer's letters to Kazim Khan had won him friends closer to home, and the Admiral wrote to Aurangzeb via Assat Khan:

> O King of kings, the English are great merchants and drive a vast trade in your country. 'Tis well, for in these days Sir John Gayer, General for the English that live in Bombay, does very good service to the subjects of your Majesty and that in every respect. There are a great many hatmen thieves in these seas, but such business is not from the English caste, nor never will be.[16]

His anger much abated by his high-ranking officials, Aurangzeb cancelled the orders to banish the English, but insisted that they, along with the Dutch and French East India Co.s, send ships out to search for the pirates, and also undertake to protect the pilgrim fleets in future years. Gayer had, in fact, already offered a similar service. He wrote that as soon as Captain Brown and his men were released from Surat the *Benjamin* would be sent out as far south as Johanna to attempt to find the pirates, and that provided the shipping expected from England arrived safely two ships would be detailed to guard the convoys to Mocha and Jeddah.

The French and Dutch, who had been enjoying watching the downfall of their English rivals, were naturally distressed to hear that they were included in the demands made by Aurangzeb. In the case of the French at least the order was probably fair since large numbers of pirates of that nation had been roving the eastern seas, and a large proportion of Every's crew were French. In any case, whether they considered the order to be fair there was little or nothing either the French or the Dutch could do but comply.

When news of Aurangzeb's change of heart reached Surat the English anticipated that their incarceration would soon be over, but the wheels of bureaucracy moved as slowly in the seventeenth century as they ever have and the official proclamation did not reach that city until the very end of the year. On 6 January 1696, after nearly four months locked up in the Company factory, Annesley sent a bond to provide ships for convoy duty to Ahmanat Khan. The sorry business having been satisfactorily concluded, the English expected to be released shortly. Sadly for the long-suffering Annesley, that was not to be the case.[17]

Now that Aurangzeb and his officials had obtained the bonds they sought from the English they were in no hurry to release their prisoners, and Annesley had little left to bargain with. A bribe of 2,000 rupees was paid, but still the prisoners remained in chains. In fact, the only real effect the bribe had was to awaken other Indian officials to the potential of extracting further bribes from the English.

Within the walls of the factory tensions mounted. Rumours began that the only reason for their continuing incarceration was the refusal of Annesley and his council to pay a further bribe of 10,000 rupees. One evening the interlopers Vaux and Uphill settled down to a mammoth drinking session with the seamen from the *Benjamin*, and as the evening wore on the conversation turned to the perceived miserliness of Annesley, and gradually became more and more mutinous, so that by the end of the evening there was open talk of Annesley's assassination.

Once clearer heads prevailed all thoughts of murder were more or less forgotten, but word of the plot reached Annesley. Throughout their imprisonment Uphill, and particularly Vaux, had been grumbling and discontent thorns in Annesley's side, and though it was probably just the drunken bravado of unhappy men Annesley was alarmed by the apparent plot against him. The secretary of the Surat Council was sent to interrogate Vaux, but the interloper refused to cooperate and merely used the interview as a platform to express his dissatisfaction and animosity towards Annesley. Uphill was similarly unhelpful when he was questioned, but rather than rail against his predicament merely told the council that he could not remember anything about the plot, having been drunk when it was discussed.

Annesley was not satisfied, but there was little he could do. The incident left an unpleasant aftertaste on the already strained atmosphere within the factory walls. Vaux walked about, no longer attempting to conceal his contempt of Annesley. Tension ran high, with tempers to match, and a few days after the discovery of the drunken plot Vaux threatened one of the Indian guards with physical violence. Ushor Beg gave Annesley full authority to punish the inhabitants of the factory at his own discretion, but aware of the strains they were all under he chose only to verbally censure Vaux.

The next mutinous plot to spread through the factory was not directed against Annesley personally, but if it had succeeded it would have put immeasurable extra strain on the negotiations which were ongoing between the East India Co. and the Indian government. The *Benjamin*'s seamen, incited by another interloper, Alexander Hamilton, began to make plans for fighting their way out of the factory. Using a great deal of diplomacy and supported by a carefully worded letter from Sir John Gayer the tired and ill Annesley managed to persuade the seamen to abandon their plan. Robbed of the opportunity to relieve their violent frustrations against their captors the prisoners soon turned on one another, and a series of fights broke out over the following days and weeks until Annesley stopped the daily ration of strong drink.

By a miracle of strong leadership Annesley succeeded in holding the little band under his command together for over six months until, on 27 June, orders arrived for their release and the resumption of trade with the English factory. For nine months the English residents at Surat had been kept shut up together, and the wounds which had been opened during that time would take much longer to heal. With the end of their imprisonment Annesley had a fresh set of concerns to worry about, not least that Vaux and his cronies continued to go about Surat inciting hatred of the Company. Nevertheless, for now the Company was free to carry on business as before.[18]

Aurangzeb's measures against the Company, particularly in the months between the arrival at Surat of the *Gang-i-Sawai* and the end of that year, might have affected English trade in India permanently, and it was only through the great efforts of diplomacy by Annesley and Gayer that the worst of their consequences were avoided. It is not too much to say that if Aurangzeb had succeeded in driving the East India Co. from the sub-continent in the closing months of 1695 the balance of power in the East might have been irrevocably changed. Over the course of the next century the international politics of the principal European nations were governed to a large extent by consideration of their colonies, and without the great wealth of India at its disposal England could not have become the great superpower it did. The actions of the pirate band led by Every over the course of a week or so very nearly tore the British Empire asunder before it had really begun. Few pirates can be credited with such an effect on the history of the world.

While Annesley and his colleagues were suffering captivity for the crimes of the pirates, Every and his men were settling down to divide their plunder. According to the promise made by Every immediately after the mutiny each man would have a share in the spoils.

While the pirates were sharing out the loot Captain Wake arrived in the *Susanna*. He and Tew had sailed in consort for a while after losing the *Fancy* and the others, but they had become separated and there was no news of the *Amity*.

The crews of the smaller vessels would as a matter of course be included in the division, but it was argued that as the *Portsmouth Adventure* had not taken part in any of the fighting Farrell's men should receive no share. In the end Farrell and four others were given a share for their part in the battle with the *Fateh Muhammad*. The men of the *Pearl*, who had joined in the battles, could expect shares equal to those received by the *Fancy*'s crew. The *Susanna*'s crew, of course, received no shares, but they had captured another ship while crossing the Indian Ocean, and shared out £100 per man amongst themselves.[19]

While the pirates had been searching the *Fateh Muhammad* and *Gang-i-Sawai* for their main cargo of valuables each man was allowed to search the ship on his own account, and take what clothing and provisions he wished.[20] Coins, specie, gems and other valuable goods were turned over to the communal pile for a fair division. Estimates of the value of the treasure varied wildly. The Indian merchants calculated the value at somewhere in the region of £600,000, but one would naturally expect them to exaggerate their losses. Englishmen in India estimated the figure to be closer to £325,000, and while it might be expected that they would deliberately seek to underestimate the value of the treasure taken by English pirates, even this figure seems a little high.[21]

John Dann deposed that 180 men each had a share of £1,000. Even taking into account the value of some goods which were not immediately divided up, the value of the provisions the pirates took, and perhaps some valuables that individual pirates managed (against the rules) to secrete away for themselves, it is difficult to reconcile the amount which was lost by the merchants with the amount the pirates took. In fact, Dann was in error in stating that each man had a share of £1,000, and later corrected himself. The shares were not a uniform size, and each man received what the rest of the crew thought fit. Phillip Middleton reckoned that each man received £970, but many of the pirates who were captured had a different story to tell. John Sparks, who claimed that he was kept aboard 'as a kind of slave to wash their clothes, sweep the decks, and light their pipes,' only admitted to receiving a little over £100. William Bishop apparently was awarded £600 or £700, while Thomas Joy estimated that the average share was only £700 or £800 per man. It might be thought that the pirates were trying to play down the enormity of their crime, and this may have been the case in some instances, but in the matter of piracy a difference of £100 or so cannot have been of much interest to the authorities.[22]

At the trial of some of his shipmates Dann testified that 'some had £1,000, some 500, others 3,000'. Every himself received two shares, and Henry Adams received one share and a half, but with such varying amounts being awarded as shares it is impossible to determine just how much Every's pile amounted to. If we assume that when Dann *et al* speak of a £1,000 share for each man they are describing an average share then Every might have received £2,000, but if some men were awarded £3,000 then Every might have been given as much as £6,000. Perhaps when Dann mentioned a figure of £3,000 he was in fact speaking of the largest share, that of Every, in which case an average share might have been as much as £1,500, which would certainly make more sense of the total estimate of the plunder being in the region of £300,000. Alas, if the pirates kept meticulous accounts they have certainly not survived, so we can have no way of knowing for sure just how rich they made themselves.[23]

The boys among the crew were given proportionally smaller shares, from £100 to £500. In 1686 a new scale of pay had been established for the Royal Navy which remained in place until 1700. According to this rate, ships' boys received £6 2s 6d per year, so even a share of £100 represented over sixteen years' pay. A pirate who received £970 as his share would have to work in the Royal Navy for nearly seventy-five years to earn an equivalent amount.[24]

But wealth provokes greed, and greed in turn provokes dishonesty and treachery. Johnson relates that after the division of the plunder Every proposed to Mace and Farrell that the plunder would be safer if it was all stored aboard the *Fancy*. If the ships were separated by bad weather and either of the smaller vessels then met with a man-of-war they would risk losing their treasure. The *Fancy* was large enough to defend herself against almost any ship then in the eastern seas so could protect the gold until such time as they all met at a safe haven to divide the loot. The gold would be locked in chests, each with three seals to prevent their being tempered with.

> Upon considering this proposal, it appeared so reasonable to them [Mace and Farrell], that they readily came into it, for they argued to themselves, that an accident might happen to one of the sloops, and the other escape, wherefore it was for the common good. The thing was done as agreed to, the treasure put on board of Every, and the chests sealed; they kept company that day and the next, the weather being fair, in which time Every tampered with his men, telling them they now had sufficient to make them all easy, and what should hinder them from going to some country, where they were not known, and living on shore all the rest of their days in plenty. They understood what he meant, and, in short, they all agreed to bilk their new allies, the sloops' men; nor do I find that any of them felt any qualms of honour rising in his stomach, to hinder them from consenting to this piece of treachery. In fine, they took advantage of the darkness of that night, steered another course, and, by morning, lost sight of them.[25]

In fact, the treachery was not Every's.

In a world before the debasing of coins even foreign currency had a value based on the fact that it was made of gold or silver, and in Europe and the colonies, particularly in port towns, coins of different nations were in widespread use. It was commonly believed that gold was more universal than silver, so when the crew of the *Pearl* offered to swap their gold coins for an equivalent value in silver the men on the *Fancy* readily agreed.

Once the exchange had been made the pirates of the *Fancy* noticed something odd about the gold coins they had been given. It transpired that Mace's men had 'clipped' the gold coins, which is to say that they had carefully cut or shaved slivers of the precious metal from the edges of the coins, thus reducing their value. Although only a small amount of gold could be taken from each coin this could add up to a significant amount if it were done to a large number of coins, as it was in this case.

Outraged at this deception, the pirates of the *Fancy* returned to the *Pearl* and retrieved their silver at gunpoint, confiscating all of the treasure then aboard the latter ship. Outnumbered by at least three to one, Mace's men could do nothing to prevent this vengeance, and almost certainly made no attempt to resist it. Every granted 2,000 pieces of eight (about £450) for the *Pearl*'s crew to buy provisions, then abandoned his faithless consorts to their fate. Mace in the *Pearl* sailed back towards the Indian coast in search of fresh prey, while the *Portsmouth Adventure* was later wrecked on the Comoros Islands. Farrell had been deposed as captain for his perceived cowardice, it is likely that his men blamed him for their not having shares of the plunder, and Captain Want had been offered command in his place. Captain Wake announced that he would sail to St Mary's, and it may have been that he and Want sailed together until the loss of the *Portsmouth Adventure*.[26]

What happened to Thomas Tew and the *Amity* is a matter for some debate. Captain Johnson is, as ever, unreliable here, for in his chapter on Every, Tew does not figure at all until well after the action is over. In his chapter on Tew himself Johnson wrote:

> they met with and attacked a ship belonging to the Great Moghul; in the engagement, a shot carried away the rim of Tew's belly, who held in his bowel with his hands some small space; when he dropped, it struck such a terror in his men, that they suffered themselves to be taken, without making resistance.[27]

This passage has led many authors to assume that the *Amity* was present at the battles with the *Fateh Muhammad* and *Gang-i-Sawai*, and that Tew was killed during one of them by an Indian cannonball. However, John Dann stated quite categorically in his depositions that the *Amity* 'fell astern and never came up'. On the other hand, even if he was not involved in the subsequent fighting alongside Every it is clear that something happened to Tew, for Adam Baldridge recorded that on 11 December the *Amity* arrived at St Mary's 'having no captain, the former captain Thomas Tew being killed by a great shot from a Moors ship'.[28]

If Tew's men arrived at St Mary's in the *Amity* then they can hardly have been so disheartened by their captain's death that they gave themselves up, but Baldridge's records do lend some credibility to Captain Johnson's assertion that he was shot in the belly by a large cannon during a sea battle. However, as well as Dann having definitely stated that the *Amity* fell behind during the chase and that it did not catch up again, there is also no mention anywhere of the *Amity*'s crew either being given or denied shares in the great plunder from the Indian ships.

The answer may lie in a letter written shortly after the pirate cruise, which states that four vessels of the pilgrim fleet were captured by the pirates. Two vessels were taken by Every and his consorts, and one was captured by Wake. Perhaps the *Amity* alone came up with a fourth vessel. More likely perhaps is that the small vessel captured at the Babs, whose captain told Every that the pilgrim fleet had passed in the night, was one of the four vessels, and that Tew and the *Amity* had still been with Wake when he took his prize. Perhaps during the engagement Tew was killed and his crew, disheartened, retired from the fight, leaving Wake and his men to capture the ship and share out the plunder alone.[29]

Tew's piratical career was one of the most interesting of the seventeenth century, and it is a great pity that so much of it, particularly his demise, is so obscure.

CHAPTER SIX

The Pirates Scatter

Once the little fleet had separated Every declared his intention to take the *Fancy* to Providence in the Bahamas. In these formative years colonial governors often found themselves struggling to keep their colonies in a viable state. Money was frequently scarce, and most of the colonies were too far away from England for them to be able to expect help when it was needed. Moreover, many of the colonies were run as semi-private concerns, so their fates were in the hands of bankers and investors as much as the government.

The result was that corruption was rife. Colonial governors not only had to consider the financial state of their little colonies, but also their own financial situations. In an age when bribery and personal connections greased the wheels of administration, even in the European homelands, backhand dealing was endemic in many of the outposts of Empire. This cannot, of course, be said of all of England's colonies at the time. The more successful and viable colonies often relied on their own merits for survival, but in many of the newer colonies, or those without any notable resources, the situation was perfect for wealthy pirates to slip into obscurity. The simple truth is that when a large number of men brought a large quantity of ready money and valuable merchandise into a second-rate port the local authorities often could not afford, literally, to enquire too deeply into the source of the wealth.

By sailing to Providence Every hoped to find a pliant governor who would, for a sizeable bribe, allow him to dispose of the *Fancy*, and step ashore unhindered, ready to start living a respectable life once more. Providence was a good choice: the Bahamas were not a particularly wealthy colony, and were a safe enough distance from the centre of English power in the Caribbean at Jamaica.

From Providence the pirates would be able to find their way back into society, and having landed quietly and broken the gang up each individual would have a good chance of remaining undiscovered.

However, despite the many points in favour of Providence as a destination, the crew was divided. Many of the men wanted instead to sail for French Guiana, perhaps for the same reason that Every had suggested Providence. In many cases the governors of French colonies were in no better position to refuse the pirates entry than their English counterparts, and it must be remembered that a large proportion of Every's crew were themselves French.[1]

In fact, the first land that the *Fancy* touched at was Rajpur, where the pirates landed seeking water and supplies. Here the pirates were engaged in a small skirmish with the locals.[2] From thence the *Fancy* sailed to the island of Bourbon (now called Réunion), which was in French hands. Sometime either just before the pirates reached Bourbon or while they were actually there, the plunder was divided up and each man was given his share. Here all of the French and most of the Danish crew left the ship, along with several of the English pirates who hoped to settle ashore, and their berths on the *Fancy* were filled by Joseph Farrell and some of his men who had made their way to the island from Mayotte after the loss of the *Portsmouth Adventure*, and a number of newly purchased slaves.[3]

The pirates who landed on Bourbon had enough money to fulfil the pirate dream. Many of them bought land on the tropical island paradise and lived out their days managing plantations and living the easy life in the sun. In time they became well-respected members of the community. One of them, Dennis Turpin, even rose to become a member of the island's council.

Although Middleton deposed that all of the French crew landed on Bourbon, the following year the commander of a French naval squadron who called at the island reported that seventy men had settled there, of whom only twenty-five were French. It may be that the French wished to play down their compatriots' part in Every's piracy, but this doesn't seem likely. Perhaps the Frenchman made a genuine mistake, or was misled by the Bourbon islanders. The most logical (but not necessarily the correct) interpretation of the discrepancy might be that the French crew members of the *Fancy* had suffered the most casualties during the battle with the *Gang-i-Sawai*, and that out of fifty-two Frenchmen aboard when the ship left Johanna only twenty-five were still alive when she arrived at Bourbon. Some may have also been left behind at Rajpur. Whatever the truth, there do not appear to have been any Frenchmen left aboard the *Fancy*.[4]

Without the influence of the French pirates the crew were now prepared to follow Every to Providence. Calling first at Ascension Island the pirates 'turned' fifty turtles, which is to say that they flipped the creatures onto their backs so that they could not escape. It was common practice for live animals to be taken aboard ships and kept alive until they were needed, thus providing a supply of fresh meat.

From Ascension the pirates sailed the *Fancy* to the Portuguese island of Sao Thomé, not far from the site of their earlier piracies at Principe, where they purchased further supplies needed for the journey to the Bahamas. Despite the fact that Every and his men were wealthy beyond the dreams of normal men they chose not to pay for the supplies they received from the Portuguese. Instead, the governor of the island was given a 'Bill of Exchange drawn on the Bank of Aldgate Pump, attested by John – a Noakes and signed by Timothy Tugmutton and Simon Whifflingpin.'[5] Tugmutton and Whifflingpin were comical fictitious names, frequently used by Englishmen in this period. The Bank of Aldgate Pump was similarly fictitious. No Englishman would have fallen for such a bill, but Every presumably got away with it because the Portuguese governor was not familiar with the English sense of humour and comical devices.

One is tempted to imagine the smirks which must have crept across the pirates' faces as they loaded their supplies bought with the bill, or the exasperation of the governor when he tried in turn to pass the bill on to an English sea-captain, or perhaps even the patient good humour of the same sea-captain as he tried to explain the joke to the hapless foreigner. Whatever the case, it is enough to know that having sailed halfway around the world, pulled off one of the greatest robberies of all time, and indulged in rape and torture, Every and his pirates still enjoyed a good joke.

When the *Fancy* reached the Caribbean in April 1696 Every anchored off the sleepy island of Eleuthera, where a letter was written to Nicholas Trott, the governor of the Bahamas. The pirates had only two days' worth of supplies to sustain them, and so sent the letter straight away. The letter stated that: '…provided he [Trott] would give them liberty to come on shore and depart when they pleased… they promised to give the said Governor twenty pieces of eight and two pieces of gold a man and the said ship [the *Fancy*], and all that was in her.'[6]

According to Nicholas Trott, when he was later answering charges levelled against him regarding his collusion with the pirates, the letter also stated that the *Fancy* was short of provisions, and that her crew had 'done nothing for which they would not answer'.

Trott called a meeting of the council of the colony, where it was agreed that the *Fancy* and her crew should be allowed in to Providence. Trott claimed that 'nothing was known against' the ship or the crew, but this is hard to believe given the notoriety which had surrounded the *Fancy* as soon as the crew had mutinied. It was at Providence that Every appears to have changed his name, and started using the alias Henry Bridgman, and it is possible that Trott was genuinely taken in by the deception. It seems more likely though that the alias simply provided a convenient excuse for Trott to allow the pirates to land, since it was noted that the pirates had a suspiciously large amount of money. When the governor of Jamaica later wrote to Trott telling him that the men who landed were the notorious pirates led by Henry Every, Trott did not deny the fact, but merely pointed out that there was 'no proof'.

Every and his men claimed that they were interlopers in the Guinea trade, illegal traders defying the Royal Africa Co.'s monopoly. The slaves aboard, and Every's own knowledge of the lucrative African trade, would have helped in this deception, made necessary by the need to explain why the pirates requested safe conduct.

In any case, the overriding factor in the council's decision seems to have been that the adult white male population of Providence at the time was only around sixty men, while the well-armed pirate ship anchored not too far away had a crew of almost double that number. Furthermore, if the pirates were going to behave themselves, and Trott had no reason to believe they were not, then their presence would serve a useful purpose. The war with France which was being fought in Europe had also found its way to the Caribbean, and the Bahamas were in no state to mount a significant resistance if the French made any attack. The presence of a large ship, mounting many guns, and manned by an English crew, would be a serious deterrent.[7]

Trott sent a letter back to the pirates assuring them that they would be made welcome at Providence, and acknowledging their requests for 'liberty'. When the pirates read the letter a collection was organised, to which every man contributed the arranged twenty pieces of eight and two gold chaquins, while Every added forty pieces of eight and four gold chaquins. This amounted to a total of 2,280 pieces of eight and 228 chaquins (a little over £100), plus the *Fancy* and her contents. The contents of the ship included not only the guns, sails, tackle and spare cordage, but also fifty tons of valuable elephant ivory. No mention is made of the fate of the slaves collected at Bourbon, but since the pirates seem only to have taken their own personal and portable wealth from the ship it is quite likely that the human cargo was included in Trott's bribe.

Of course, the payment was not called a 'bribe': each man gave money as a bond or 'security' for his good behaviour. In the normal run of things such a bond should have been returned to each pirate when he left the island, but in practice Trott kept the money and shared it with his deputy. Whatever the pirates or Trott called the payment it was a bribe. Even in an age famous for its bribes this was an excessively large amount for a band of interlopers to pay. In particular, the gift of the ship itself must have made the Bahamians realise that Every and his men were no traders.

When the pieces of eight and chaquins had been collected a deputation led by quartermaster Henry Adams and consisting of Robert Chinton, Thomas Hollingsworth and possibly one other was sent to Providence to hand over the cash. Every and the *Fancy* followed, and on arrival at Providence handed the ship and her contents over to Governor Trott. Trott left his boatswain in command of the ship with a small crew of blacks, and started to unload the cargo of elephant tusks, 100 barrels of gunpowder, 'several chests of buccaneer guns', a (presumably large) quantity of 'small arms which were for the ship's use', as well as most of the ship's stores of sails, blocks and cordage. The value of the ship's cargo was estimated at £1,000.

It is possible that Trott also ordered the *Fancy*'s anchors to be removed to shore, and that this was the cause of the ship running aground two days after the pirates' arrival. There is, however, some suspicion that Trott secretly ordered the ship to be deliberately run aground, for when James Brown and other members of the crew (as well as some other men from Providence) offered to attempt to float her free their offers went unheeded. Trott concentrated instead on completing stripping the ship of anything of value. It may have been that the ship was in such a poor state after her long journey that it was not considered worth the effort to save her. Trott himself maintained that one of the reasons given by the supposed interlopers for wanting to anchor at Providence was the damage done by teredo worms, but Phillip Middleton later stated quite clearly that the ship 'was firm and tight' and he 'could not perceive she made the least water'. Interesting though this speculation is, the cause of the *Fancy*'s loss and Trott's subsequent attitude must remain something of a mystery.[8]

Once the pirates were ashore Trott repeated to them his promises of safe conduct, and even entertained them in his own home. While there, one of the pirates broke a glass and was made to pay eight chaquins. Most of the crew of the *Fancy* stayed at Providence only for a short time; many of them joined together to form three bands, each of which bought a small vessel. The *Isaac*, commanded by Thomas Hollingsworth, departed Providence in mid-May bound for Ireland; Every in the *Sea Flower* followed a few weeks later at the beginning of June. Many of the pirates preferred to take their loot and go their own way.[9]

Several of the crew of the *Fancy* remained at Providence. When John Graves arrived at the island a year later he reported that seven of Every's men were still living there, and that most of them had married. Amongst those who stayed at Providence was John Devin, the surgeon of the *Fancy*. He was put on trial by Trott's successors, but was found not guilty in August 1698. Only a few months later Devin travelled to New England – where he was again arrested and brought to trial at Boston. Fortunately he had been given a certificate declaring his innocence after his trial at Providence, and by producing it in court secured his release. Others of the crew remained in the Caribbean, but travelled to other islands, particularly Jamaica (where Edward Short was eaten by a shark).[10]

Three men, Daniel Smith and the brothers William and Benjamin Griffin, came from Bermuda, and returned there from Providence. With their plunder they bought large amounts of property. Smith and Benjamin Griffin were later arrested, though Griffin managed to escape jail with the help of the jailer William Brice. One of their friends and former shipmates, John Birch, had also been part of the gang that robbed the *Gang-i-Sawai*, but it seems that he had been aboard the *Pearl* for 'Griffin and Smith owned that their company robbed all the ship's company that Birch was in'. Smith and Griffin approached Birch's wife, Sarah, before their arrest, and offered her 'ten or a dozen pounds' in lieu of what had been taken from the husband.[11]

It will be recalled that the veteran buccaneer William Dampier had been one of the officers of the Spanish Expedition at the time of the mutiny. In 1699 he had the opportunity to meet three or four of the pirates for a second time when he sailed into Bahia, Brazil, in command of the Royal Navy vessel HMS *Roebuck*. During an acrimonious investigation following this voyage, the ship's lieutenant claimed that Dampier had met and fraternised with four of Every's men. Dampier himself claimed that there were only three: John Guy, the *Fancy*'s carpenter who had cut the anchor cables and perhaps threatened to hack Thomas Joy's leg off; Broadneck, a carpenter's mate; and Wastcoate, one of the seamen. Dampier's sympathy for the pirates is perhaps shown by the lieutenant's allegation that Dampier 'had promised not to hurt a hair of [Guy's] head'.[12]

Several of the crew made their way to North America, including William May, who travelled to Virginia and there took a ship for England. Welshman David Evans, who had joined the pirates from the *James and Thomas* at the Isle of May, made for Pennsylvania where he took ship for England, but was press-ganged en route and forced to join HMS *Tiger*. Edward Carwitheris, also originally of the *James and Thomas*, went further north, and in New England was recognised, and so changed his name to Edward Thomas and went to ground in the wooded wilderness which covered most of the province at that time. Eventually he made his way to Salem, Massachusetts, and got a job as a seaman on a ship bound for Bilboa. From there he sailed to England where in 1699 a game of skittles turned nasty and the two men he was playing with turned him in to the authorities. He was imprisoned in Newgate, but later released.[13]

Evans was also discovered, and when HMS *Tiger* arrived in England he was handed over to the authorities and was committed to Newgate prison at the end of January 1697. He remained in Newgate until he was brought to trial six months later on 12 July, and while there was joined by Henry Adams who had also been captured. When their case came to trial there could be found no evidence against them except the testimony of Phillip Middleton who, despite being a very able and intelligent lad, was too young for his evidence alone to convict them, and they were released.[14]

Josiah Raynor landed at Long Island, New York, with a chest containing over £1,000. A £50 bribe to Governor Benjamin Fletcher not only ensured his own protection, but also secured the return of his chest with its contents intact. John Elston, a cabin boy, was arrested in New Jersey, but was released on account of his tender years. Two pirates named Cornish and Downe were arrested and imprisoned in Rhode Island, but managed to escape. Rhode Island had long been known as a colony friendly towards pirates, and there is some suspicion that the pirates' escape was aided by the sheriff.[15]

Of the pirates who went to America, perhaps those who settled in Philadelphia had the best luck. Rumour had it that Governor Markham had received £100 from each of Every's men who sought his protection, and if true, it was certainly money well spent by them. Plantation owner and magistrate Robert Snead, newly arrived in the colony from Jamaica (where he had perhaps had enough of pirates), was horrified at the apparent collusion between the pirates and highest authorities, and his indignant letters provide us with many details. On 20 September 1697 he wrote to Sir James Houblon, owner of the *Charles II*:

> On the 10th of August 1696, a proclamation came into my hands and another to Mr Penn's deputy, William Markham, who took no notice of it… I went at once to the governor and told him that several of Every's men were here, well known to him and all persons… We all knew he had a great present made to him and his family by them and others of the same crew though not in the same ship, which they sank or burned. I… called upon two of my fellow justices to join me, who knowing the Governor's inclination at first refused, but on my threatening to send to England if they did not, at last consented. Three of the pirates were brought before us and there was sufficient proof that they belonged to the *Fancy*. I ordered them to be sent to jail, but one of my fellows went to the Governor, and he and the others were for bailing them, which they did, though I declared against it, and one pirate for another.[16]

In another letter written at about the same time to Edward Randolph, he complained that Markham's wife and daughter had overheard the meeting between himself and the governor, and that they had then gone personally to warn some of the pirates. The welcome given to the pirates, and the hostility shown to those who, like Snead, would oppose them, reached such a level that Snead was openly insulted and called 'informer' in the streets.

The letter continued, detailing again the coercion of the two magistrates, and the arrest and bailing of three pirates who put up bonds for one another. Apparently it was not just money which influenced the authorities in Philadelphia: magistrate Anthony Maurice ran to Governor Markham after Snead approached him, and it was noted that one of Maurice's family was married to one the pirates in question, Peter Claus.

A short while later Snead tried to arrest the three pirates, Claus, Robert Chinton, and Edmund Lassells, on the evidence of James Brown. Brown claimed not to have been a pirate, but merely to have hitched a ride on the *Fancy*'s voyage to Providence, and further claimed that he could identify Claus, Chinton, and Lassells as having been aboard. Even if this was true (which it was not, as he had presumably been aboard the *Susanna* when it took an Indian vessel before catching up with the *Fancy*), even if he hadn't been a pirate, he was certainly a disreputable rascal. Whether Brown's story was true, or whether he had in fact been a pirate, could have been easily checked, and the fact that it wasn't checked may owe something to the fact that he had married Governor Markham's daughter.

The three pirates were arrested and locked up, 'but soon after they were at liberty and went to their own houses'. Snead then went after some of the other pirates (who he unfortunately does not name), but again the governor intervened. Markham sneered at Snead and told him that the pirates he had arrested would not be kept in prison without good evidence. Snead assured Markham that he had the evidence, but was not prepared to divulge its nature until the trial. Markham replied that Snead was a rascal, and ordered the constables that Snead's commands need no longer be obeyed. He added an order to Under-Sheriff Curtis to strip Snead of his arms. Given the general violence of the times, and particularly the number of people who would happily have seen Snead dead, one must wonder at Markham's motives for the order.

There were however still some pirates in jail whom Snead had arrested before Markham stopped him, and they needed to be dealt with. Markham brought the matter up with the council, but the problem was a slightly complex one. At that time the American colonies did not have the power to hold Admiralty Courts, and piracy was a crime in the jurisdiction of the Admiralty, therefore the pirates could not be tried in Philadelphia. For the pirates to face trial they would need to be sent back to England, but that would only be done at the colony's expense, which the council agreed to pay. Since Markham was not much inclined to see the pirates brought to justice, and he certainly didn't want to pay for the privilege, he immediately dismissed the council.

But the council was not Markham's last obstacle. While the pirates remained in jail and Markham pondered on what to do with them, a messenger arrived from neighbouring Maryland. Snead had been corresponding for some time with Governor Nicholson of Maryland, who Edward Randolph claimed 'is really zealous to suppress piracy and illegal trade and was formerly very severe to those that were even suspected of countenancing pirates, so that not one of Every's men came to Maryland'. Nicholson had been kept appraised of Markham's actions by the wily magistrate Snead.

All of the governors and councils of the American colonies had earlier been sent a proclamation concerning the apprehension of Every's men, and only by pretending to be ignorant of this document could Markham maintain his charade. Markham had been shown the proclamation as soon as it had arrived in Philadelphia, but kept this fact a secret. When Snead tried to show the governor a copy he claimed that since Snead had no official status to present proclamations to the governor he was not obliged to pay it any attention. Now though, the messenger from Maryland brought a copy of the proclamation direct from Governor Nicholson, and Markham could not maintain his ignorance of its contents any longer:

> Proclamation by the Lords Justices of England for the apprehension of Henry Every, as in the proclamation of 17th July last.
>
> The East India Company reports that the said Every has changed his name, and now goes by the name of Henry Bridgman, and that among his crew are James Cray, Thomas Somerton, Edward Kirkwood, William Down, John Reddy, John Strousier, Nathaniel Pike, Peter Soames, Henry Adams, Francis Frennier, Thomas Johnson, Joseph Dawson, Samuel Dawson, James Lewis, John Sparks, Joseph Goss, Charles Faulkner, James Murray, Robert Richie, John Miller, John King, Edward Saville, William Phillips, Thomas Jope and Thomas Belisha, with fifty-two Frenchmen and fourteen Danes.
>
> They have taken plunder to the amount of about £1,000 a man.
>
> The said Every is reported to have left the ship in the island of Providence, and arrived with several of the persons above named in two small sloops in Ireland; some have stayed there, some have come to England and Scotland, as has been confessed by two of their accomplices, now in custody. They may probably be discovered by the great quantities of gold and silver of foreign coinage which they have with them.

Markham sent Under-Sheriff Curtis to the prison. What passed between him and the pirates will never be known, but the meeting went on for a 'considerable time', and the subsequent events enable us to make a reasonable guess.

When Snead heard that Governor Markham had officially received a copy of the proclamation he went to the prison and offered to order some extra men to guard the pirates if the prison was not strong enough. The sheriff refused Snead's offer. On the same day a prize-agent named Thomas Robinson, who had an interest in the fate of the pirates, told Markham that he thought the prison was not strong enough to hold the prisoners. Markham replied that the prisoners would be better secured in the very near future.

The following morning it was discovered that Chinton and Lassells had escaped. Robinson wrote:

> I waited on the Governor and complained of this, but was answered that he was
> not sheriff nor jailer… On that same day or next I went down to the jail and saw
> where a board of about fourteen inches by ten had been ripped off, but could not
> believe that men of their bulk could have crept through such a place, especially
> Chinton, who was a very fat gross man.

The implication was clearly that Markham had arranged the men's escape from
the prison before he had to relent and send them for trial. With the sheriff's
help 'Every's chief lieutenant' Chinton, and Lassells, who was 'some sort of
officer', had probably walked out of the front door of the prison. All Markham
had to do now was to go through the motions of pursuing them, without actually catching them.

On the morning of the pirates' escape Governor Markham called out the
law keepers and offered a reward of £5 for the apprehension of the two men.
By lunchtime they had been spotted hiding in some bushes in town, Chinton
apparently well armed with a sword, musket, and two pistols. Robinson rushed
to the sheriff with the news, but the sheriff dismissed the witness as mistaken.
Not to be deterred, Robinson next went to Markham and begged for a warrant to be issued against the pirates. Markham at first demurred, but eventually
agreed to sign a warrant filled with blank spaces which the sheriff could fill
in later. The sheriff in turn refused to fill in the blanks, so the warrant went
unexecuted.

A short while later the pirates remaining in prison were released without
bail, and Chinton and Lassells remained at large in Philadelphia, making little
attempt to hide their presence. Snead once more went to the governor requesting that action be taken against them, but Markham once again did nothing.

On 19 June one of the pirates, John Mathias, approached Robinson and
confessed to being one of Every's men. Two days later he was taken before
Markham and told the governor that apart from himself, Chinton, Claus,
Lassells and Brown there were none of Every's men in Philadelphia. He
added that a 'privateer' from Carolina was waiting to take some of the pirates
away: Robert Snead believed the captain of the privateer to have also been
one of Every's men. Mathias was released, Chinton and Lassells sailed on the
Carolina ship to obscurity and freedom, while Claus and Brown presumably
remained at home with their new wives. Brown's story was not quite over,
though. He remained in Pennsylvania until some more pirates, men that had
sailed with Captain Kidd, arrived in the colony seeking shelter. Kidd's robberies in the Indian Ocean had caused as great a stir as Every's and the authorities
were determined not to allow any of his men to escape as they had Every's.
Governor Markham could not afford to have questions asked about his protection of Brown, so Brown was sent with some of Kidd's men to Governor

Bellomont at New York, and thence to England where Brown was released for lack of any evidence against him.[17]

For most of the crew of the *Fancy* though, it was not the New World that they looked to – the voyage they had just completed had shown them enough new lands. With their fortunes in their pockets they wanted to return home. For a large number of them home was Britain: records often do not make clear where in Britain many of the pirates came from, as 'English' frequently might mean Scottish, Irish or Welsh. We know that some of the crew were definitely from Scotland, Ireland, or Wales, and it seems reasonable to suppose that some of the other 'English' crew whose exact origins are unknown may not have been English in the proper sense.

But to return to England as a group would mean landing somewhere together, and having to have a good cover story to prevent being immediately arrested. For each to travel independently or in small groups or pairs might have been easier in terms of slipping home without explanations, but given the sheer number of pirates compared with the number of England-bound vessels on which passage could be had the task would have taken years. The pirates needed a place they could land and then quickly separate, each man going his own way. They needed somewhere fairly close to home, where port officials were not likely to be too efficient or over-zealous, and where there was enough country for all the pirates to make themselves disappear. Ireland seemed ideal. Dublin was a long way from London, and the Atlantic coast of Ireland was a long way from Dublin. The pirates could land in Ireland, and should have no difficulty making their way home to England, Scotland or Wales.

The first vessel to leave for Ireland was the *Isaac*, commanded by Thomas Hollingsworth, which departed Providence about the middle of May. Aboard the *Isaac* were Robert Richie, sailing master of the *Fancy*, Robert Ogilby, Patrick Lawson, Thomas Johnson, James Stevenson, Edward Forseith, Thomas Castleton, William Bishop, Jacob Game, Richard Chope, Dennis Merrick, John King, Richard Saville, Edward Saville, John Miller, William Phillips, Thomas Joy, and an unfortunate man named James Trumble who was not one of the pirates but had come with them from Providence as a passenger. Off the Irish coast the *Isaac* was chased by a French privateer ship, and ran for the harbour at Westport, Co. Mayo. There is a certain delightful irony about the way the tables had turned on the pirates – no longer the desperate freebooters that had once been, they were now wealthy men forced to run from some other brigand.

Two or three weeks later a second vessel, the *Sea Flower*, commanded by Captain Farrell of the *Portsmouth Adventure* and bought by some of the crew for £600, set sail from Providence for Ireland, arriving less than a month later. The *Isaac* had made a similar time and had landed at Westport on 7 June. Aboard the *Sea Flower* were Henry Every himself, Henry Adams and Joseph Dawson, quartermasters of the *Fancy*, Thomas Johnson, ship's cook, Samuel Dawson, John Down, Peter Soames, Francis Wilson, James Hammond, Joseph Roy, John Sparks, James Grey, Charles Faulkner, John Reidy, John Dann, James Cragget, Nathaniel Pike, John Strousier, Robert Seely, James Lewis, Joseph Goss, James Murray, Thomas Somerton, Phillip Middleton, and at least one woman – the newlywed Mrs Henry Adams.[18]

The pirates were right to have chosen Ireland as a landing place. The *Isaac* had been lying at Westport for a full week before Thomas Bell, Sheriff of Mayo, was told of her presence. He rushed to Westport, but by the time he arrived only Hollingsworth and two others remained aboard. Bell's first concerns were about the cargo of the vessel: had she been carrying taxable goods? For some time following the landing of the *Isaac* the authorities were most concerned with the issue of taxable goods. Ready money was not taxable, but before sailing into Westport Hollingsworth had landed on the small island of Achill, where about a dozen men and a large quantity of baled goods had been put ashore. In fact one witness had seen eight pieces of muslin in the pirates' possession at Achill, and one of the pirates who had landed there was later apprehended with striped muslin, cottoned cloth, quilted linen, and a number of cravats and kerchiefs. All of these fabric goods were liable to duty, but there were no customs officers on Achill.

Hollingsworth told Bell that the only cargo had been gold and silver, which explained the lack of crew and passengers. Having been chased into port by a privateer the men on his ship had not wanted to put back out to sea with their pockets full of gold and so had all gone ashore. Once ashore they had scattered to the four winds. Horse traders had done a roaring business around Westport – so desperate were the pirates to break up and get as far away as possible that they paid 'ten pounds for a [horse] not worth forty shillings'.[19]

Ogilby, Lawson, Johnson, and Stevenson had all made for Scotland. Castleton, Bishop, and Merrick had gone to York, Exeter, and Bristol respectively. Richard Chope had perhaps intended to return to London to be with his wife, but on reaching Dublin decided instead to bigamously marry a local girl. William Phillips turned King's Evidence and gave information against his fellow pirates. Edward Saville eventually made his way to visit his wife in Wales, but on trying to return to Ireland was captured at Holyhead. From there he was sent to the prison at Beaumaris, but was later pardoned in exchange for appearing as a prosecution witness at the trial of some of his shipmates in Dublin. The King made a bad deal, for the pirates on trial were acquitted.

Sheriff Bell was able to redeem himself a little for his earlier misfortune in missing the pirates when he captured Edward Forseith and James Trumble. Bell found £200 in the men's possession and rushed to inform his superiors. Forseith and Trumble were sent before Sir Henry Bingham, but were released. Trumble had been entirely innocent of piracy, and was perhaps by now regretting his choice of travelling companions. Forseith headed for England, where he was arrested in Newcastle and sent to London for trial.[20]

John Miller eventually made his way to New England, where in 1703 he joined the crew of a Marblehead privateer, the *Charles*. The *Charles*, under the command of Captain Daniel Plowman, had been commissioned to attack French and Spanish shipping, particularly off the coast of Nova Scotia. New England had long borne the brunt of French aggression in America thanks to the colony's proximity to Canada. Many New England ships had been lost to French privateers, and Plowman and the *Charles* were sent out to settle the score a little.

However, Plowman was dangerously ill at the start of the voyage, and within the first few days had died. Command fell to the lieutenant, John Quelch, who instead of sailing north to Newfoundland set a course for the south. Off the coast of Brazil Quelch captured a number of Portuguese vessels, far exceeding the privateer commission in his possession, and all the worse for the fact that Portugal was England's newest ally in the war against France and Spain. The *Charles* sailed back to New England in the spring of 1703, and the company broke up. Almost immediately questions were asked about the large numbers of Portuguese coins Quelch had brought back, and arrest warrants quickly followed. Many of the crew escaped, but Miller was one of the unlucky ones who was taken and brought to trial at Boston. (Incidentally, while Chinton and the rest of Every's crew had escaped trial in Philadelphia because the colonies had no power to hold Admiralty Courts, legislation passed in the intervening years had made such courts legal, and the trial of Quelch's crew was the first such trial held in any colony under the new laws.)

Miller might still have escaped execution, as did many of his shipmates from the *Charles*, had he not bragged of his association with Every during the voyage. During his examination it was revealed that he had told others that he had been one of Every's crew. Although Miller denied that he had been aboard the *Fancy*, the double piracy secured his fate and he was hanged with Quelch and four others on 30 June 1704.[21]

Hollingsworth sold the *Isaac* to a pair of Galway merchants, Thomas Yeeden and Lawrence Deane, but retained his captaincy of her. He presumably took on some extra hands at Westport for the journey he made to Galway. At Galway there was more paperwork to be filled in or presented: clearance from the customs officers at Providence, customs declarations for the Irish authorities, bonds to be handed in against the ship leaving without proper permission. By August Hollingsworth had sailed again in the *Isaac*, steering back for Providence where he was to meet Thomas Wake of the *Susanna*. It would be a fruitless trip, for when his ship had been left behind in the chase of the *Gang-i-Sawai* Wake had sailed for the pirate haven at St Mary's and died there early in 1696.[22]

The pirates in the *Sea Flower* sailed for the north of Ireland, and landed at Dunfanaghy, Co. Donegal. At Dunfanaghy the pirates found an unscrupulous port official, Maurice Cuttle, who gave many of the crew passes to go to Dublin. John Dann deposed that he and his travelling companion, Thomas Johnson, gave Cuttle 3lb of gold for their passes, and that other members of the crew had made similar arrangements. If even half the pirates of the *Sea Flower* had paid a similar sum to Dann then Cuttle must have made a small fortune out of his blind eye.

Dann made his way to Londonderry, and from there to Dublin where he met up with several of his old shipmates. During the weeks following the pirates' landing many of them ended up in Dublin where their presence caused something of a stir. Thanks to the weight of money in their pockets the authorities had a hard time rounding them up, and in the event only a few were apprehended. Rumours abounded that Every himself was in Dublin, but nobody appears to have seen him personally. From Dublin Dann and Johnson sailed for Holyhead, and from thence went to Chester where Johnson lived. Dann continued alone to London, then on to Rochester where he was captured. Thomas Somerton and Nathaniel Pike also remained in Ireland for a while, but perhaps then made their way to Chatham, following a similar route to Dann. We shall meet Dann again in the next chapter.

Samuel Dawson was arrested in Dublin and released on bail. Brother Joseph tried to return home to Yarmouth in Suffolk, but was captured and taken to London for trial. John Strousier was also a Yarmouth man, but wisely remained in Ireland (though he was probably ignorant of Joseph Dawson's fate). The boy Robert Seely stayed in Ireland with Strousier.

Joseph Goss and James Lewis travelled together to Dublin and lodged at an inn there. When the proclamation against the pirates was read Goss and Lewis went to the authorities and volunteered large sums of cash and paper bills as a bond. They must have had second thoughts, and realising that their freedom in Ireland was far from guaranteed by the bonds they had given, made to leave. Goss was captured in Ireland, while Lewis managed to escape to England but was captured at Wapping.

Informer William Phillips believed that Henry Adams had remained in Ireland, but he also said the same of Thomas Johnson. When Adams left Ireland he probably went to Deptford where it was reported that he had friends living. Not far from Deptford was another of the slums of the metropolis which was a popular lodging place for seamen, Ratcliffe Highway. While James Cragget stayed for a while in Castle Street, Dublin, his wife waited for him at their home in Ratcliffe Highway. Cragget's story is one of the most interesting of the *Sea Flower* pirates'.[23]

The *Fancy*'s cooper, Thomas Joy, who had arrived in Ireland aboard the *Isaac*, eventually made his way to Wapping, and in 1699 gave information that he had recently seen another of the *Fancy*'s crew, James Cragget, in Norwich. Cragget had already been arrested the previous year and had spent three months in prison. Cragget's wife wrote to him, and in her missive mentioned various members of the *Fancy*'s crew, without naming names, and stated that several of them had managed to purchase pardons for cash. The authorities knew that Cragget was guilty: several people had mentioned his name in connection with the return voyage to Ireland, and the letter from his wife appeared to confirm his guilt. However, when he was interrogated he told a story which could not be disproved and he was released on the order of the secretary of state, there being no solid evidence against him.

When Joy brought Cragget to the attention of the authorities again the news was passed along to Norwich and Cragget found himself once more in prison. From Norwich he was sent to Newgate, where he was interrogated a second time. Cragget denied ever having been aboard the *Fancy*, but said that he knew Thomas Joy from when they had served together in the Royal Navy aboard HMS *Royal Sovereign* in 1692. With not enough evidence to convict him Cragget was released once more.[24]

The fates of most of Every's pirates have been lost to time, if they were ever known. Various reports exist of pirates being arrested and released, particularly in the colonies, but for the most part the pirates eventually found the quiet anonymity that they craved. Their success at going to ground can be attributed to a number of factors: the easy-going attitude of colonial governors and authorities towards men with money was certainly of great help to Every's men, and the tardiness of communication in the late seventeenth century made life difficult for those authorities who were zealous enough to pursue the pirates. Perhaps the greatest advantage the pirates had was the relative ease with which seamen could move from ship to ship, from port to port. The seafaring community of Europe and the colonies was huge and relatively fluid, making it easy for a man to 'lose' himself without too much difficulty provided he knew to keep his mouth shut and had a little bit of luck on his side.

Before leaving the pirates it is worth listing some of those whose fates can be roughly ascertained. On 27 August 1696 William Phillips and Edward Saville reported that a sloop had arrived at Kinsale bearing some of the pirates of the *Fancy*. James Brown, Chinton, Lassells and Claus had been aboard the sloop but had left it in America. From America it had then sailed to Ireland carrying William Caddy, Thomas Anderson, Edward Kirkwood, William Down, boatswain Robert Prince, James Cray, John Reddy and others. Despite several of them having been named in the Government's proclamation, these men disappeared across Ireland and were not heard of again.[25]

CHAPTER SEVEN

The Trial

O f the crew of the *Fancy* only six men were arrested and tried by the
Admiralty Court in London. John Sparks, Joseph Dawson and James
Lewis had sailed to Ireland with Every in the *Sea Flower* before making their
way to England. Dawson was taken at Yarmouth and Lewis was arrested in the
sailors' district of Wapping. William May had made his way from Providence to
Virginia, from whence he had taken ship for Bristol. From Bristol he travelled
by coach towards London, but only a short way into the journey he was arrested
and taken back to Bath. From Bath he was then sent under guard to London.
Edward Forseith and William Bishop were aboard Captain Hollingsworth's sloop
Isaac when she arrived in Ireland. Forseith was arrested in Ireland with £200 in
his possession, but was released and made for Newcastle, where he was arrested a
second time and brought to trial with the others. William Bishop made his way
from Ireland back to his native Devon where he appears to have tried to slip into
quiet obscurity as a tobacconist in Exeter before he was arrested.[1]

All six of the prisoners brought to trial had been part of the *Fancy*'s crew
since the mutiny at Corunna, and so they were tried for activities which had
taken place during the whole of the piratical cruise. The six men were tried
together, as was customary at the time.

On 19 October 1696 they were brought before several important and influential Admiralty and legal officials, and indicted for the piracy committed against the
Gang-i-Sawai. Prosecution witnesses included two former crew members, John
Dann and Phillip Middleton, and in fact, so important was their testimony that
the whole case virtually hinged on them. Among the witnesses for the defence
was William Dampier, along with other officers of the Spanish Expedition.

Both Dann and Middleton had sailed from Providence to Ireland on the *Sea Flower*. In Dublin Dann had met some of the men from the *Isaac*, and had then made his way via Holyhead to London, and then to Rochester. At Rochester a maid became suspicious of the weight of his jacket, and discovered that a large number of gold coins were sewn into the lining. The mayor of Rochester was alerted and Dann was arrested, but by turning King's Evidence was able to procure his eventual release. Middleton had only been a boy during the *Fancy's* cruise, indeed he was only thirteen years old at the time of the trial.[2]

Sadly the records of that trial have been lost and we are only able to reconstruct certain elements of it from peripheral documents, such as the subpoenas relating to witnesses and a brief summary recorded at the beginning of the published account of the second trial. Dr Newton, King's Counsel, began the trial with a stirring speech, designed to turn the jurors against the defendants, and filled with a mixture of patriotism and racism:

> Their last piracy was this in the Indies, the greatest in itself, and like to be the most pernicious in its consequences, especially as to trade, considering the power of the Great Moghul, and the natural inclination of the Indians to revenge: But they are now brought hither on their trial, and if the matters they are charged with shall be proved, to receive that judgement from you, [that] their crime deserves; and that is piracy, which by so much exceeds theft or robbery at land; as the interest and concerns of kingdoms and nations, are above those of private families, or particular persons: For suffer pirates, and the commerce of the world must cease, which this nation has deservedly so great a share in, and reaps such mighty advantage by: And if they shall go away unpunished, when it is known whose subjects they are, the consequence may be, to involve the nations concerned, in war and blood, to the destruction of the innocent English in those countries, the total loss of the Indian trade, and thereby, the impoverishment of this kingdom.[3]

Dawson, who had been a quartermaster aboard the *Fancy*, seems to have been despondent about the position he was in, and pleaded guilty. In an earlier statement he wished he had 'never gone [on] the voyage',[4] and was reticent about the taking of the *Gang-i-Sawai*. The other five defendants pleaded not guilty, and so the trial began. If the evidence given by Dann and Middleton elsewhere is anything to go by the case for the prosecution must have been damning. Conversely, since none of the defence witnesses had been present at the capture of the *Gang-i-Sawai* their testimony must have been of little relevance. It therefore came as a great shock to everyone – probably including the defendants – when all were acquitted by the jury.

The six men were not released however. Since they had only been tried for the taking of the *Gang-i-Sawai* they might yet be tried and found guilty of the other piracies they had committed, as well as for the mutiny and theft of the *Charles II*. It was on this last charge that they were brought back to the Old Bailey on 31 October and indicted before a different jury. Again Dawson pleaded guilty, while the rest pleaded not guilty, and the second trial began.

Sir Charles Hedges, the Admiralty judge, opened the proceedings by making clear what the charges against the defendants were, reiterating the importance of trade and sea-commerce, and reminding the jury of the grave responsibility to justice which they held. Further impassioned speeches were made by the prosecution, and the first witness, John Gravet, second mate of the *Charles II*, was sworn.

Gravet stated that on the night of the mutiny he was on watch on the deck when the boat arrived from the *James*. He was grabbed by the throat and threatened with a pistol, before being confined in his cabin. When Captain Gibson and the rest of the loyal crew were released into the pinnace Gravet was allowed to join them, but was prevented from taking any of his possessions. Every gave him a coat and waistcoat, and May shook his hand before he was sent over the side into the boat. The key pieces of information offered by Gravet were that nobody was held aboard the *Charles II* against their will, and that there was plenty of room in the boat for those who wanted it. Dawson, May, and Sparks were identified as having been aboard the *Charles II* at the time of the mutiny, though Gravet could not specify to what extent they were involved.

The next witness called was Mr Druit, mate of the *James*, who testified that Forseith, Lewis and Bishop had all been in the boat which went from that ship to the *Charles II*. When asked if the three defendants had been ordered into the boat or whether they had gone of their own accord he stated that they had been acting on orders.

The third witness, David Creagh, caused some concern when it was pointed out that he was currently a prisoner on a charge of treason. Lord Chief Justice Holt, one of the judges, ruled that his confinement for a crime for which he had not yet been tried did not necessarily impair his reliability as a witness. Creagh described the events which culminated in the mutiny, and in particular played up William May's part in the affair. Like Gravet he stated that nobody was refused entry to the pinnace, but noted that an exception was made for the ship's doctor, who was forced to remain aboard the *Charles II*.

John Dann, whose testimony had failed to secure a conviction during the first trial, was called next. He testified that word had been passed around the ship calling anyone who wished to go ashore to the boat. He, too, noted that the doctor was forced to remain aboard, but that 'no [other] man's name was mentioned to be stopped'. Dann identified May, Sparks, Forseith, Lewis and Bishop as having taken part in the mutiny, and most importantly when asked if they knew of the intention to mutiny replied, 'Yes, sir, they knew to be sure.'

What then followed must be of interest to students of law. Dann was extensively interrogated about the subsequent piracies committed by Every's crew, and in particular the defendants' part in them, including the taking of the *Gang-i-Sawai*. Yet the defendants were being tried on this occasion for their parts in the mutiny on the *Charles II* – they had already been tried and acquitted of the taking of the *Gang-i-Sawai*, and had not yet been indicted for the capture of any other vessels. When William May asked whether Dann could identify him as having taken part in the mutiny, the reply was negative.

Following Dann's testimony Phillip Middleton was called, and immediately stated that he knew nothing of the mutiny because he was asleep. He was then questioned about the subsequent activities of the defendants during the piratical cruise. Finally, when asked if any of the prisoners had been present on deck when Every gave leave to those who wanted it to go ashore, Middleton could not say that any of them had been.

The evidence given by Dann and Middleton regarding the piracies committed by the crew of the *Fancy* following the mutiny was succinct and damning, but the defendants were not on trial for those piracies. Having failed to obtain a satisfactory verdict in the original trial the authorities were taking no chances in the second.

With Middleton's evidence finished, the defendants were given the opportunity to speak. No witnesses were called for the defence, but the defendants were given the opportunity to cross-examine the prosecution witnesses. Forseith questioned Druit, who admitted that he, Forseith, was sent into the boat from the *James*, rather than having gone of his own accord. In an attempt to prove that the *Charles II*'s pinnace could not safely hold more men than had gone ashore May questioned Dann, who said that a bucket was given to the pinnace's crew to bail with.

Apart from those two incidents the defendants' case was mostly taken up with claims that they were forced to join the mutineers. Forseith claimed that he had held water with his oar (that is, he held the blade of his oar still in the water so that it acted as a brake), but could do no more by himself to prevent his being taken aboard the *Charles II*; Bishop also claimed that he had originally been ordered into the *James*'s boat by Druit, but when he was given the opportunity to question Druit he declined. Lewis also claimed to have been ordered into the *James*'s boat, and further stated that once aboard the *Charles II* he was forced into the forecastle by armed men. Sparks told the court that he had been beaten over the head when he came on deck during the mutiny. Only William May made any serious attempt to prove his innocence. He explained at some length that he had not been party to the plotting, and had not taken an active part in the mutiny, then continued to tell the story of his illness at Johanna, and his meeting with Captain Edgecomb.

The claim of having been forced into mutiny and piracy was frequently used by pirates brought to trial. In later years 'forcing' was a common way for pirates to recruit crew, especially artisans, and became almost a standard defence in court. Perhaps because it was so commonly used, but more likely because it was difficult to prove, it was rarely a successful course of action. For desperate men with their lives at stake it must have offered a glimmer of hope. The great difficulty was that even if a man could prove that he had been forced to join the pirates unwillingly (which he might be able to do by producing a witness in his defence), it still left open the question of whether he had always been unwilling or whether he had changed his mind later and joined in the subsequent piracies. Indeed, cases of men deliberately pretending to be forced, despite their actual willingness to join a pirate crew, just so they could use the plea of 'forcing' if they were ever captured, were not unknown.

In many cases the question hinged on whether or not the supposedly forced man had taken any part of the plunder. Whatever his original intentions, if he had joined in with piratical attacks and had profited by them then he was as guilty of piracy as a willing volunteer. Very occasionally a man was acquitted on the grounds that he had taken no share, but on the whole the plea of having been forced was rarely successful.

Like these other cases the question of whether any of the five defendants had received a share of the plunder was raised by the prosecution on this occasion. Dann categorically stated that all five defendants received a share of the profit. In fact, four of the defendants had earlier admitted to having received a share: May and Lewis each received about £500, Bishop had between £600 and £700, while Sparks claimed to have only been given a little over £100. Forseith had not admitted receiving a share, but as we have seen was taken with £200 in his possession.[5]

When the defendants had finished their case the King's Counsel summed up for the jury. His summation is worth reproducing in part here:

> ...It has been very plainly proved against the prisoners, that the ship *Charles* was run away with from the Groyn. And it is plain by two witnesses that all the prisoners at the bar were in this ship; by three [Gravet, Creagh, and Dann] that William May in particular was one of them; and by one that William May was so far concerned, that because J. Gravet seemed to dislike it, he said he deserved to be shot through the head: so that he that would make himself the most innocent of the five, is most guilty.
>
> Now they have only this to say for themselves, that they were forced to do what they did. But it has been proved to you that they were not forced; it was said, all might go that would. And it is not proved on their side, that any one of the prisoners did seem to dissent from their going away. It is proved that they all made

use of this ship to very bad purposes; that they took and plundered several ships, and shared the booty. We do not produce this to prove them guilty, but to show that they made use of this ship to this very purpose… They have said a great deal indeed, but without any manner of probability of truth. They have produced no witnesses for themselves, to prove any thing they have said. And the witnesses for the King have given testimony without any exception.

Lord Chief Justice Holt then added his comments before the jury withdrew. He reminded the jury of the basic facts of the case, and noted the apparent involvement of the five defendants, but then went on to say:

There was a consult, it seems, by some particular persons, of which Every was the ringleader, how to effect this design [the mutiny], Captain Every, as they call him; though he was no captain, but was under the command of Captain Gibson that had the conduct of this ship. It's true, it is not proved to you that these men were at the consult.

Holt then reiterated the evidence against each of the men, paying particular attention to that against William May, before telling the jury:

You have a great trust reposed in you, for you are not to act arbitrarily, but you are accountable to God Almighty, to whom you are sworn, and to the Government for the verdict you give. If you are not satisfied in your consciences that the evidence is sufficient to find these men guilty, in God's name, Acquit them.

But if you are satisfied in the sufficiency of the evidence to convict them, you must find them guilty.

The jury left the court room to consider their verdict, but returned only a short while later to ask, 'If there be any evidence to prove that John Sparks consented to the running away of the ship, we desire it may be heard again.'

In fact, there was very little evidence against Sparks, excepting the fact that he was aboard the *Charles II* at the time of the mutiny. Sparks claimed to have been knocked unconscious, and Dann testified that he could not remember seeing Sparks at all that night. The jury's interest in Sparks may have been because he was the youngest of the defendants – he was only sixteen or seventeen at the time of the mutiny – but more likely it was because the case against him appeared to be the weakest.

In response to their question the jury were told that the fact that he did not leave the ship with Captain Gibson and the others indicated his complicity. The jury went back to their deliberations, and after another short pause returned their verdict. All five defendants were guilty.

Sentence was not passed immediately, and the defendants were returned to their cells to await a third trial on 6 November 1696. This time the indictment against them was for the seizure of the two Danish ships at the Isle of Principe, and for the capture of the *Fateh Mohammed*.

Again, the star witnesses for the prosecution were John Dann and Phillip Middleton and, curiously, David Creagh. Since Creagh had been among those who departed in the pinnace with Captain Gibson after the mutiny his testimony can hardly have been relevant to the later piracies. The third trial was something of a formality, the defendants 'appearing to be very weak' did not put up much of a fight, and were found guilty. Dawson, Bishop, Lewis and Sparks threw themselves on 'the King's mercy' and the mercy of the court. Forseith protested his innocence, was told that he had received a fair trial, and eventually begged, along with May, to be allowed to be sent to India for punishment. Finally Sir Charles Hedges, the Admiralty judge, passed sentence:

> Joseph Dawson, you stand convicted upon four indictments, by your own confession, for piracy and robbery. And you Edward Forseith, William May, William Bishop, James Lewis, and John Sparks, having put ourselves upon your trials according to the customs and laws of your own country, have been found guilty upon three several indictments, for the same detestable crimes committed upon the ships and goods of Indians, of Danes, and of your own fellow subjects.
>
> The law for the heinousness of your crime hath appointed a severe punishment, by an ignominious death; and the judgement which the law awards, is this, that you and every one of you be taken from hence to the place from whence you came, and from thence to the place of execution, and that there you, and every one of you be hanged by the necks, until you, and every one of you be dead. And the Lord have mercy upon you.

The trials of the six men of Every's crew were marked by curious choices of witnesses, dubious and irrelevant testimony, and weak defence tactics. No doubt a modern barrister would balk at the procedures found in the Old Bailey in the autumn of 1696, and indeed it might be argued that the Admiralty acted more in the interests of expedience than justice. Had Dawson and co. escaped punishment the consequences, particularly in India, might have been severe, but whether that fear excuses the irregularity of the trials is open to debate.

Only in the first trial, for the seizing of the *Gang-i-Sawai*, were any witnesses called by the defence, and since those witnesses were not present at the event their testimony must have been of little relevance, except perhaps for establishing the good character of the defendants. Their absence in the second trial might be easily explained: if Dampier and his colleagues from the Spanish Expedition were sympathetic to the defendants' cause they may have felt that they would do more harm than good during the trial for mutiny. They might have provided good character references, perhaps even made the court aware of the unsatisfactory circumstances which led to the mutiny, but they could not have denied that the defendants took part in that mutiny.

David Creagh's presence at the third trial is harder to explain. He cannot have been able to give any first-hand testimony about the piracies mentioned in the third indictment, and the defendants had already been found guilty of the mutiny. The Admiralty were perhaps taking no chances.

Despite the fact that the defendants were tried three times for crimes covered by three separate indictments, constant references and witness testimonies were made regarding all the crimes, regardless of which particular indictment the pirates were on trial for. The fact that the capture of the *Gang-i-Sawai* was repeatedly brought home to the defendants, even after they had been legally absolved from it, would certainly cause raised eyebrows, and even censure of the prosecution by the judges in a modern court.

Neither are these points only relevant with hindsight. After sentencing the defendants were returned to Newgate to await execution, from where William May wrote a letter, or 'petition', with hopes that it would save his neck. He did not proclaim his innocence as he had during the trial, but merely tried to discredit the testimony of David Creagh, and thus the verdict of the court. May claimed that he was 'condemned to die merely upon the testimony of David Creagh', which in fact was not true, and proceeded to cast doubt on Creagh's honesty. May listed a number of incidents when Creagh had stolen from his employers and patrons, and more seriously stated that Creagh had joined the notorious French corsair Jean Bart. Bart was a Dunkirk privateer who had been ravaging merchant shipping in the Channel and North Sea. Creagh was captured and arrested, and it was for this treason that he was awaiting trial when he acted as a witness against Every's men. May named several people who could show that Creagh could not be trusted, and ended by stating that, 'the said Creagh's testimony is false, and not sufficient to hang a dog.'[6]

It was, however, enough to hang William May. Intriguing though these legal quibbles may be, they are academic: the six men brought to trial had all been present at the mutiny, and if they were not all active in those events they made no attempt to oppose them. They had then all taken part in the piracies which followed, and had all profited from a share in the loot. In short, they were undoubtedly guilty of the crimes of which they were accused. If the first trial was a triumph for law over justice the second trial, more specifically its verdict, was a triumph for justice over law.

According to the published version of the trial, 'Edward Forseith and the rest were executed. On Wednesday, November the 25th 1696, at Execution Dock, that being the usual place of execution of pirates.'

Whether that statement was deliberate deception or honest mistake is unclear, but it was not true. Only five of the six men, May, Sparks, Forseith, Bishop and Lewis, were hanged. Joseph Dawson, the only man to admit his guilt, remained in Newgate at least until the following February. Perhaps it was his honesty and apparent penitence that saved him. Bail was taken and he was allowed to plead for a pardon. Amongst the contributors towards Dawson's bail was William Dampier, who gave the pirate £20. Dawson's plea was successful and he received not only a pardon, but also a protection from impressments into the Royal Navy.[7]

This last reward is particularly interesting. Impressment (or 'pressing') into the Royal Navy was one of the hazards of a seaman's life in the seventeenth and eighteenth centuries, and 'protections' were highly sought after. Certain classes or groups of people, apprentices for example, were generally exempt from the press, but a protection granted to an individual was rare and usually indicated some meritorious act, or individual achievement. What the cause for Dawson's exemption might have been is a mystery. One historian has suggested that it may have been a 'payoff for services rendered'[8], but is unable to elaborate on what those services might have been.

Whatever the case, Dawson was pardoned on 28 May 1697, and perhaps remained a tool of the Government for some time afterwards. In December 1698 Dawson was called upon to provide information during the investigation of James Cragget mentioned in the previous chapter. Strangely, despite Cragget's apparent guilt Dawson could not, or would not, give any evidence against him.[9]

For the five men who did not escape the noose their last days must have been a stark contrast to the months spent cruising in the Indian Ocean. For three of these men – May, Sparks and Lewis – the desire to escape the slums of London had perhaps played a part in their decision to turn pirate. For Devon man Bishop, and Newcastle man Forseith, life at home had probably been no better. Now, in the gloomy rain of autumnal London they sat languishing in prison awaiting execution. It was a far cry from the warm days they had spent lounging on the deck of the *Fancy*, surrounded by their booty, the sun turning their skins browner and browner. The air had been clear and clean, and they had seen exotic sights which most of the people in Newgate with them would never experience. If they had risked tropical diseases and fever in the Indies, then they risked no less unpleasant infections in prison. Still, with death looming so imminent the threat of disease can have held little terror for the five condemned men.[10]

Public executions were a popular spectacle of the time, and the notoriety of Every's crew must have drawn considerable crowds. Wapping was one of the principal resorts of sea-faring men in London, and Execution Dock was located on the edge of the Thames, just off the main thoroughfare in the area. The proximity of the gallows to the lodgings of countless sailors was perhaps designed deliberately to remind the seamen of the fate which awaited them if they turned pirate. It had been used as the site of Admiralty executions for centuries by the time Every's men met their end there.

The procession of the condemned men from Newgate to Wapping was led by an Admiralty official carrying a silver oar, the symbolic badge of Admiralty justice. The prisoners followed behind, probably closely guarded as escape attempts were not uncommon. Once they reached Wapping the prisoners were herded onto a temporary gallows, where they were attended usually by a chaplain and given an opportunity to say a few last words – a public acknowledgement of the wickedness of their crimes was hoped for by the authorities – before the supported blocks were pulled out, the ropes tautened, and slowly the prisoners choked to death. There was no dignity in their end: their spasming bodies jerked at the end of the ropes, 'dancing the hempen jig'; their muscles relaxed and their bladders opened. Finally, when the body could not sustain life any longer it hung limp, the breeches soaked with urine and the face blackened and distorted.

Once all the prisoners were dead their bodies were taken down and tied to posts in the ground between the high and low water marks. There they remained until three tides had washed over them. The bodies of notable prisoners, like Captain Kidd for example, were then prepared for public display in an iron gibbet to remind passers-by of the penalty of lawlessness. Lesser criminals like the wretches of Every's crew were simply cut down and buried in a common grave.

Before the first tide had washed over the body, often before the noose had been placed around the condemned man's neck, the pamphleteers and balladeers were scribbling notes to be hastily sent to the printers. 'Dying Speeches' were particularly popular, and were often used as media to bring to mind the evils and apparent repentance of the dead men. John Sparks' 'dying words' (which Sparks himself may have had nothing to do with), included the statement, ' He declared that he justly suffered death for such inhumanity even more than for his crime in running away with the Charles…'[11]

Similar sentiments were expressed in ballad form, such as this one, which appeared in print shortly after the execution:

Well may the world against us cry; for these our deeds most base,
For which alas! We now must die, death looks us in the face,
Which is no more than what's our due, since we so wicked were,
As here shall be declar'd to you. Let pirates then take care.

King of the Pirates: The Swashbuckling Life of Henry Every

We with our comrades, not yet ta'en, together did agree,
And stole a ship out of the Groyne, to roam upon the sea;
With which we robb'd and plundered too, no ship that we did spare.
Thus many a one we did undo. Let pirates then take care.

Our ship being well stored then for this enterprise,
One hundred and men there was in her likewise:
We pillag'd all we could come nigh, no nation did we spare,
For which a shameful death we die. Let pirates then take care.

We robb'd a ship upon the seas, the Gunsway call'd by name,
Which we met near the East Indies, and rifled the same;
In it was gold and silver store, of which all had a share;
Each man 600 pounds and more. Let pirates then take care.

Thus for some time we liv'd and reign'd as master of the sea;
Every merchant we detained and us'd most cruelly.
The treasures took, we sunk the ship, and those that in it were
That would not unto us submit. Let pirates then take care.

Thus wickedly we every day liv'd upon others' good,
The which, alas! we must repay now with our dearest blood;
For we on no one mercy took, nor any did we spare.
How can we then for mercy look? Let pirates then take care.

We thus did live most cruelly, and of no danger thought,
But we at last, as you may see, are unto justice brought
For outrages of villainy, of which we guilty are,
And now this very day must die. Let pirates then take care.

Now farewell to this wicked world, and our companions too;
From hence we quickly shall be hurl'd to clear the way for you;
For certainly if e're you come to justice, as we are,
Deserved death will be your doom. Then pirates all take care.[12]

CHAPTER EIGHT

Every's Disappearance

The biggest question about the case of Henry Every has always, since 1696, been, 'What happened to the arch-pirate himself?' Although many of the crew of the *Fancy* found their way into custody one way or another, none of them were so sought after as their captain. Yet despite the best efforts of the government and the East India Co. he was never captured.

Once solid news of Every's piracy reached England the Lords Justices moved quickly and on 17 July 1696 issued a proclamation for his arrest. As more news seeped back, including the names of some of his crew, a second proclamation was issued on 10 August:

Whereas we formerly received information from the Governor and Company of Merchants of London Trading to the East Indies, that one Henry Every, Commander of the Ship called the *Fancy* alias *Charles*, of forty-six Guns, and one hundred and thirty men, had, under English Colours, committed several acts of piracy upon the seas of India or Persia, whereupon we issued a Proclamation, bearing date the 17th day of July last, for the taking and apprehending the said Henry Every, and such other persons as were with him in the Ship in order to have them punished as pirates and common robbers upon the high seas; And whereas we have since the issuing the said Proclamation received further information from the said Governor and Company of Merchants Trading to the East Indies, that the said Hen: Every hath changed his name, and now goes by the name of Henry Bridgman, and that James Cray, Thomas Somerton, Edward Kirkwood, Wm Down, John Reddy, John Strousier, Nath: Pike, Peter Loanes, Henry Adams, Fran: Frennier, Thomas Johnson, Jos: Dawson, Samll Dawson,

James Lewis, John Sparks, Joseph Goss, Charles Faulkner, James Murray, Robert Rich, John Miller, John King, Edward Saville, William Philips, Thomas Jope, and Thomas Belisha, together with several others whose names are not yet discovered (amongst whom were fifty-two Frenchmen, fourteen Danes, & others of other nations) were with the said Henry Every alias Bridgman in the said Ship *Fancy*, when the several acts of piracy were committed, and were aiding and assisting therein and shared in the plunder so by them piratically taken, to the amount of one thousand pounds a man or thereabouts; And whereas we are Informed, That the said Henry Every alias Bridgman, with several other persons above named, have since they committed such acts of piracy left the said ship in the Island of Providence, and are arrived in Ireland in two small sloops and have there dispersed themselves, some of which persons remain there and others are come into this Kingdom and the Kingdom of Scotland, as two of their accomplices, who are now taken and in custody, have confessed and declared: We have therefore thought fit (by the advice of his Majesty's most honourable Privy Council) to issue this Proclamation, hereby declaring that the said Henry Every alias Bridgman, together with the said several persons above named, and others Englishmen, Scotchmen & foreigners to the number of about one hundred and thirty, did steal and run away with the said ship from the port of Corunna in Spain; and that neither the said Henry Every alias Bridgman, nor any of the persons above named had any commission or authority from his Majesty to command the said ship or the men therein; but that the said Henry Every alias Bridgman, and the several other persons above named and such others as were with them in the said ship are pirates and robbers upon the high seas, and we do hereby charge and command all his Majesty's Admirals, Captains and other officers at Sea, and all his Majesty's Governrs and Commanders of any forts, castles or other places in his Majesty's plantations and all other officers and persons whatsoever, to seize and apprehend the said Henry Every alias Bridgman, James Cray, Thomas Somerton, Edward Kirkwood, Wm Down, John Reddy, John Strousier, Nathaniel Pike, Peter Loans, Henry Adams, Francis Frennier, Thomas Johnson, Joseph Dawson, Samll Dawson, James Lewis, John Sparks, Joseph Goss, Charles Faulkner, James Murray, Robert Rich, John Miller, John King, Edward Saville, Wm Philips, Thomas Jope, and Thomas Belisha, and such others, as were with them in the said ship (who may probably be known and discovered by the great quantities of gold and silver of foreign coins which they have with them) in order that they may be brought to justice and suffer the just punishment of the law, as pirates upon the high seas.

And we do hereby further declare, That in case any of the persons above named (except the said Henry Every alias Bridgman) or any other persons who were in the said ship with the said Henry Every alias Bridgman shall discover the said Henry Every alias Bridgman or any other of the persons above named, so as they may be seized and taken, in order to be brought to justice, he and they making such discovery shall have his Majesty's gracious pardon for their offences, and we do hereby further declare, that such person or persons, or any other person or persons who shall discover the said Henry Every alias Bridgman, so as he may be seized or taken or shall be otherwise instrumental in seizing the said Henry Every alias Bridgman, so as he may be seized or taken, he or they making such discovery or seizure, shall have the reward of five-hundred pounds promised in the said former Proclamation, for the discovery and seizure of the said Henry Every, and that in case any person or persons shall discover of the other persons above named, so as they may be seized or taken, or shall be otherwise instrumental in seizing any of the said persons, he or they making such discovery or seizure, shall have a reward of fifty pounds for every of the said persons, whom he or they shall so discover or seize, which several sums of five-hundred pounds and fifty pounds, the Lords Commissioners of his Majesty's Treasury are hereby required and directed to pay accordingly; Given at the Council Chamber in Whitehall, the Tenth day of August 1696. In the eighth year of his Majesty's reign.[1]

The reward of £500 offered for Every's apprehension was unprecedented – even the infamous Blackbeard would only have a reward of £100 offered for his capture twenty years later. The proclamation, and the ones which followed it, were sent by ship all around the globe, to every English colony in the world. In every corner of the world men sought Henry Every. Never before had the hunt for one man extended across four continents, as the hunt for Every did, and there can have been few criminals since who have been so sought after.[2]

It must be marvelled at that a subject of such a manhunt and with such a reward on his head could have escaped detection for any length of time, but Every had two factors in his favour. Most importantly, the authorities did not know where to look for him. It was assumed, based on the testimony of some of his crew, that he was in England, but even in 1700 it was estimated that London had a population of 550,000, and England ten times that number. It might have been thought that Every made his way to one of the country's major sea ports, which would have been natural for a seaman, but much of the population of port towns was itinerant so it was almost impossible to keep tabs on them.

The other factor in Every's favour was that nobody knew what name he was using. As well as his own name Every is known definitely to have used two aliases. As we have seen, when the *Fancy* arrived at Providence Every assumed the name Bridgman, but we have also seen that that name became well known to the authorities fairly early on. The other name which Every is known to have used earlier in his career was Long Ben Every, less an alias than a nickname. Thomas Phillips knew Every by this name, and it seems likely that his other contemporaries did too. That he was still using the name during his piratical career is shown by the news brought back from the East by a merchantman in which the arch-pirate is described as, 'one who goes by the name of Long Ben'.[3]

However, little or none of the official correspondence relating to the Every case mentions the name Long Ben, so it may be that the authorities were unaware of it, or perhaps though it a frivolous nickname not worth mentioning.

Every must have known that there was a chance that at least some of his men would be captured, and that one or two of them might attempt to give him away. Therefore, if he were going to use an alias in England as he had in the Bahamas, it would have to be a new one.

Unfortunately, like the authorities in his own day, we do not know what alias he chose. A tantalising possibility is offered by the 1732 publication *History and Lives of all the Most Notorious Pirates, and their Crews*, a book clearly based heavily on the earlier *General History of the Robberies and Murders of the Most Notorious Pirates* by the pseudonymous Captain Charles Johnson, 1724. Most of the text of the 1732 anonymous book is plagiarised directly from Johnson's work; in fact, only two chapters contain any noticeable differences, and one of them was that of Henry Every.

The differences between the two texts suggest that the later author had access to information which was unavailable to Johnson, and was able to make corrections and additions to Johnson's text. The extra details in the later work thus have, on the face of it, a ring of authenticity. However, it must be borne in mind that these extra details did not surface until nearly forty years after Every ran off with the *Charles II*, and that the author gives no indication as to the source of his information. Furthermore, since the author of the additions remains anonymous it is impossible to ascertain the likelihood of his having obtained extra details. Finally, it must be noted that some of the additional details found in the later text are demonstrably correct. Others, however, are certainly incorrect.

Thus, when the author of the *History and Lives* wrote that Every, once in England, changed his name to Johnson, we can only admit that it is a possibility that he was correct. If Every had a third alias, and it seem likely that he did, there is nothing at all unlikely about 'Johnson'. Alternatively it may have been a mistake, or a deliberate fabrication, perhaps as a tacit nod to Captain Charles Johnson.[4]

Every's story as told in the *General History*, and later in the *History and Lives*, is particularly significant as it details the pirate's last years following his disappearance, and although there is no corroborating evidence to prove its accuracy Captain Johnson's version of Every's end has persisted into our own time as the most popular theory.

Briefly, Captain Johnson supposed that Every had returned to his native Devon, where he lived quietly at Bideford. He was possessed of great wealth, but much of it was in the form of diamonds. Seeking a way to turn his diamonds into ready cash he approached some Bristol merchants via a middleman. The merchants gave Every a small deposit of money to tide him over while they disposed of the plunder, but once Every's money had run out they refused to give him any more. Every of course could not seek any legal recompense without revealing his identity and so, after all his adventures, was reduced to poverty. He went over again to Ireland, but after a while returned to Bideford where he died penniless, unable even to buy a coffin.[5]

Before the publication of the *General History*, however, a different theory was prevalent. In the years immediately after Every's disappearance it was widely believed that he had stayed at Madagascar, and was ruling the island of St Mary's as a king. So widely was the rumour believed that mutinous seamen in the Indian Ocean believed they would be protected by Every if they went to St Mary's; Tsar Peter the Great of Russia hoped to ally himself with Every and his men in order to give his own country a naval presence in eastern waters; and from time to time adventurers turned up in the courts of European princes claiming to be ambassadors of Every's kingdom – many were believed at face value.[6]

Throughout the 1690s the genuine pirate settlement at St Mary's grew in size and importance, and although Every himself had nothing to do with the pseudo-nation of pirates he was widely believed to be its leader. Even as late as 1722 a Royal Navy seaman described the fortifications built by the merchant Adam Baldridge as 'Captain Avery's Fortifications'. This seaman, Clement Downing of HMS *Salisbury*, went on to tell the interesting story of John Plantain who became a King of a Malagasy tribe, and made war on several other kings and their tribes. His general, Downing tells us, was called Mulatto Tom, and claimed to be the son of Henry Every. In fact, the man was far too old to have been Every's son – not to mention the fact that Every did not visit St Mary's.[7]

The legend of Every's pirate kingdom at St Mary's went into print in 1709 in a highly fictionalised account entitled *The Life and Adventures of Captain John Avery*. This work, which did not even get the arch-pirate's name correct, was anonymously written but attributed to Captain Adrian van Broeck, an invented Dutchman. The book was (and to some extent, still is) widely believed to be an accurate account of Every's life. So fantastic were some elements of the *Life and Adventures of Captain John Avery* that when a second account of Every's life, *The King of the Pirates*, appeared in 1720 it took the form of a correction of the earlier work, supposedly written by Every himself, but in fact probably penned by Daniel Defoe. In *The King of the Pirates* Every's fortification and kingdom were moved from St Mary's to Madagascar.

However attractive the idea of Every's Madagascan pirate kingdom may be, it is the theory which we can discard easiest. Whatever did eventually become of

Every there is no evidence that the *Fancy* touched at St Mary's or the Madagascan mainland following the attack on the *Gang-i-Sawai*, and plenty of witnesses stated that he had remained with the ship until it reached the Bahamas.

From the Bahamas Every sailed with Farrell in the *Sea Flower* and landed in the north of Ireland. As the company of the *Sea Flower* made their way across Ireland Every remained with them for a while, but parted company with the rest about six miles into the voyage at Ray on the banks of Lough Swilly. As he parted from his band he told them that he would make his way to Dunaghedee, Co. Down, and from there go to Scotland.

Scotland would have been a good place for Every to hide. It contained great expanses of untamed land, far from the law, in which Every could lose himself. Furthermore, although Scotland was ruled by William III, it was still a distinct country, separate from England until the Act of Union was passed in 1707. Hiding in Scotland was by no means failsafe, but even if he had been found extradition was not a certainty, and with anti-English feeling still strong it was unlikely that the Scots would have brought Every to trial themselves, preferring instead to watch the reputation of the East India Co. (who were widely held to blame for the disastrous failure of the Scottish 'Darien Scheme' and the resulting decline of Scottish economy) suffer.

It seems more likely, though, that Every was deliberately trying to put any pursuers off his trail. He must have known that some of his men were likely to be captured, and that if they were some might try to give him away in order to obtain their own pardons. By feeding his men false information, which he perhaps anticipated would reach the ears of the authorities, he hoped to send the ensuing manhunt in completely the wrong direction.

John Dann, who told his interrogators of Every's intention to make for Scotland, later made his way to Dublin where he ran into several of his old shipmates. Some of them told him that far from being safe in Scotland Every was in fact in Dublin at that very time. Dann also mentioned this in his examination, but added that if Every had been in Dublin he had not seen him.

Perhaps out of loyalty to his captain, or perhaps simply from a desire to give as much information as possible to save his own neck, Dann muddied the waters still further by saying that Every had also earlier spoken of returning to Devon, specifically to Exeter. Exeter was by no means as populous as London, or even Bristol or Plymouth, but it was still a city with a thriving sea trade and a population of several thousand inhabitants. The idea of hiding in Exeter may possibly have entered Every's head as it seems likely that some of his wife's extended family lived in the area, and as a Devon seaman he undoubtedly had friends there himself.[8]

William Phillips, who travelled to Ireland with Hollingsworth in the *Isaac*, also stated that Every had often spoken of his plan to return to Devon and his family there. It seems likely that during the voyage when all was going well and the pirates freely discussed their pasts and their plans for the future, Every was quite open about his true intentions, but that when the reality that they were wanted criminals dawned on them Every set about laying false trails.[9]

There was one person aboard the *Sea Flower* though who was let in to Every's plans. The woman Henry Adams had married in the Bahamas evidently decided during the voyage to Ireland that she preferred the charms of Henry Every. The journey must have been an uncomfortable one for Mrs Adams, and an unpleasant one for her husband, and one must wonder at the tensions that must have existed aboard the little sloop. When exactly Mrs Adams left her husband is unclear, but when Every split from the group and headed for Dunaghedee she went with him.

If the *Sea Flower* landed in Ireland at the end of June 1696 then Every and Mrs Adams presumably left the rest in either the closing days of June or the first few days of July. Phillips believed Dann was still in Dublin on 8 August, but in fact he had left that city around 13 July and travelled via Holyhead to London, where he arrived on 28 July. As he was passing through the town of St Albans in Hertfordshire, probably on 27 July, he met Mrs Adams as she was climbing into a stage coach. The coincidence of the meeting is remarkable, since a few seconds later Mrs Adams would have been inside the coach and all but invisible to Dann as he strolled past.

If Mrs Adams told Dann why she was no longer travelling with Every then he chose not to mention it later. Mrs Adams stopped to talk in hushed tones to Dann, who she would have known well after several weeks together on a small vessel crossing the Atlantic. Dann evidently asked her where she was going, to which she replied that she was journeying to meet 'Captain Bridgman', but in response to Dann's questions about where Every was hiding she refused to answer. Dann continued on to London, and then Rochester where he was arrested. Mrs Adams got into the stagecoach and travelled off to join Every.[10]

Unfortunately, the meeting of Dann and Mrs Adams, though interesting, does not help much in the search for Henry Every, primarily because Dann did not think to disclose in which direction the stagecoach carrying Mrs Adams was travelling. If Mrs Adams was travelling away from London then we might infer that Every was hiding somewhere in the North as St Albans lies on the Great North Road and was a staging point on the voyage in that direction from London. However, it is equally likely that Mrs Adams was travelling into London, then, as now, the hub of England's infrastructure. If Every and Mrs Adams had crossed from Ireland into Scotland, or directly into England via an Irish Sea port such as Chester, then St Albans would have been a likely place for Mrs Adams to have broken her journey to London. Once in London she could have taken a coach for almost any part of the kingdom.

Every may well have been hiding in London. As already noted, the city had a large population which was difficult to keep track of, and it would have been an excellent place for the arch-pirate to go to ground. Furthermore, it was the home of his wife, who had kept at her business of selling wigs in one of the slummiest districts while Every was at sea making a name for himself under the tropical sun.

Quite apart from the fact that he now had another man's wife in tow, it would have been dangerous for Every to have returned to Ratcliffe Highway. As early as 1694 the Committee of Trade and Plantations had been aware of Mrs Every's existence and whereabouts when they summoned her to appear before a council hearing concerning the petition of Jane May and the wives of other seamen aboard the *Fancy*. Every would not have known for sure that the authorities knew about his wife, but to return to her would have been foolhardy nonetheless. There were undoubtedly other people living in Ratcliffe Highway who would have been able to recognise Every, and with such a reward offered for his apprehension, would surely have done so. Perhaps it was the realisation that he could never return to his wife that convinced Every to throw in his lot with Mrs Adams.

As in Ratcliffe Highway, there would have been plenty of people who knew Every and would be happy to claim the reward for his capture in Plymouth and the surrounding regions – Every's home. However, since two other places in Devon have been put forward independently as Every's hiding place there is a strong likelihood that he made his way back to his home county.

The Devon town most associated with Every's disappearance is Bideford, which deserves examination. In the sixteenth century Bideford was one of the most important ports in England, and legend has it that Sir Walter Raleigh landed his first shipment of tobacco on the town's quay. By Every's day Bideford was declining in importance, but was still a major port with strong trade links with Ireland. For a retiring pirate crossing from Ireland and looking for quiet anonymity Bideford would have been ideal. Like the larger port cities many of the inhabitants of Bideford were seamen, and there would have been nothing strange about a seaman of Every's age retiring from the sea and settling in the town. Bideford is close enough to Plymouth and Exeter that it would have been easy for Every's relatives to visit him there, but there is little to connect Every to the town so fewer, if any, of the local people might have been able to recognise and denounce him.

One strong piece of circumstantial evidence links Every with Bideford. On 15 November 1719 one 'Henry Everey' married Mary Evans in Bideford; the following year, on 14 September, John Every married Joan Cann in the same church. John Every was probably the brother (born 1686) or cousin (born 1692) of Henry Everey, and had two sons: John, born in 1724; and Henry, born in 1729. There is nothing at all to link this Every family with the arch-pirate, but John and Henry seem to have been common family names, and the pirate Every's father's name was John. This might be nothing more than coincidence, but it is a strange coincidence to find in the very town which was widely believed to be the pirate's last refuge.

According to the *History and Lives of all the Most Notorious Pirates*, Every lived at Bideford under the name Johnson until his death, and was buried on 10 June 1728.[11] The parish registers of Bideford contain no record of the burial of anyone named Every, Bridgman, or Johnson on that date, or even in that year, but that does not necessarily prove the story wrong. It was not until many years later that the keeping of parish records became standardised across the country. In Every's day the detail and completeness of the records kept depended very much on the fastidiousness of the individual responsible for each one. In many cases the records list only burial services so if Every died a pauper, as both the *History and Lives* and Captain Johnson's *General History* maintain, his death and interment might easily have not been recorded. Also, if, in his last years, Every had practised a nonconformist form of worship, which was not at all uncommon (and nonconformists included fairly significant sects such as Quakers and Presbyterians), his burial could not have been conducted by the minister of the church and so might not have been recorded in the register.

So, if Every lived into the eighteenth century what was he doing during the years following his disappearance? From time to time reports were made of Every being at sea once more, in command of a pirate ship. Most of these reports were inaccurate and Every's name was simply inserted to sensationalise an otherwise trivial attack by pirates, but there was an underlying belief that Every was still alive and potentially active. By 1698 the depredations of English pirates (amongst others) in the eastern seas had become so serious that William III issued an 'Act of Grace', a free pardon to pirates who surrendered to the Royal Navy. The Navy and the East India Co. simply did not have the resources to effectively suppress piracy in the region, and so it was hoped that the pirates could be persuaded to retire peacefully by means of a general pardon. Only two men were excepted from the pardon: the infamous Captain William Kidd and Henry Every.[12]

In 1731 a notorious smuggler named Joseph Avery was executed at Oystermouth in Wales. Since this Avery had also at times apparently indulged in piracy it has been suggested that he was the arch-pirate. Oystermouth is situated almost directly across the Bristol Channel from Bideford, no more than forty miles away, but since Henry Every would have been seventy-two in 1731 (if he had lived that long) it is very unlikely that he was the same person hanged for smuggling in that year. More plausible perhaps is a report received by the Royal African Co. in March 1699 from one of their captains, William Burrough:

This is to acquaint the Royal African Company of my misfortune in being taken by a pirate under English colours in the Lat. Of 7' 15', they being a ship of 14 guns and 6 patereroes [small swivel guns mounted on the gunwales] and 50 men, he being a consort of Avery, and they told us likewise that there was 10 sail upon the coast of Africa and that Avery was the head of them in a ship of 24 guns and 100 men. They told us that they had fought the *Bedford Galley* at the Isle of May and that she had disabled their mast, by which reason they took my ship, which I have brought to Sierra Leone and delivered her to Agent Corker.[13]

It is possible, perhaps even likely, that the pirates who attacked Burrough's ship mentioned Every's name to deliberately frighten Burrough, but the report was taken seriously in London. Samuel Heron, the merchant of the Royal African Co. to whom the report was addressed, forwarded it on to James Vernon, secretary of state, who was commanded by the King to send it on to the Council of Trade and Plantations with a request for advice on how to protect shipping against this new threat from Every.

It is quite conceivable that Every returned to the sea after his disappearance, though his share of the *Gang-i-Sawai* plunder was more than enough to have kept him in quiet anonymity for the rest of his life. Burrough's report is to some extent credible because the seventh degree of latitude lies almost midway between the Isle of May and the Isle of Principe, hunting grounds which Every knew well both from his days as a slave-ship captain and from the cruise of the *Fancy*. Sadly, the matter ended with Vernon's note to the Council of Trade and Plantations.

Three centuries after Every's disappearance we are only a little closer to finding him than his contemporaries were. We know he did not build a fort and kingdom at St Mary's or on the Madagascan mainland, and we have seen some evidence that he may have settled in Bideford as Captain Charles Johnson suggested, perhaps using the name Johnson as an alias. But there we must draw the line. Possibly Every's talk of returning to Devon was a trick, like his talk of going to Scotland. Possibly he was using an alias other than Bridgman or Johnson. In that case he might have gone anywhere in the world under any name, and we cannot hope to find any trace of him.

Perhaps in the future some document will come to light which allows us to reaffirm one of the theories surrounding his disappearance, or form a new one, but if that happens it is unlikely to be possible to prove conclusively that it relates to Every the arch-pirate, or to prove that it is accurate. In all probability, future theories will never make the transition from theory to fact, and so will get us no nearer to solving the mystery. The only thing we know for sure about Every's disappearance is that having sailed halfway around the world, pulled off one of the most profitable criminal raids in history, come within a hair's breadth of destroying the British Empire before it began in earnest, and returned to England, he was never heard of again and never brought to justice. That in itself makes him one of the most successful pirates in history, and one of the most fascinating.

EPILOGUE

Flotsam and Jetsam

Henry Every's piracies in the Indian Ocean had a lasting effect on trade in the region, and opened the government's eyes to the dangers of allowing the pirates to become too powerful, but he also had a distinct effect on the pirates who followed him. If he was vilified by the establishment he was at least an inspiration to subsequent generations of pirates. He had shown that it was possible, by picking the right targets and quitting while the going was good, to make a fortune quickly and get away with it. Few of the pirates of later years were so successful, and most were caught or retired penniless, but Every had shown the way.

In the years following the capture of the *Gang-i-Sawai* hundreds of men flocked into the eastern seas and made their base at St Mary's Island for raids in the Indian Ocean and Red Sea. Robert Culliver in the *Mocha* and Dirk Chivers in the *Soldado*, sailing in consort, took the wealthy *Great Muhammad* in 1698; the following year George Booth and John Bowen took control of the *Speaker* and used her to prey on Indian shipping, and in the opening years of the eighteenth century pirate captains such as Thomas Howard, Nathaniel North, Thomas White, and John Halsey all sailed in the area.[1]

One pirate who deserves further investigation, if only because his own pirate cruise mirrored Every's so closely, is Captain William Kidd. Kidd was an adventurer who in 1695 was commissioned to sail to the Indian Ocean as a pirate hunter, and among the pirates specifically targeted in Kidd's commission were Every's consorts Tew, Wake, and Mace. In April 1696, just as Every was reaching the Bahamas, Kidd left England in the *Adventure Galley*, and sailed first for New York, where he picked up extra crew, and then for the Red Sea, where he arrived in August 1697. Like Every before him, Kidd landed at Mayd to gather supplies and then sailed for the Babs where he waited for the pilgrim fleet to pass. Mindful of the success of the ruse against Every, the pilgrim fleet made the passage through the Babs by night, hoping to escape detection, but when dawn came the following day they discovered the *Adventure Galley* sailing amongst them. One ship of the fleet had chosen to sail early and alone, hoping to be able to slip through the Babs unnoticed, and so Kidd missed his chance of capturing the *Gang-i-Sawai*, which had been repaired since the fight with Every and was plying the ocean once again.

Since Every's raid the pilgrim fleet had been to some extent protected by European ships belonging to the various East Indian Co.s, and as soon as the extra ship in the convoy was spotted the English East Indiaman *Sceptre*, commanded by Edward Barlow, sailed out to investigate. Seeing no flag on the *Adventure Galley* but the red flag of 'no quarter', Barlow assumed the newcomer was a pirate and fired a few cannons at her. For the rest of the day the *Sceptre* and *Adventure Galley* played cat and mouse, resorting to oars in the unreliable winds, until Kidd realised that he could not risk a broadside-to-broadside engagement and sailed away from the pilgrim fleet.

Kidd then sailed for the Highlands of St John, where Every had captured the *Gang-i-Sawai*, and lay in wait for the pilgrim fleet, just as Every had done. Failing to meet any prizes at the Highlands, Kidd then sailed down the coast of India and took several rich ships on the way, before sailing for St Mary's. When he returned to New York Kidd was arrested and sent to London, where he was tried and executed.[2]

When John Rose Archer joined the pirate crew commanded by John Phillips in 1723 he, 'having been a pirate under the famous Blackbeard, was immediately preferred over the other people's heads', but in the last years of the seventeenth century and early years of the eighteenth it was Every's name which gave a pirate a pedigree. John Miller was looked up to in Quelch's crew because he had sailed on the *Fancy*, and amongst several other examples a gang of men who claimed to have been in Every's crew were welcomed aboard a pirate brigantine sailing out of Jamaica in 1699, until they quarrelled with the captain and were set adrift in an open boat. Perhaps the greatest testament to Every's reverence by other pirates is the tale of Walter Kennedy, hanged for piracy in 1721, but born in the year of Every's raids in the Indian Ocean. We are told that Kennedy in his youth, 'became acquainted with the principal expeditions of these maritime desperadoes [and]... Captain Avery's... exploits at Madagascar; his fancy insinuating to him continually that he might be able to make as great a figure... whenever a proper opportunity offered'.[3]

The Bit-Players

No biography can be written without the intrusion of other characters, who come into the story after it has begun and leave before it is finished. These characters, though incidental to the main story, each had stories of their own and the parts they played in Every's tale often had a profound effect on their lives. It may be of interest, therefore, to the reader to know something of what befell these men after their brush with Every.

Thomas Wake

Before parting company with Every and the *Fancy* in the region of Rajpur, Thomas Wake and the crew of the *Susanna* announced their intention to sail for St Mary's, having heard of a large and powerful ship for sale there. They intended to buy the twenty-two gun ship and continue their piracy in the eastern seas. They arrived at the island on 7 December 1695, but the vessel they had hoped to meet there was not to be found, so they set about preparing the *Susanna* for sea again. They careened and cleaned their ship, bought supplies from the natives, and approached Adam Baldridge for some necessities. Baldridge supplied them with goods he had bought from the *Charming Mary* some months before, and some cattle which were probably slaughtered and salted for the voyage ahead. The crew of the *Susanna* remained on St Mary's until the middle of April 1696 – when Wake and many of the crew died.

What remained of the crew sailed the *Susanna* to St Augustine's Bay in the hope of meeting a ship there. When the *John and Rebecca*, commanded by Captain John Hore, arrived in the bay, the *Susanna*'s men all signed aboard. In August the *John and Rebecca* captured two ships, the *Ruparell* and *Calicut*, which belonged to the East India Co. The pirates found some cash aboard the two ships, but it was a disappointingly small amount, so they tried to ransom the vessels at Aden. No ransom was paid and so the pirates set the ships on fire and sailed for the Persian Gulf. In the Gulf, Hore captured a wealthy merchantman laden with printed fabrics which would fetch a high price in the markets of Europe and the Americas. A prize crew was put aboard and the two ships sailed back to St Mary's together where the fabrics were sold to Adam Baldridge.

In the summer of 1697 the natives of St Mary's and Madagascar rose against the pirate community there and killed a number of the pirates, including men from Hore's crew. The pirate community was destroyed by the attack and most of the men, including the crew of the *John and Rebecca*, sailed home for the

Americas. The *John and Rebecca* itself was wrecked at Port Dauphin, but most of the crew were able to join other ships and so get home.[4]

Thomas Tew's Men

With their famous commander killed by an Indian cannonball, the *Amity* was thrown into disarray and sailed for St Mary's where her crew could refit, re-supply, and reorganise. John Yarland, who had been sailing master under Tew, remained in that post, but no new captain was elected.

When they arrived at St Mary's Adam Baldridge told them of a wealthy ship which had recently called at the pirate settlement and had since sailed for the Madagascan mainland to load a cargo of rice and slaves. The *Charming Mary*, commanded by Richard Glover, was a large ship of sixteen guns which had been sent out by a consortium of Barbadian merchants. The crew of the *Amity* remained at St Mary's long enough to deal with their immediate needs and then sailed in chase of the *Charming Mary*. They quickly caught the larger vessel, and appear to have taken it without a fight. Captain Glover was given the *Amity*, while the pirates transferred themselves to the *Charming Mary*.

With a newer and stronger ship at their disposal the pirates elected a new captain named Bobbington, and sailed to St Augustine's Bay, where they were able to obtain the supplies they needed to continue cruising in the eastern seas. The *Charming Mary* sailed once more for the Red Sea, but does not appear to have found any ships worth the taking there, and so sailed for the coast of India where, off Rajpur in September 1696, they met with a rich prize. The prize put up a stiff fight and ten of the pirates were killed before they were able to overcome the Indian crew. Once aboard their prize the pirates laid about the Indians with their cutlasses in revenge for the deaths of their comrades. Twenty Indians were killed, and many more wounded, before the pirates set them ashore and sailed off with both ships.

In December the *Charming Mary* was in the Gulf of Persia and a landing party under Captain Bobbington went ashore, but were surprised by a group of soldiers. The East India Co. recorded that:

> The Persians fought with them and after killing three of the pirates took their commander and the rest prisoners. This Bobbington says that he is an Irishman though his father was Dutch and his mother English. He confesses the crew are of all nations, but that the ship comes from English Dominions. For this reason the Persians say that the English are the only sea robbers. The English [i.e. the East India Co.] demanded that Bobbington be given up by the Persian government to

be sent to Bombay to answer for his great roguery in burning two ships belonging to the Great Moghul in the Gulf of Mocha.

The crew of the *Charming Mary* sailed away, making no attempt to rescue their comrades. After the loss of their second captain the pirates made no moves to elect a new one, and it appears that John Yarland shared the running of the ship with Henry Smith, the quartermaster. The *Charming Mary* cruised in the eastern seas a little longer, sometime in cohort with other pirate ships, but in October 1697 returned to Barbados where the crew shared out the plunder, which amounted to around £700 per man.[5]

William Mace

Following their dishonesty over the clipped gold William Mace and the crew of the *Pearl* said they, too, would sail for Madagascar, and there try to find some more men. Adam Baldridge made no mention of the arrival of the *Pearl*, so if Mace did sail for Madagascar it seems likely that he landed on the mainland rather than at St Mary's. In early 1696 the *Pearl* was once more off the Indian coast where it was reported, 'this pirate ship, the *Pearl*, hath taken two rich moors ships off Cape Comorin, and, after heaving the crews overboard, hath burnt both vessels'. These two vessels, whose crews Mace and his men treated no better than they had the crew of the *Gang-i-Sawai*, were probably the ships whose loss was blamed on Bobbington and the *Amity*'s men.

Mace and his crew went on to take two or three more prizes over the next two months, but thereafter the *Pearl* disappears from the historical record, leading some to assume that she was wrecked. Mace and some of his men seem to have found their way back to Madagascar. In Rhode Island, where no news of Mace's activities had been heard for some time, an altogether different opinion was prevalent.

> William Mace had his clearance here for Madagascar and a commission from this government to fight the French. By the best information that we have Captain Every plundered him, and we very much suspect has destroyed him and his company, for none of them are returned and there is no news of any one of them.

While Mace and his men were making their way to Madagascar some of Tew's old crew were preparing at Barbados to take the *Charming Mary* back to sea. When the ship called at Madagascar William Mace joined the crew, and was obviously remembered well by the men who had sailed with Tew, for in January

1699 he was elected captain. Several rich prizes were taken and in December 1699 the *Charming Mary* arrived at New York where the crew shared out £3,000 per man.[6]

Some men – who had supposedly sailed with Tew, but were more likely to have been members of Mace's original crew of the *Pearl* – remained on Madagascar where their superior knowledge of firearms enabled them to become warlords with large numbers of slaves and wives. They took part in various native wars and started large families. Woodes Rogers, a Bristol sea captain, arrived at Madagascar aboard the *Delicia* in 1714 to collect slaves to sell in the Dutch colonies. When he landed at Madagascar he came across some of the survivors of this band who had lived on the island for nearly twenty years. There were only eleven of the original pirates left alive, but they were surrounded by children and grandchildren.

When the pirates saw the *Delicia* they thought her to be a Royal Navy ship and so hid in the jungle. When they realised Rogers was there to trade they left their hiding places and went to meet him. They were dressed in animal skins and their beards were long, but they traded their slaves for European commodities and clothing, and so shortly looked like their former selves again.

The pirates often visited the *Delicia* and formed a plan to capture her during the night when there was just a token watch on deck. Rogers heard of the plan and increased the watch, but some of his crew were taken with the idea of piracy and so conspired with the pirates to take the ship by mutiny. Again Rogers heard of the plot and prevented his men having any contact with the pirates. When the trading was complete the *Delicia* sailed away, leaving the pirates once more to their kingdoms.

This chance meeting had a most profound effect on Rogers, who at his return to England wrote a proposal setting out how the pirate communities on Madagascar might be destroyed. His scheme was never enacted at Madagascar, but it did secure him the government of the Bahamas, which was at that time infested with pirates as St Mary's had been in the 1690s.[7]

The End of the Spanish Expedition

And what of the rest of the ships and men of the Spanish Expedition left at Corunna? Every's mutiny on the *Charles II* took place in May 1694, but after he and his co-conspirators had run away with the ship, Admiral Arturo O'Bourne still intended to proceed on the voyage to the West Indies.

Mutiny was a desperate act, seen by seamen and ship-owners alike as a heinous crime. For abused and disillusioned seamen it was the last resort, only to be considered in the most desperate circumstances. It must not be imagined then that the seamen who did not join Every's mutiny were content with their lot at Corunna; for the most part they were just unable or unwilling to literally risk their necks by taking part. Therefore, even after the *Charles II* had sailed from Corunna with the most desperate of the men aboard, ill will still ran strong on the remaining ships. Wages remained unpaid, and Houblon's consortium was more stubborn than ever: who was to say that the rest of the ships' crews would remain loyal once they had been paid? Supplies remained inadequate, the food was bad, and there was still a deep suspicion that Houblon had sold the men into Spanish service.

Thus, as the weeks rolled on the seamen refused to budge and their stubbornness was matched only by that of their employers. Admiral O'Bourne, caught between the two, became more and more despondent and convinced that mutiny was afoot. Following the loss of the *Charles II*, O'Bourne shifted his flag into the *James*, the second largest (the largest in the *Charles II*'s absence) ship in the squadron.

At the beginning of July, sensing mutiny everywhere, O'Bourne ordered the ships to take down their sails and send them on shore. Without their sails the ships could not leave Corunna until all of the difficulties had been resolved to the owners' satisfaction, and until O'Bourne gave the order. Captain Street of the *James* and Captain Humphreys of the *Dove* both refused to obey, perhaps fearing that the removal of sails was a prelude to the ships being handed over to the Spanish. The wages of the officers and men were also tied up in the value of the ships, since they were to be paid from the stock of the company (which at that time consisted only of the vessels). They were naturally opposed to any move which might lower the value of the ships, and refused to allow any part of the vessels or their equipment to be removed.

To O'Bourne, the outright refusal by two of his captains to obey his order was proof that mutiny was afoot. When O'Bourne upbraided them for their refusal they both promised that if he could show them the order from Houblon and the other owners for the removal of their sails they would at once obey. All of the men, they pointed out, had entered £100 bonds for their good behaviour during the voyage, and they themselves had entered bonds of £1,000. They would not do anything to risk their bonds if they could help it. Furthermore, since they only had provisions aboard to last four days, as O'Bourne well knew, for them to think of running off as Every had done would be ridiculous.

O'Bourne's response to this measured argument was to have Street and other officers arrested and thrown into jail ashore. Street, realising that O'Bourne was not to be reasoned with, wrote to the English consul at Corunna, pointing out the reasons for his refusal and begging him to intercede. Once again the old issue cropped up. The consul would perhaps have helped Street, since he must have been well aware of the grievances of the sailors, but since the ships were under Spanish colours the crews were technically the subjects of Spain and he had no authority over them or their treatment.

Street, undaunted, wrote next to the Secretary of State, Sir John Trenchard. Street was a Poole man, and Trenchard came from an old local family from Lytchett Matravers, which lies seven miles from Poole. The two men may have known one another personally since Street's letter begins, 'having from your own mouth received encouragement to trouble Your Honour when urgent occasions should require', and Street had corresponded with Trenchard on an earlier occasion. Street laid out the dispute between Admiral O'Bourne and the captains, related how he had been imprisoned, and concluded:

> so that here [in prison] we are all like to remain unless assisted by Your Honour's favour in this most unfortunate affair, wherein you will create to yourself a last-ing name in defending their Majesties' subjects from the wrongs of a most unjust crew, who I much fear, if we are not soon delivered out of their hands, will not boggle to swear us out of our lives.

O'Bourne's own report of the situation must have reached Houblon in England some time earlier, while Street was writing to the English consul. On the same day that Street wrote to the Secretary of State, Houblon also wrote to him requesting, 'assistance in quelling mutinies on the ships *James*, Captain Street, the *Dove*, Captain Humphreys, and the *Seventh Son*, Captain Thomas, who will not obey the commands of General Don Arturo O'Bourne'.[8]

The spirit of mutual distrust which had increased with the imprisonment of Street and the other officers was in no way diminished when they were eventually released. No lasting resolutions could be found and the squadron lay idle at anchor at Corunna until the following February, in which month the contracts of employment which all the men had signed expired. When the Spanish Expedition finally weighed anchor from Corunna it was not to sail to the West Indies, but to sail home to London, where they arrived on 10 February.

In London many of the officers and men petitioned for their wages, but since the Spanish Expedition had proved a complete failure Houblon's consortium were in no mood to hand over what little cash remained to the seamen whom they saw as the cause of the disaster. The men were forced to take their claim to the courts, but Houblon and his associates levelled counter-charges that the men making the claim had all assisted or conspired with Every and his muti-neers and had thus forfeited not only their wages but also their bonds. Since the crews of all four ships had freely mingled ashore for several weeks before Every's mutiny, it was an easy charge to make and an impossible one to disprove. The men's refusal to obey Admiral O'Bourne's order was also cited as evidence of their misbehaviour, and the court ruled that the seamen did not have sufficient evidence to win the case. Despite further suits none of the seamen of the Spanish Expedition received their wages, and they eventually gave up.[9]

William Dampier

One of the officers who went without his wages from the Spanish Expedition, of course, was William Dampier. Dampier had been virtually penniless when he had enlisted on the *Dove*, and this further calamity cannot have helped his situation. In 1697 he published his *New Voyage Around the World*, the manuscript of which he had perhaps been working on during his enforced idleness at Corunna. In August 1698 the diarist John Evelyn dined at the house of fellow diarist Samuel Pepys where he met 'Capt. Dampier, who had been a famous buccaneer… He was now going abroad again by the King's encouragement, who furnished a ship of 290 tons. He seemed a more modest man than one would imagine by the relation of the crew he had assorted with.'[10]

Dampier sailed in HMS *Roebuck* in January 1699, and called at the Canary Islands, Brazil, and the Cape Verde Islands on his way to the Cape of Good Hope. It was during this passage that Dampier again met John Guy and two others of Every's crew at Bahia, Brazil. Having passed the Cape he then sailed to the western coast of Australia, reaching there in July 1699. Dampier had already visited Australia while sailing with John Read in the *Cygnet* in 1687, but on this occasion he carefully explored the coast, searching for a good harbour.

The *Roebuck* remained on the Australian coast until September, but being unable to find either a good harbour or a supply of provisions set sail for New Guinea, where they arrived in December after a brief call at Timor. For most of 1700 the *Roebuck* remained in the Pacific while Dampier charted coastlines, but when mutiny nearly broke out he turned back towards the Cape of Good Hope and home. In February 1701 the leaking *Roebuck* foundered and the crew had to get ashore on Ascension Island where they remained for two months until being rescued by a homeward-bound East Indiaman.

Dampier was court-martialled on his return, but even while he was still at sea the Admiralty had had doubts placed in their minds about his suitability for command. Since almost the beginning of the voyage Dampier had been at loggerheads with his second in command, Lieutenant Fisher. Fisher had been turned ashore at Bahia, and from there had written to the Admiralty listing his grievances against Dampier, including the incident with Every's men. At the court martial Dampier was declared to be unfit to command a naval ship, and found himself unemployed once more.

In 1703 Dampier was appointed to command a private venture into the Pacific. The venture consisted of two ships and its purpose was privateering. Dampier's consort ship set sail without him, but after he set sail from Bristol in the *St George* he met with another privateer ship, the *Cinque Ports*, at Ireland and the two ships sailed together. Again Dampier quarrelled with his officers, and two of them left the ship at the Cape Verde Islands and at Brazil. In January 1704 the ships lost each other while rounding Cape Horn, but met again at their rendezvous at Juan Fernandez at the beginning of the following month.

At Juan Fernandez the privateers shied away from fighting two large French ships, but over the following days captured two Spanish merchantmen. On the pretext of wanting to save room for the gold and silver he hoped to capture later in the voyage Dampier refused to allow his men to take much in the way of plunder from the Spanish ships, and once more his crew started to turn against him.

After a sojourn at the Galapagos Islands and a disastrous attack on the town of Santa Maria a third Spanish ship was taken. This time Dampier allowed his men to plunder her before they returned to Juan Fernandez to refit. When the ships came to sail from the island the master of the *Cinque Ports*, Alexander Selkirk, elected to remain, not having any confidence in his ship.

On the coast of Peru Dampier fought an inconclusive action with a Spanish man-of-war, and a small Spanish ship which they later captured was stolen by some of his mutinous crew. Dampier then sailed north to wait for the fabled *Manila Galleon* coming from the East, but he failed to capture her and some more of his crew later mutinied and went off with another small prize. A short while later Dampier and his remaining crew left the sea-worn *St George* and transferred themselves to a prize in which they sailed across the Pacific.

In the Dutch East Indies Dampier was arrested and thrown into prison. Somehow he managed to get out and returned home towards the end of 1707. Shortly afterwards he found employment as navigator of another Bristol privateering expedition under the command of Woodes Rogers. Rogers followed a similar route to Dampier's previous cruise and at Juan Fernandez they rescued Alexander Selkirk, who had been alone on the island for four years and four months. Selkirk's story would later be transformed by Daniel Defoe into the novel *Robinson Crusoe*. Rogers' privateers also failed to capture the *Manila Galleon*, but returned to England in 1711 with a decent profit nonetheless.

Dampier had circumnavigated the world three times, and did not go to sea again before his death in 1715. In an interesting circle which perhaps began with the arch-pirate Every quizzing Dampier about the best routes through the eastern seas, Woodes Rogers went on to become famous as the man who expelled the pirates from the Bahamas. The greatest pirate and the greatest pirate-hunter of the age perhaps both learned something from William Dampier.[11]

Samuel Annesley and the East India Co. at Surat

The piracies of Mace and others in the years following Every's cruise did nothing to improve the reputation of the East India Co. with the Indians. Captain Farrell's old mate Dirk Chivers had also become a notorious pirate, and when the crews of two East India Co. ships, the *Mocha* and *Josiah*, mutinied and turned to piracy their reputation suffered further. Robert Culliver, who had sailed with Kidd early in his career and had first entered the eastern seas as a pirate, but who had served the East India Co. for some years past, rose to become one of the most important of the pirate commanders in the region.

Following the release of Samuel Annesley and the others at Surat the activities of these English pirates caused such a fear amongst Company officials in India that Sir John Gayer wrote to London that:

> If there be not care taken to suppress pirates in India, and to empower your servants there to punish them according to their deserts, without fear of being traduced for what they have done when they return to their native country, it's probable their throats will be all cut in a little time by malefactors and the natives of the country in revenge for their frequent losses, as well as your Honour's; trade in India wholly lost.[12]

The reports of Kidd's piratical intentions, which had circulated in India before he had actually committed any piracy, did nothing to help the cause of the East India Co. At about the time that news reached the Company and the Great Moghul of Kidd's capture of the *Quedah Merchant*, his richest prize, the King's proclamation of July 1696, arrived. Gayer and Annesley must have been flattered and pleased that their frequent letters home regarding the pirates had had such an effect, but the timing of the proclamation's arrival was as bad as it could be. On the one hand the Company officers were keen to show Aurangzeb that the matter was being dealt with, but on the other the proclamation appeared, and to some extent was, an admission that the pirates who infested the area were English. In light of the then current circumstances such an admission might have had disastrous consequences, so Annesley and Sir John Gayer did not immediately publish the proclamation.

When the first reports of the capture of the *Quedah Merchant* filtered through to Surat, Annesley feared a repetition of the event which had followed the loss of the *Gang-i-Sawai*. The *Quedah Merchant* was Indian-owned, and carried merchandise belonging to Indian and Armenian merchants – but the Captain, Wright, was English, and there were a handful of European officers aboard (though most of the crew were native). Some of the merchants had travelled aboard the ship, and when their reports reached Aurangzeb they accused

Wright of colluding with Kidd. Wright had refused to fight, Kidd had shown his English commission, and it was suggested that the two ships met by a prior agreement of their captains.

Once again it was in everyone's minds that the worst of the pirates were English, and that the East India Co. was to blame. Aurangzeb did not, on this occasion, order the imprisonment of the English at Surat but, frightened by an angry populace, Annesley though it wisest to remain in the English factory with the doors shut. Aurangzeb sent orders to stop European trade until hefty bribes were paid and an undertaking was made to hunt down the pirates. In Surat he demanded the largest bribe and forbade the selling of food to the English. Annesley begged Gayer to allow him to come to an arrangement with the Indian governor, but Gayer, in his typical fashion, refused. When he did finally give permission for Annesley to seek a deal he placed such restrictions on Annesley's offers and requests that the Indians refused. Against Gayer's wishes, Annesley submitted to the demands made by the Indian government and all restrictions were lifted. Gayer had never been a friend of Annesley's, and this incident of disobedience enabled Gayer to remove Annesley from his post. Annesley remained at Surat in various capacities until his death in 1732.[13]

The Early Accounts

Every's piracy and the furore which followed made his name a household word. Before he had even taken the *Gang-i-Sawai* broadside ballads about the mutiny at Corunna were circulating in England, and the trial of six of his crew was headline news. The reputedly fabulous value of his treasure gave his story a romantic quality which was only enhanced by his successful disappearance. It is not surprising therefore that within a generation of his disappearance his story had been told in popular print more than any other pirate of the age. These stories have formed the basis for many subsequent histories of Every's life, despite their largely fictional content, and so a brief overview of them might be of interest.

'The Life and Adventures of Captain John Avery'

The first major work narrating the supposed history of Every's life was published in 1709, apparently written by Adrian van Broeck, a Dutchman held prisoner aboard the *Fancy*. Van Broeck himself was a fictional character, created to explain away the mystery of how the otherwise anonymous author knew so many of the details of Every's life and career. According to the book's preface, van Broeck was captured by some of 'Avery's* band' who took him to be presented to the arch-pirate in his stronghold at Madagascar. Every took a liking to van Broeck and the two men spent much time in each other's company until finally Every allowed the Dutchman to leave Madagascar aboard an English East Indiaman.

According to van Broeck, John Avery was born at Plymouth in 1653 to hardworking parents. His father had served with Admiral Blake before the civil war, but on the outbreak of the conflict had left the Navy to sail on merchantmen. By hard work and careful saving he amassed a small estate and a good reputation. While his father was at sea young Avery was cared for by his mother until her death in 1659, whereupon the boy was taken into the care of his aunt. This aunt sent John to school, where he excelled and even outshone boys older than himself. John's intelligence made him unpopular amongst his school fellows, who accused him of bullying, and indeed he showed a great intolerance for authority and was often beaten for it.

Eventually Avery's father returned from the sea and settled at Cat-down, a village on the outskirts of Plymouth, until his own death in 1663. John returned once more to the care of his aunt, who shared the responsibility with Bartholomew Knowles. In 1667 John's doting aunt died, and Knowles sent John to sea aboard a man-of-war sailing to fight pirates in the Mediterranean. While John was away Knowles conspired with a local lawyer to gain possession of Avery's estate at Cat-down. In the Mediterranean John proved himself, gained the favour of his Admiral, and despite fighting a duel with a bullying lieutenant managed to secure a post on a ship sailing for the West Indies.

At Port Royal, Jamaica, John left the Navy and signed aboard one of the many buccaneer vessels that infested the Caribbean at that time. For two years Avery sailed with the buccaneers, and at the end of that time returned to England where he found that his lands and possessions had been tricked from him. He used what pay he had to fight a lawsuit against Knowles, but was unsuccessful and so returned to sea once more. He fought through the Dutch War, and at its conclusion was given command of a merchant ship bound for the West Indies once more.

After several successful trading voyages Avery made something of a name for himself, and eventually settled down to marry a farmer's daughter. However,

---

Since the authors of the early accounts of Every's life detailed here all used the spelling 'Avery' I have used the different versions of his name to signify the difference between the genuine historical pirate and the semi-fictional one described in the accounts. Throughout this chapter 'Every' refers to the genuine pirate, while 'Avery' refers to his popular fictional counterparts.

six months after the wedding Avery's wife gave birth to a baby boy with a striking resemblance to a local innkeeper, and Avery left the marital home for London. There he met with some merchants who had employed him on a previous occasion, and persuaded them to make him commander of a large merchantman, heavily armed and with a crew of brave ruffians. Once at sea Avery gathered his crew round and suggested to them that if they continued on their trading voyage they would run great risks for a meagre reward, and so their minds turned instead to piracy. They sailed first to Jamaica, where they disposed of some of their cargo in exchange for provisions, and recruited a few of Avery's old buccaneer cronies, and then set sail for the Indian Ocean.

After several months sailing back and forth in the Indian Ocean without finding any prize of value they finally came across a great ship with 1,000 men aboard, belonging to the Great Moghul. Avery was reluctant at first to attempt to capture such a prize, but his men were battle-hardened rogues, spoiling for a fight, while the Indians were virtually untrained. After only one or two broadsides the Indians struck their colours and surrendered. The pirates plundered the Indian ship of its gold and jewels, but Avery was more interested in a young lady, the daughter of the Grand Moghul himself, who was among the passengers. Taken with the princess, Avery did not immediately ravish her, but instead carried her aboard his own ship and treated her with great respect. The princess was being carried to a Persian ruler to be married, but she was so enamoured of Avery that she had her attending priest perform a marriage between herself and the pirate instead.

Along with the princess the ship contained a great number of her female servants, but instead of passing the young women around, as one might have expected the pirates to do, they drew lots and the priest performed several more marriages. Laden with riches and wives, the pirates sailed for Madagascar.

When they reached the island the inhabitants came down to the shore to watch the strange newcomers' arrival, and there was some consternation aboard the pirate ship. Some of the old buccaneers who had joined Avery at Jamaica had visited the island before though, and persuaded their captain that a gift of some presents would assure their safety. Avery was introduced to the local King and explained to him that he wished to set up a base on the island from which he could attack European trade. An alliance was forged between Avery and the natives and the pirates set about refitting their ship and establishing themselves on a small islet with a good harbour.

During a second brief cruise Avery captured two Indian vessels, and English East Indiaman, and a French pirate ship. Realising that he could not return to Europe in safety Avery and his pirates decided to build a permanent colony at Madagascar. They built a small fort, armed it with cannon from the captured ships, and named it 'Fort Avery', but realising that the threat of anarchy from within was greater than the threat of attack from without next settled down to draw up a set of laws for the new kingdom which were so fair that all of the pirate inhabitant agreed to them.

Several more adventures followed, including an unwelcome visit by the Royal Navy and a foiled mutiny by the treacherous French pirates, but Avery managed to survive all of them with great flair and genius until, tiring a little of his outcast life, he wrote to the East India Co., offering millions of pounds for a pardon. For unknown reasons the offer was ignored, and so Avery set himself to strengthening his colony and lived, more or less, happily ever after with his Indian bride.

Much of van Broeck's story was drawn from the folklore that already surrounded Every, even at that early date, but its appearance in print gave it a solid respectability that assured its continuing credibility. The year 1653 has, for example, been cited as the year of Every's birth in countless books since, without any more evidence than van Broeck's assertion that it was so. The story was written at a time when it was widely believed that Every had indeed built a fort and settlement on St Mary's Island and was the leader of the pirates based there, so it is no surprise to find that much is made of his kingdom there. It also appears to be from this story that the popular myth of Every having approached the English government with an offer to pay off the national debt sprang. Students of social history might find it interesting to note the very sympathetic way in which Avery is treated by the anonymous author: despite his faults he is hard working and successful, forced into piracy by the cupidity of his wicked guardian and faithlessness of his wife and her family; honourable in his treatment of female prisoners; a beloved and fair ruler of his little kingdom; and an enemy of the French, with whom England was at war at the time of publication.

'The Successful Pirate'

In 1712 a play opened on Drury Lane, loosely based on van Broeck's version of Every's story. The central character is Arviragus, a pirate king who has settled on Madagascar and tries to force the captured Indian princess Zaida to marry him. Zaida, though, is in love with Aranes, who, it transpires, is the long-lost son of Arviragus. The French pirates on the island try to overthrow Arviragus but are foiled.

The author of the play, Charles Johnson (not to be confused with Captain Charles Johnson, author of the *General History of the Robberies and Murders of the Most Notorious Pirates*) is generally believed to have been one of the worst playwrights in English history, and *The Successful Pirate* is excruciating to read, and must have been excruciating to watch performed. The plot is haphazard and the jokes are not particularly funny. Nevertheless, thanks to complaints that the play glamorised Every's piracy, it became somewhat controversial and thus enjoyed some success. Once the controversy has dissipated the play's popularity fell and it can hardly be considered a classic work today.

The play adds nothing to the myth of Every, and the essentials of its plot mirror van Broeck's work so closely that there is little point in describing it further. It is bad enough that this author should have to read the terrible script: I see no reason to burden anyone else with details.

'The King of the Pirates: Being an Account of the Famous Enterprises of Captain Avery'

The *King of the Pirates* was published in 1719 and can be read as a response to van Broeck's story. It purports to be written by Every himself in the form of two letters correcting earlier versions of his story, but was probably written by the great novelist of the early eighteenth century, Daniel Defoe. Like the earlier works it assumes that Every was responsible for the fortification of the pirate settlement of St Mary's, and was so clearly influenced by the then current folklore that it mirrors fairly closely the earlier works while describing them as 'ridiculous and extravagant accounts'.

The *King of the Pirates* makes no attempt to describe Every's birth and early life:

> only this I enjoin you to take notice of, that the account printed of me, with all the particulars of my marriage, my being defrauded, and leaving my family and native country on that account, is mere fable…
>
> …I shall, without any circumlocutions, give you leave to tell the world, that being bred to the sea from a youth, none of those romantic introductions published had any share in my adventures, or were any way the cause of my taking the courses I have since been embarked in.

For some years Avery, it claimed, was a logwood cutter in the Bay of Campeche, but had an ambition to become master of a ship in which he might take up piracy, having seen the wealth amassed by the buccaneers who sometimes resided in the bay. Avery sailed alongside Captain Sharp on his voyage into the South Seas (on which voyage, incidentally, Every's real-life acquaintance William Dampier sailed), but eventually found himself stranded once more at Campeche. After two years Avery and two other buccaneers decided to bury their gold and make the best of their way along the coast.

After five days travelling Avery and his companions met with some Englishmen in a small boat who took them aboard their ship. The ship turned out to be a pirate commanded by Captain 'Redhand' Nichols, a Scotsman who had earned his nickname through his savagery in battle. The pirates were short of supplies so Avery suggested they should sail for Cuba where they could hunt wild cattle, and once there he instructed them in the art of salting meat. Avery slowly gained the confidence of Captain Nichols and tried to persuade him to take the ship into the Pacific where he had earlier been so successful with Captain Sharp. Nichols approved of the idea, but his ship was too small for the voyage so the pirates cruised in the Gulf of Mexico in search of a larger ship. The first ship they captured was a large English merchantman, but was not suitable for their purposes so they continued to cruise until they took a large Irish ship, which they refitted to their own designs.

Nichols and his pirates took several prizes in the Caribbean, then made their way to the coast of Brazil where they took further prizes before sailing south, and towards the end of 1690 rounded Cape Horn and entered the Pacific. A band of buccaneers who had crossed overland from the Caribbean had put the Spanish into a fright, but Nichols and Avery were able to capture one or two small prizes on the coast of South America. Nichols was killed in an engagement with a large Spanish ship, and Avery was elected the new captain.

After taking several more prizes Avery's men began to fall out about where they should go next, until an old buccaneer suggested they should sail for Madagascar where they would be safe from the authorities and would find plentiful provisions and many rich ships to plunder. The pirates all agreed, and so they set course back round Cape Horn, across the Atlantic, and round the Cape of Good Hope to St Augustine's Bay, where by misfortune their ship was wrecked. As well as their large ship, the pirates also had a small sloop which escaped being wrecked, so after eight months on Madagascar, during which time they built a strong fort, it was decided that Avery should take some of the men to sea in the sloop in the hope of capturing another large ship which could carry the rest of the stranded crew.

Avery's intention, however, was to abandon his shipmates and sail the sloop back to England. In February 1694 the sloop reached the Caribbean. After loading supplies at Tobago, Avery then proposed that they should sail for Campeche and load logwood, with which they could sail anywhere under the pretence of being traders – though his real objective was to recover the gold he had buried there years before. Eventually Avery and his men managed to make their way back to London, where there was great disagreement about what to do next – until Avery managed to get himself appointed first mate of a 'stout ship' bound for Spain.

Avery and seven of his men were joined by three others. In the dead of night, they rose up and took control of the ship. The captain and nine of the crew refused to join the mutineers so were put ashore, but the rest agreed to join Avery. At the Canary Islands the pirates took three English ships, from which twelve seamen joined the pirates. Avery then sailed down the coast of Africa, around the Cape of Good Hope, and returned once more to Madagascar.

At Madagascar Avery was joined by the men he had left behind, as well as some other seamen whose ships had been wrecked on the island. After a fortnight or so Avery sailed for the Arabian coast, where he captured two small prizes, and then to the Indian coast. On the Indian coast the pirates heard news that two rich ships belonging to the Great Moghul were due to arrive shortly. Eventually the expected ships hove into view, and after a brief fight were taken. As in van Broeck's tale, one of the passengers on the largest vessel was a daughter of the Moghul himself, but Avery, 'like a true pirate, soon let her see that I had more mind to the jewels than the lady'. In his 'letter', Avery maintained his innocence on the count of rape: not only did he not ravish the young princess – he set a guard over her to ensure that none of his pirates did either.

Laden with riches (but no beautiful wives) the pirates sailed back to Madagascar. The story of the pirates' stay at Madagascar contained in *The King of the Pirates* is far more prosaic than van Broeck's version. There is a fort which attracts other pirate crews, but there are no fabulous Indian beauties, no mention of any laws, and no mutiny by the villainous French. In fact, a good portion of the book is taken up with Avery's attempts to leave the island.

Having made their fortunes, the pirates on Madagascar settled down to peaceful living, safe from interference thanks to the great strength they were reputed to have. But slowly the men trickled away, until it was feared that if some of them found their way back to Europe it would become known that they were not nearly as formidable as they were reputed to be. Avery thus had to use guile to effect his escape: he managed to get aboard a sloop destined for India to buy rice. The crew of the sloop put him and his followers ashore in Persia, and they travelled overland to Baghdad. There they assumed the disguise of Armenian merchants and invested their treasure in silks and other commodities. By caravan they travelled to Constantinople where Avery wrote the second of his letters, detailing his adventures thus far and announcing his intention to make the best of his way to Marseilles, and then to settle in anonymity in the south of France.

Defoe's account is far more believable than *The Life and Adventures of Captain John Avery*. The hero is far less heroic, and pours such scorn on the more romantic earlier story that it would be easy to imagine it might really have been written by Every himself, were it not for the many glaring inconsistencies with the known facts of Every's life. It is interesting therefore that the 'corrections' contained in *The King of the Pirates* have done little to dispel the myths created or perpetuated by the earlier work, even three centuries later.

'The General History of the Robberies and Murders of the Most Notorious Pirates' and 'The History and Lives of all the Most Notorious Pirates and their Crews'

The versions of Henry Every's career found in the *General History* and the *History and Lives* are so similar, more or less word for word, that they must be dealt with together. The bare bones of the story were written in the *General History*, and were copied out almost verbatim but with several significant details added in the later *History and Lives*. The similarity of the two books has led some bibliographers to assume that they are in fact merely different editions of the same work issued under slightly different titles, but this is not the case.

The *General History* was published in 1724 and such was its popularity that it enjoyed several new editions in English and other languages over the following years, and was augmented by a second volume in 1728. The *History and Lives* for the most part is an almost verbatim transcript of the *General History*, but in the chapters concerning Henry Every and Mary Read there are significant additions, and it also contains extra chapters not to be found in any earlier editions of the *General History*. The account of Every's life printed in the *History and Lives* follows the *General History*'s version fairly closely, but is considerable enlarged by the additional details. Many of these details appear to have been based loosely on the 1709 *Life and Adventures*.

The *General History* was an immediate bestseller and in the intervening centuries had been reprinted numerous times. It has formed the basis for much of the research of the last centuries and has been the principal source of information for countless books. Robert Louis Stevenson drew heavily from the *General History* when writing *Treasure Island*, and it has shaped our perception of pirates immeasurably. As a result of the book some fairly insignificant and unsuccessful pirates are better known today than some of their more important counterparts whose lives were not described by its author, Captain Charles Johnson.

The identity of the Captain Charles Johnson, for that name is a pseudonym, has perplexed and divided scholars since the 1930s. Most historians were content to reflect on the contents of the book rather than its author until John Robert Moore announced that no less a person than Daniel Defoe had penned the seminal work on pirates. Moore's arguments were compelling and led to many libraries re-cataloguing the work under Defoe's name, and though not everyone was convinced it was not until the 1980s that any serious argument against Moore's hypothesis was presented. In recent years it has been suggested, with some good reason, that the journalist Nathaniel Mist was behind the book, but he is one of several proposed candidates. This is not the place for an in-depth investigation into the authorship of the book: suffice it to say that I believe it was the work of more than one author, possibly including Defoe, and edited by one person, possibly Nathaniel Mist.

The crucial question about the *General History* concerns its accuracy: much of the second volume can be shown (by comparison to other historical records) to be seriously flawed, and this has led in turn to many people dismissing the book as largely inaccurate. However, much of the book, including the larger part of the first volume, is borne out by historical records where available. Johnson is often vague and inaccurate about dates and ship names, but frequently the outlines of the stories he presents are fairly accurate. There are exceptions, of course, but from the information contained in the text several scholars have concluded that a number of eye-witnesses and experienced experts were consulted. Of the chapters in the first volume perhaps the least accurate is that concerning Henry Every: however, it is still the most accurate version of that pirate's life published in the period.

According to Johnson, Avery was born near Plymouth and went to sea early, eventually becoming mate of a successful merchantman. A group of merchants of Bristol fitted out two privateers to sail in the service of the Spanish. One of the ships was called the *Duchess*, and other ship, commanded by Captain Gibson and with Avery as mate, was the *Duke*.

At Corunna Avery plotted amongst his fellows to run away with the *Duke* to go pirating on the coast of India, so one night when Captain Gibson – a notorious drunkard – lay in a stupor, the mutineers took over. Some men from the *Duchess*, who were privy to the plan, appeared in their longboat and gave the password, 'Is your drunken boatswain aboard?' When the mutineers were all aboard they loosed the sails and put out to sea. The captain woke from his dozing and was informed that command of the ship had been taken from him. Despite protesting he was given a boat and with five or six of his loyal men returned to shore.

Avery sailed to Madagascar without taking any prizes on the way, but upon arrival found two sloops at anchor. The crews of the sloops ran ashore in fear of Avery, thinking his was a Royal Navy ship, but Avery sent two or three unarmed men ashore to convince them of his friendship. The two sloops turned out to be pirates from the West Indies who agreed to join with Avery.

The three ships sailed together towards Arabia and eventually spotted a large prize. Avery kept his large ship at a distance from the prize and bombarded her while he sent the two smaller vessels in close to board. The prize turned out to belong to the Great Moghul himself, and was carrying pilgrims home from Mecca with a rich cargo of jewels, plate and money.

The pirates then sailed back for Madagascar where they intended to build a fort to protect themselves and their treasure, but on the way Avery suggested that all the plunder should be placed aboard his own ship. If they should encounter a storm, he told them, his larger ship would be better able to survive it, and if they were separated he was more able to resist any large ships they might meet than the smaller pirate vessels. Thus, all the plunder was brought aboard Avery's ship, and each chest was sealed with three seals to prevent any tampering.

Avery, however, was beyond mere tampering, and in the dead of night altered his course away from his companions and escaped with the whole of the treasure. He sailed for the Bahamas, where he sold his ship and bought a small sloop. In this sloop he sailed for New England, and arrived at Boston where he might have settled had not many of his men gone ashore there. Instead he sailed for Ireland, and from thence went to Bideford. From Bideford he wrote to a group of Bristol merchants asking whether they could dispose of his diamonds. Once he had handed the diamonds over to the merchants they duped him and refused to pay him anything for them. Unable to complain to the authorities he returned to Ireland, from where he worked a passage on a trading vessel to Plymouth. Intending to return to Bristol and have it out with the merchants he began to walk there, but on arrival at Bideford sickened and died.

One can see that the basic story of Every's career is reasonably well told in the *General History*, but that several of the details are wrong. For example, we know that Every took several ships between Corunna and Madagascar, and that while the *Duke* and *Duchess* were indeed Bristol privateers they were actually fitted out under the command of Woodes Rogers almost twenty years later. Johnson's story of Avery deliberately tricking his consorts out of their gold, and of failing to support them during the battle, is at direct odds with the historical record. However, the *General History* has been so important in the creation of pirate lore that his version of events has long been believed.

Crying for mercy.

Appendices

1. Every's 'Declaration' at Corunna

Houblon's assertion that the ballad was actually composed by Every is, on the face of it, absurd. However, the fact that his response to the wives' petition was the second time he made the claim makes it worthy of investigation.

He first claimed that Every and his men had left behind a declaration of their intent at Corunna on 14 July in a note to the Secretary of State.[1] Therefore, we can be sure he was aware of the verses' existence by that date at the very latest. If the name of the *Charles II* was changed to the *Fancy* after the mutiny then the first people who might have carried news of the ship's new name would have been the crews of the English ships Every subsequently met at the Isle of May (see chapter three), who remained there with Every until 9 or 10 June. Even if they sailed immediately the *Fancy* had departed, it would have been fast work for them to sail back to England and report their experiences, then for details of those experiences to have reached a song-smith, for him to have written and printed a ballad, and for that ballad to have reached the desk of Sir James Houblon – all in thirty-four days. It would not have been impossible, but it seems unlikely. Also possible perhaps is that the mutineers started calling the ship *Fancy* during the mutiny, and news of it was carried back by one of Gibson's men.

Several parts of the ballad mirror very closely what Every actually did next (honouring the English flag, and sailing for the East, for example), so the possibility remains that Every announced more of his plans to Gibson and his men than the historical record suggests. It must also be noted, however, that neither of those activities were unique to Every and the ballad writer may just have been drawing from a stock of recent news concerning pirates.

The similarity between the 'shield' described in the ballad and the actual arms of Baronet Every's family is noted in the next appendix. Since Baronet Every's family were on the rise in the 1690s it is not impossible, or even unlikely, that the writer had seen the coat of arms somewhere and incorporated it into the ballad. It is, nonetheless, an interesting coincidence for the writer to have included it.

On the other hand, we also know that parts of the ballad are entirely inaccurate. For example, in July 1694 there were not 150 men aboard the *Fancy*. When Every left a message for East India Co. ships at Johanna later in the cruise, his estimate of the number of men aboard tallies with the estimates of others, such as Phillip Middleton. It would have been no great matter for Every to have over-exaggerated his strength in the note left at Johanna, for nobody except those aboard the *Fancy* would have had enough reliable information to contradict him, yet he did not. It is unlikely in the extreme then that he would have so wildly over-exaggerated his strength in any ballad that he left at Corunna when there were so many people who knew his true strength. This, more than anything perhaps, must count against any possibility that Every wrote the verses himself.

There are, then, three possibilities about the origin of the information contained in the ballad, namely: that it was brought to England by some crewman of one of the English ships Every met at the Isle of May; that it was brought by one of the men who had been present at the mutiny and had returned with Captain Gibson; or that it was supplied by Every himself, that the ballad represents in some form, a written declaration left by Every at Corunna as maintained by Sir James Houblon.

I personally think it unlikely that Every left a declaration at Corunna. Between agreeing to the conspiracy on Sunday afternoon and carrying it out on Monday afternoon he would have been very busy! He would not have dared to leave a declaration ashore before the mutiny took place, and could not have left it there afterwards. It is possible that he left it with one of Gibson's men, but in that case one must ask why he refused to discuss his intentions with David Creagh.

Upon consideration there is nothing in the ballad which convinces me that it was indeed written by Every himself, but despite the circumstantial evidence I can see no definite proof that he did not write it. Although unlikely for reasons given here it must, therefore, remain a possibility (though a slight one) that Sir James Houblon was telling the truth about the verses.

2. Henry Every and the Derbyshire Everys

When *A Copy of Verses Composed by Captain Henry Every* was published in 1694 its mention of his supposed flag of 'four cheveralls of gold in a bloody field / Environed with green' suggested a connection between the pirate and the powerful Every family of Eggington, Derbyshire. The coat of arms of the Every baronets of Eggington was remarkably similar, bearing four red chevronels on a gold field. *The Life and Adventures of Captain John Avery* later added to the idea by suggesting that Henry Every's father had fought alongside General-at-Sea Robert Blake in the English civil war. In fact, it was a member of the Eggington family who had stood beside Blake at the siege of Taunton, and who was remembered in the general's will.

The supposed connection between the pirate and the baronets is further enhanced by the fact that the Every family had only lived at Eggington for two generations by the 1690s, and had previously been an important family in north Devon. Furthermore, the names 'John' and 'Henry' were both used by the pirate's family, and were also common names in the Eggington family.

Unfortunately, that is as far as the connection can be taken. There is no evidence that the information from either the ballad or the *Life and Adventures* is based on fact, and in truth we know that the Every who fought with Blake was not the pirate's father. Neither John nor Henry were uncommon names in seventeenth-century England, and the fact that two families sharing the same name once lived at opposite ends of the same county should not surprise us.

The Everys of Eggington did have some naval connections. Sir Henry Every, baronet in the pirate's day, had married Vere, daughter of Admiral Russell, and his younger brother, Sir John, served for many years in the Royal Navy. However, there appears to be no naval connection between Captain Sir John Every and Henry Every, master's mate. It is just possible that the Every family secured a midshipman's post for their poor cousin, but no evidence exists that this was the case.

3. Wages and Money

As noted earlier, any attempt to calculate the value of historical sums of money into modern currency is fraught with difficulty and is bound to be unreliable anyway. There are just too many factors to take into consideration. Calculations based on inflation might be mathematically accurate, but would not reflect reliably, say, the relationship between the wages of a seaman in 1695 and a seaman today. The general reduction of the prices of 'essential goods' such as clothing by the industrial revolution of the nineteenth century and subsequent reductions in prices caused by technological advance and the advent of cheap imported goods make any calculations based on the buying power of money redundant. The futility of trying to convert historical sums into modern ones is illustrated amply by the attempt made by Jan Rogozinski in *Honor Among Thieves*, in which he calculates that the plunder from the *Gang-i-Sawai* would be worth £37 million or $188 million today, without noting that those two sums are not comparable with one another (at the time of writing £37 million is worth approximately $76 million, $188 million is worth around £91.5 million).[2]

Appendices

The conversion of different currencies in use at the end of the seventeenth century presents fewer difficulties, particularly as the most widely accepted currency worldwide was the Spanish 'piece of eight' (a silver coin worth eight reales). In 1704 Queen Anne issued a proclamation regulating the value in pounds sterling of foreign coins. The value of a piece of eight varied depending on when and where it was minted, but mostly they were valued at 4s 6d. In the English colonies where ready cash was scarcer, the value of the silver coin might have been as much as 6s.[3]

The best way of examining and understanding the sums of money mentioned throughout the text is probably to compare them with each other, and with other sums from the same period. Every's wages, for example, can be compared easily. When he joined the Navy in 1689 the wage of a midshipman on a third-rate ship (such as HMS *Rupert*) was £1 17s 6d per lunar month. Every's promotion to master's mate increased his wages to £2 16s 2d, and his transfer to the larger, second rate, HMS *Albemarle* in 1690 increased it further to £3 per month, or £39 per annum. When Every was discharged from HMS *Albemarle* he was owed £7 3s 6d, of which 2s 6d was to be paid to the Chatham Chest, a sailors' welfare fund. As first mate of the *Charles II*, Every was promised around £5 per month, or £65 per annum. Thus, if Every's share of the pirates' plunder was £3,000 after two years at sea he earned forty-six times what he could have earned as a mate in the Spanish Expedition, and almost seventy-seven times what he earned as mate in a second-rate ship of the Royal Navy. A ship the size of the *Fancy* would have been regarded as a fourth-rate vessel had she been employed by the Royal Navy. The captain of a fourth rate vessel was paid £10 10s per month, £136 10s per annum, or a little under one tenth of what Every earned as captain of the *Fancy*.[4]

The common crewmen of the *Fancy* fared similarly well. A seaman in the Royal Navy was paid 19s per month, or £12 7s per annum, while the seamen of the Spanish Expedition were contracted at more than twice that wage: £2 per month, £26 per annum. A share of £1,000 from the plunder of the *Fancy*'s voyage represented almost eighty years' wages to a Navy seaman – or thirty-eight years' worth of wages in the Spanish Expedition. Since none of the seamen of the Spanish Expedition ever actually received more than a few pounds of wages, the latter comparison is purely academic. The lower-ranking officers did not do quite so well from the piracy by comparison. Had, for example, the steward William May served in that rank on a fourth-rate ship of the Royal Navy he would have received £1 3s 4d per month, £15 3s 4d per annum, or had he remained in his post as a steward on the Spanish Expedition (and been paid for it), he would have received £3 per month, £39 per annum. May claimed only to have been given a share of £500, but this was probably a deliberate underestimate, and if we assume that he received a share of £1,000 it would have been the equivalent of over twenty-five years service on the *Charles II* or nearly sixty-six years of Royal Navy pay.[5]

The pirates, of course, were not the only ones to profit from the plunder of the *Fateh Muhammad* and *Gang-i-Sawai*. The bribe collected by the pirates before landing at Nassau amounted to approximately £600, and the value of the cargo and gear left aboard the *Fancy* when the pirates donated it to Governor Trott was estimated at £1,000. The total profit to Trott was therefore more than five times his annual wage of £300 for literally doing nothing – enough to buy about eighty-four slaves if he was so inclined, the cost of a slave being less than double the £10 paid by the pirates for horses in Ireland. Examination of the governor's wage also puts into perspective the £100 protection money each pirate who settled in Philadelphia paid to Governor Markham.

The reward offered for each of the pirates was a mere £50, the cost of two slaves and an Irish horse. The £500 offered for the apprehension of Every himself was not enough to buy a colonial sloop: the *Sea Flower* cost £600.

4. Every and Kidd

In recent years it has been suggested by several theorists that Henry Every was a some-time associate of William Kidd, usually leading to the conclusion that Kidd was really sailing in search of Every's hidden treasure, or that the two men buried their treasure together on a desert island, sometimes suggested as Oak Island off the coast of Nova Scotia. The discussion of the mythical Oak Island treasure has no place here, but the supposed relationship between Every and Kidd is worth examination.

The evidence presented in favour of the relationship can be summed up in three points:
1. When Kidd sailed in to New York he called first at Gardiner's Island where he was entertained by John Gardiner, the island's owner. From Gardiner Kidd bought supplies: he also arranged to leave some of his plunder there for safekeeping. Legend has it that Kidd asked Mrs Gardiner to roast him a pig, and because of her generosity he made her a present of various articles, including some cloth inlaid with gold thread, known as 'cloth of gold'. Subsequent generations have divided the cloth up, and most of it has since been lost, but a small fragment of it can be seen on public display at a local library.

The theorists have concluded that the cloth of gold was not part of the cargo carried by the *Quedah Merchant*, and so must have come from some other source, namely the plunder of the *Gang-i-Sawai*.
2. During Every's homeward-bound voyage in 1696 he called into the New York region and spent some time there. At around the same time, Kidd arrived in New York on his outward-bound voyage. There is therefore a time lasting several days, perhaps even weeks, during which Kidd and Every met over a tankard of beer or glass of wine and discussed their plans. The certificate issued to John Devin, surgeon of the *Fancy*, states that Every's ship arrived in Providence, Rhode Island in April 1696.
3. It is remarkable that after such a successful career Every should have died in poverty. The story about the treachery of the Bristol merchants is clearly false: since Every had stolen the *Charles II* from a consortium of Bristol merchants in the first place they

would be the last group of people he would entrust his fortune to. He must therefore have lost his fortune some other way. The theory goes that the unexpected arrest of Captain Kidd in 1699 prevented Every from retrieving the treasure they had conspired to hide, and so when his immediate ready cash ran out he was destitute.

Other spurious ideas have been put forward in support of the theory, but these three points, and in particular the first two, are the important ones on which the theory relies.

To take the first point, I have been unable to discover the origin of the notion that the cloth of gold was not originally taken by Kidd. In the years immediately following Kidd's trial and execution Cogi Baba, one of the Armenian merchants whose goods were shipped on the *Quedah Merchant*, petitioned for the return of his goods or restitution from the Admiralty, who had sold Kidd's plunder at auction. Among the goods listed by Cogi Baba were muslins, silks, and calicoes. Since Kidd himself described the present to Mrs Gardiner as 'several pieces of silk stript with silver and gold' it is entirely reasonable to assume that they came from among the silks stolen from Cogi Baba or one of his associates.[6]

However, the question of whether they might have been stolen from the *Gang-i-Sawai* still remains. In the absence of any detailed manifest the theorists turn instead to fiction, maintaining that Daniel Defoe's *The Life, Adventures and Piracies of the Famous Captain Singleton* is a thinly disguised but factually accurate biography of Henry Every. However, Singleton's story does not tally with Every's known life – and at one point in the story Singleton actually meets Every. The novel was published twenty-four years after Every's disappearance, so even if Every or one of his crew did lend a hand providing background information it is unreasonable to assume that any of the details are accurate, let alone to use those details as though they were historical fact. Defoe's novel does not contain an accurate record of Every's plunder, and there is evidence that the Gardiner cloth was indeed among the cargo of the *Quedah Merchant* taken by Kidd, so the first argument in favour of a Kidd-Every union can be disregarded.

The idea that Kidd and Every may have met in New York while the former was outbound and the latter was homebound is even simpler to dispel. Every's movements during the spring and summer of 1696 are well documented in several sources. Every arrived in the Bahamas around the beginning of April, and remained there until the beginning of June, at which time he set sail for Ireland. At the end of June the pirates arrived in Ireland and a short while later Every split off from the group (with Mrs Adams in tow). In fact, Every was never in New York. The certificate of John Devin which has been used to suggest that Every landed at Providence, Rhode Island, was actually made out at New Providence, Bahamas.

At about the time Every arrived in the Bahamas Kidd was weighing anchor in the Downs and sailing for Plymouth. After a short stop in that city, Kidd set sail on 23 April: he reached New York on 4 July. Kidd remained in New York until 6 September. By the time Kidd was in New York Every was in Ireland; he did not call in to North America on the homeward voyage, but if he had he would have been long gone by the time Kidd got there anyway. Thus, the theorists' second argument is dismissed. [7]

Regarding the third point, that Every's poverty can only be explained by Kidd's arrest, the theorists labour under two misapprehensions: firstly, that it is certain Every died in poverty, and secondly, that he could not have approached merchants of Bristol to fence his jewels because he had previously stolen the *Charles II* from their community. In fact, the Spanish Expedition was sent forth by London merchants: the association of Bristol with the enterprise is an error which can be laid at the door of Captain Charles Johnson. Every's death in poverty, though credible, is only one of several theories regarding his end, and is plausibly explained by the story of the Bristol merchants.

There is, therefore, no evidence at all that Kidd and Every had anything to do with one another, that they ever met, or even that one had heard of the other until Kidd heard Every's name in the eastern seas, while there is plenty of evidence against their having had any piratical association. It remains a possibility that they met briefly at sea when they were both crossing the North Atlantic in June 1696, but since they were sailing in opposite directions on different courses across an area of sea measuring approximately 5 million square miles, it is unlikely in the extreme.

5. Legends of Every's Buried Treasure

Like all the best pirates, Henry Every has attracted legends of hidden or buried treasure. Of the many hundreds of pirates who sailed the seas throughout the centuries only a few can be shown to have buried any part of their treasure. The best-known example is that of William Kidd, who is believed to have buried some of his loot on Gardiner's Island, and who certainly claimed before his execution to have buried thousands of pounds. Other examples may include Jack Rackham and Blackbeard, both of whom are described as hiding some of their plunder by Captain Johnson, and Peter Easton, who was believed by the authorities in his own time to have buried thousands of pounds in Ireland. Lady Elizabeth Killigrew ordered six plundered chairs to be buried in her garden following a piratical raid by some of her servants. Thanks no doubt to the literature of Robert Louis Stevenson and Edgar Allen Poe, stories of buried treasure are now an essential part of any pirate yarn.

One of the Every legends places some of his loot on Gallops Island in Boston harbour. In some versions of the legend Every himself buried stolen diamonds on the island, while in other versions the diamonds were buried by Every's second in command, 'Hendricks'. A third version has Every burying the treasure and drawing a map which he subsequently gave to Hendricks. This supposed map eventually found its way into the collection of New England historian Edward Rowe Snow. Snow is rightly remembered for his tireless conservation work on historical monuments, but as an historian he was lacking, for he was far too ready to believe all that he heard or read.

The Hendricks map is certainly a hoax, perpetrated by persons unknown for similarly obscure reasons.

Every himself was never in the Boston region during the immediate aftermath of his piracy, and there is no other mention of his second in command being called Hendricks. On some pirate ships the post of second in command was assumed by the quartermaster, in this case Henry Adams or Joseph Dawson, but aboard the *Fancy* the second in command was probably either Robert Richie, the sailing master or, more likely, Robert Chinton, the lieutenant. Despite the apparent aid of the treasure map no diamonds have been found on Gallops Island.

More plausible, but not necessarily any more accurate, is the legend that Every buried some of his treasure near the Lizard in Cornwall. Some of the treasure is said to be hidden at Kennack Cove near Cadgwith on the eastern side of the Lizard peninsula, while the rest is supposed to be hidden at Gunwalloe on the western side. The legends vary as to whether the treasure is split between these two sites, or whether the two sites are rivals to the claim of hiding the whole amount. In the nineteenth century the legend was embellished to include mysterious references to three grass-covered stones on a high promontory, and the treasure was itemised:

1st chest. Haslar wood 2ft long and 1ft wide. In it were precious stones and bracelets, large rubies, sapphires, emeralds, topazes and diamonds.

2nd chest. Almost the same size and make as the first. 120 ingots of gold, 40 thick flat pieces of gold as large as a round tobacco box, with various characters on some of them, 25 bars of gold, some of which was 4 or 5 inches long.

3rd chest has 3,000 pieces of eight besides bullion, not weighed but crammed in with pieces of brocades.'[8]

In fact, the legend of Every's treasure buried in Cornwall goes back to his own time. In February 1701, information reached a Mr St Lo that Every or some of his men had hidden treasure in the county. St Lo wrote to Secretary of State James Vernon, who replied that King William himself had taken an interest and that St Lo should instigate a search. An unspecified reward was offered to the finder, but if anyone did discover Every's treasure in the caves around the Lizard they very sensibly kept it to themselves.[9]

6. The Crew of the *Fancy*

Sadly it is impossible to compile a complete list of the pirates who sailed aboard the *Fancy*. Many of the crew joined after the ship left Corunna and before she reached the Bahamas, and so managed to escape mention by name in the records of the time. Nevertheless, a significant proportion of the crew are named in the various documents relating to Every and his piracy, so a partial muster list is possible. Officers are listed in descending order of rank, crewmen are listed alphabetically:

Henry Every – captain
Robert Clinton – lieutenant
Robert Richie – sailing master
Edmund Lassells – officer of unspecified rank
Henry Adams – quartermaster
Joseph Dawson – quartermaster
Robert Prince – boatswain
John Guy – carpenter
Thomas Joy – cooper
Broadneck – carpenter's mate
Thomas Johnson – cook
John Devin – surgeon
Thomas Anderson
Thomas Belisha
William Bishop
Thomas Bolitho
James Brown
William Caddy
Edward Carwitheris
Thomas Castleton
Richard Chope
Peter Claus
Cornish
James Craggett
James Cray
Samuel Dawson
John Dann
John Down
William Downe
John Elston
David Evans
Charles Faulkner
Edward Forseith
Francis Frennier
Jacob Game
Joseph Goss
Benjamin Griffin
William Griffin
James Grey

James Hammond
Thomas Hollingsworth
Thomas Johnson
Thomas Jope
Thomas Joyce
John King
Edward Kirkwood
Thomas Lane
Patrick Lawson
James Lewis
William May
John Mathias
Dennis Merrick
Phillip Middleton
John Miller
Joseph Morris
James Murray
Robert Ogilby
William Phillips
Nathaniel Pike
Josiah Rayner
John Reddy
John Reidy
Joseph Roy
Edward Saville
Richard Saville
Robert Seely
Edward Short
Daniel Smith
Peter Soames
Thomas Somerton
John Sparks
James Stevenson
John Strousier
Turlagh Sullivan
Dennis Turpin
Wastcoate
Francis Wilson

Notes

The most commonly used source for the history of Every's life is Captain Charles Johnson's *General History of the Robberies and Murders of the Most Notorious Pirates*, though in some histories the other publications of the 1696-1732 period listed elsewhere in this book have also been used. Unfortunately, all of those sources contain factual errors to a greater or lesser degree. Captain Johnson's account is more or less correct in its outline, but many of the details are incorrect. The version of the story found in the *History and Lives of all the Most Notorious Pirates and their Crews* closely follows Captain Johnson's version and so is no more or less reliable. The other accounts written in the early eighteenth century are all more fiction than fact. Of the many brief accounts published in more modern books only a few are drawn from sources other than Johnson's account, and of these the one found in Charles Grey's *Pirates of the Eastern Seas* (1933) was probably the best until the publication of Joel Baer's *Pirates* (2007). Professor Baer has made a long study of Every's life and career, and it is no surprise to find that his account is excellent, marred only by its brevity. Professor Baer has also written three articles examining aspects of Every's story in considerable detail.

A wide variety of sources have been used in the compilation of this book. Documents contained in the various *Calendars of State Papers* for the relevant years, Domestic, Ireland, and Colonial (America and West Indies) series, give a very good outline of the events of 1694 and the following years. The documents contained in John Jameson's *Privateering and Piracy in the Colonial Period* have been invaluable, particularly in the study of the arrival of the pirates in Ireland in the summer of 1696.

The National Archives, Kew, hold many of the original documents relating to Every's career and piracy. Among the Admiralty papers are the muster books, pay books, and log books from which much of my account of Every's service in the Royal Navy has been drawn. Various sets of documents relating to the Spanish Expedition are housed at Kew, and of these the papers relating to the petition of the seamen's wives and to the subsequent petitions for wages by the seamen themselves are the most useful.

The bulk of Every's story from the time of the mutiny at Corunna to his disappearance in Ireland has been reconstructed from information provided by the pirates themselves. John Dann and Phillip Middleton both gave numerous depositions, but they were only two among many of the pirates who told their stories to the authorities. Most of the depositions can be found in the bound volume pertaining to the High Court of the Admiralty numbered 1/53. Along with Dann's testimony the best of the accounts is the confession of William Phillips, made in Dublin in August 1696 and found among the State Papers.

Too many other documents have been used to list them all here – they are all cited in the end notes – but special mention should be made of the published version of the trial notes of Joseph Dawson and the others. While no record remains of the proceedings of the pirates' first and third trials, which dealt with the piracy against the *Gang-i-Sawai* and other vessels, these matters were touched on during the pirates' second trial, for the mutiny at Corunna. It is a great pity that the testimony given at the first and third trial is no longer available to us, because the second trial sheds so much light on the details of the events of the mutiny that I suspect the missing testimony might tell us far more about the piracy committed during the cruise of the *Fancy* than I have been able to reconstruct from all of the depositions together. The testimony given at the trial is, I believe, the only source which directly quotes any dialogue between Henry Every and his associates, and even if we cannot assume that the witnesses remembered it word perfectly two years later it does at least convey a sense of the style of the archpirate's speech. More than any other source, the trial conveys the way the pirates felt, and captures some of the confusion which existed in the moment. If the glimpse into the pirates' lives afforded by the trial is brief, it is also deep.

ADM. Admiralty papers held at the National Archives, Kew.

Baer (1994). Baer, J.H., ''Captain John Avery' and the Anatomy of a Mutiny'. Published in *Eighteenth Century Life* 18 (February 1994), pp. 1-20

Baer (1996). Baer, J.H., 'William Dampier at the Crossroads: New Light on the 'Missing Years,' 1691-1697'. Published in the *International Journal of Maritime History*, VIII, No. 2 (December 1996), pp. 97-117

Earle. Earle, P., *Sailors: English Merchant Seamen 1650-1775*. Methuen, 1998

Grey. Grey, C., *Pirates of the Eastern Seas*. Sampson Low, Marston and Co., 1933

Hannibal. Phillips, T., *A Journal of a Voyage Made in the Hannibal of London, Ann. 1693, 1694*. Reprinted in *A Collection of Voyages and Travels,* vol. 6 (London, 1746), pp. 189-255

HCA. Papers relating to the High Court of the Admiralty held at the National Archives, Kew.

History and Lives. Anon. *The History and Lives of all the Most Notorious Pirates, and their*

Crews, (fourth edition). London, 1732

Jameson. Jameson, J.F. (ed.), *Privateering and Piracy in the Colonial Period: Illustrative Documents.* Macmillan, 1923

Naval Documents. Hodges, H.W. and Hughes, E.A. (eds), *Select Naval Documents.* Cambridge University Press, 1922

Phillips. *The Voluntary Confession and Discovery of William Phillips*, 8 August 1696. National Archives SP 63/358, fols. 127-32

Rodger. Rodger, N.A.M., *The Command of the Ocean.* Allen Lane, 2004

Rogozinski. Rogozinski, J., *Honor Among Thieves.* Stackpole Books, 2000

SP. State Papers held at the National Archives, Kew.

Talboys-Wheeler. Talboys-Wheeler, J., *A History of the English Settlements in India.* Curzon Press, 1878 (1972 reprint)

Teonge. Teonge, H., Manwaring, G.E. (ed), *The Diary.* Routledge, 1927

Trial. The published version of *The Tryals of Joseph Dawson, Edward Forseith, William May, William Bishop, James Lewis, and John Sparks: For several Piracies and Robberies.* Reprinted in *A Compleat Collection of State-Tryals, and Proceedings… From the Reign of King Henry the Fourth to the End of the Reign of Queen Anne.* London, 1719. Volume 4, pp. 217-32

Wives' Petition. Papers relating to the petition of Jane May, Ann Johnson, Mary Gulston, Mary Guyham, Ann Joy, and Several Others. National Archives, CO 388/4 fols. 48-62

Prologue

[1] Phillips, fol. 131; Baptism records of Newton Ferrers, West Devon Record Office. This identification was, I believe, first noted by Professor Joel Baer.

[2] Phillips, fol. 131.

[3] For examples of the signatures of Every's men see the depositions contained in *HCA* 1/53; letter at Johanna, Jameson, p. 154; Every's letters to his wife, Wives Petition, fol. 52; for general seamen's literacy, see Earle, pp. 20-1.

[4] Stackhouse, A., *Holy Cross Parish Church.* Newton Ferrers, 1998. pp. 3-4.

[5] Earle, p. 20.

[6] Trial, p. 223.

Chapter One

[1] Lloyd, C., *The Nation and the Navy* (The Cresset Press, 1954), pp. 74-6; Rodger, pp. 138-41

[2] Baer (1994), pp. 3-4; ADM 36/3148. Professor Baer claims to have found no documentation of Every's career prior to his enlistment on HMS *Rupert*, and despite searching through numerous muster books and pay books of the Royal Navy prior to that date

I cannot add anything. It remains a possibility that in the future more information will come to light, probably in the form of Every's name in the books of some merchant vessel or other. Although the *Rupert's* muster book does not specifically name Every as a midshipman, Professor Baer believes it to be the case and I am entirely in agreement. Every's wages and subsequent promotion are certainly suggestive of his having been a midshipman. Assuming that Every was a midshipman it is surprising that no record of earlier service in the Royal Navy has yet been found, as it was usual for a man to be made midshipman once he had served a year or more in the Navy. Occasionally men who had long service in merchant ships might be admitted to the Royal Navy as petty officers, and in the absence of evidence to the contrary we can only assume that Every was one of them. While not explicit evidence, Every's presence in the paybook of HMS *Rupert* is certainly very suggestive indeed of earlier sailing experience.

[3] *Naval Documents*, pp. 52-53.

[4] ibid, p. 110.

[5] ibid, p. 75.

[6] ibid, pp. 72-3; ADM 107/1.

[7] ADM 36/3148.

[8] Quoted in Lloyd, C., *The British Seaman* (Collins, 1968), p. 96.

[9] Teonge, pp. 22-3.

[10] Rodger, p. 214.

[11] Baer (1994), p. 4; ADM 33/136.

[12] Rodger, p. 620.

[13] Monson, W., *The Naval Tracts*, reprint, vol. 4 (Navy Records Society, 1913), p. 23.

[14] ADM 51/55.

[15] Rodger, p. 611.

[16] ibid, p. 145; ADM 51/55.

[17] ADM 51/55.

[18] *Naval Documents*, pp. 90-1.

[19] ibid, p. 92.

[20] Rodger, p. 145.

[21] ADM 51/55.

[22] Hoste, Père P., *L'Art des Armées Navales*, 1697, quoted in *Naval Documents*, pp. 103-4. Paul Hoste was a professor of mathematics at the Royal College of Marine, Toulon, and he associated with Admirals Tourville and D'Estrées. He was present at the Battle of Beachy Head, and his generous assessment of Torrington's tactics can be taken as typical.

[23] ADM 51/55; ADM 33/127.

[24] Several records state that Henry Every was married, and despite an exhaustive search I have only succeeded in finding one record of marriage which could possibly be that of Henry Every the pirate. Corroborating evidence that this marriage record does indeed refer to the correct Henry Every is non-existent, but Henry Every was known to be ashore near London less than a month before 11 September, and

the east London area in which the marriage took place would be the natural place for discharged seamen in the region like Every to gravitate towards. The church of St James was also, as noted in the text, only a short distance from Mrs Every's known home on Ratcliffe Highway. Sadly, none of the documents which mention Every's wife give her first name, so some doubt must remain.

[25] Grey, pp. 152-3.

[26] Merriman, R.D. (ed.), *The Sergison Papers* (Navy Records Society, 1950), pp. 285-6.

[27] Hannibal, p. 222.

[28] ibid, p. 234.

[29] ibid, p. 235.

[30] ibid, p. 245.

[31] ibid, p. 253.

Chapter Two

[1] For an excellent study of the Spanish Expedition and subsequent mutiny see Baer (1994).

[2] *CSPD* 1693, p. 44.

[3] For an excellent account of Phips' 1686-7 expedition see Earle, P., *The Wreck of the Almirante* (MacMillan, 1979).

[4] Dyer, F.E., 'Captain John Strong, privateer and treasure hunter', *Mariners' Mirror*, XIII (1927), pp. 145-59.

[5] Fox, E.T., *Pirates of the West Country* (Tempus, 2007), pp. 87-94.

[6] Charnock, J., *Biographia Navalis*, vol. 2 (London 1795), p. 76.

[7] *CSPD* 1693, p. 164.

[8] *Wives' Petition*, 55.

[9] *CSPD* 1693, p. 5.

[10] Baer (1994), p. 5.

[11] *HCA* 13/82, fol. 106.

[12] See, for examples, the contract of William May, *Wives' Petition*, 61; William Street, SP 42/3 fol. 702; Robert Strong, SP 42/3 fol. 704.

[13] *Wives' Petition*, 49.

[14] *HCA* 13/82 fol. 106.

[15] *Wives' Petition*, 49.

[16] Phillips.

[17] *Wives' Petition*, 49.

[18] The Examination of John Sparks, 10 September 1696.

[19] *HCA* 13/81 fol. 256.

[20] The events of 7 May 1694 were complex and confusing, and can hardly be understood from only one or two sources. The mutiny and the following departure of Gibson and his men have been reconstructed from various witness accounts, particularly Phillips;

The Information of Phillip Middleton, 8 September 1696; *The Examination of John Sparks*, 10 September 1696; *The Information of Thomas Joy*, 16 August 1699; Jameson, p. 165; and the testimony of John Gravet, David Creagh, T. Druit, and John Dann in Trial, pp. 221-4.

21 *Wives' Petition.*

22 The version of the ballad given here is that which was presented by Sir James Houblon (*Wives' Petition*, 59), but it is subtly different from the printed version entitled *A Copy of Verses composed by Captain Henry Every, lately Gone to Sea to seek his Fortune* (London 1694).

Chapter Three

1 Trial, p. 225; Grey, p. 155.

2 Hannibal, p. 204.

3 Phillips.

4 The account of the three English ships at the Isle of May has been reconstructed using information from The *Examination of David Evans*, 27 January 1697; *The Examination of Edward Carwitheris*, 12 July 1699; Grey, p. 155; 'Narrative of Phillip Middleton', 4 August 1696, *CSPC 1696*, pp. 260-1; *The Examination of John Sparks*, 10 September 1696; *The Examination of James Lewis*, 13 October 1696.

5 *The Examination of John Sparks*, 10 September 1696; Jameson, p. 166; Phillips.

6 Hannibal, pp. 227-8.

7 Johnson, pp. 180-91.

8 'Examination of Peter Claus', *CSPC 1697-98*, p. 184.

9 ibid; Jameson, p. 166; Trial, p. 225; Grey, pp. 155-6; *Proceedings of the Council of Maryland, 1698-1731* (Baltimore, 1905), vol. 25, p. 562.

10 Butler, Nathaniel, *Boteler's Dialogues* (Navy Records Society, 1929), p. 132.

11 Jameson, p. 156.

12 Ibid, p. 166.

13 Johnson, pp. 130-1.

14 For havens on Madagascar see Rogozinski.

15 Rogozinski, p. 81; *Deposition of Adam Baldridge*, Jameson, pp. 180-7.

16 Trial, p. 225; Jameson, p. 166.

17 Trial, pp. 224-7; Jameson, p. 166-7; *The Examination of William May*, 10 September 1696.

18 Ibid; *The Examination of John Sparks*, 10 September 1696; Grey, p. 157.

19 John Leckie to Leonard Edgecomb, 24 August 1695, reprinted in Grey, pp. 133-5.

20 Trial, pp. 227-8.

21 Jameson, p. 154.

22 Ibid, p. 155; Trial, pp. 224-5.

Chapter Four

1 Grey, pp. 81-8, 90, 196-7.

2 Trial, pp. 224-5.

3 Jameson, p. 167; Rogozinski, pp. 71; *CSPC* 1696-7, p. 260; Phillips

4 For early colonial privateering and piracy see *Pirates of the New England Coast*; for the careers of the Blessed William and Jacob see Ritchie, pp. 31-8; Zacks, pp. 72-6.

5 The meeting of the three ships is recorded in several depositions and other sources, but the most detailed is Phillips.

6 Jameson, pp. 167-8, 183-5.

7 'The Examination of James Brown, 17 October 1700' (*HCA* 1/26 fol. 16). Although the muster books and pay books of HMS *Rupert* and *Albemarle* from Every's time contain several names similar to or the same as those of some of the pirates who sailed with Every in the *Fancy*, James Brown is the only one whose connection I have found solid evidence for. It may well be that some of the other pirates had sailed with Every during his Royal Navy days, but this must remain speculation, for such intense biographical research lies outside the scope of this book.

8 *CSPC* 1696-7, p. 260; Grey, pp. 130-1.

9 Dow, G.F., and Edmonds, J. H., *Pirates of the New England Coast* (Dover reprint, 1996), p. 84; *CSPC* 1699, p. 44; ibid 1696-7, p. 744.

10 Johnson, p. 423.

11 Jameson, p. 183; *CSPC* 1696-7, p. 260.

12 *CSPC* 1697-8, p. 587.

13 *CSPC* 1696-7, p. 260; *Pirates of the New England Coast*, pp. 94-5.

14 *The Examination of James Lewis*, 13 October 1696.

15 Jameson, p. 168; *CSPC* 1696-7, p. 262.

16 Trial, p. 225.

17 Jameson, p. 168; *CSPC* 1696-7, p. 262.

18 For example, *The Examination of James Lewis*, 13 October 1696.

19 Ibid; *The Examination of John Sparks*, 10 September 1696; *The Examination of James Lewis*, 13 October 1696.

20 Hamilton, Alexander. *A New Account of the East Indies, volume 1* (reprint, London, 1930), p. 89.

21 Richie, pp. 102-3.

22 Trial, p. 224.

23 Jameson, p. 168; *CSPC* 1696-7, p262; *The Examination of John Sparks*, 10 September 1696; *The Examination of James Lewis*, 13 October 1696; Trial, pp. 224, 226.

24 Jameson, p. 168; Grey, pp. 159-60.

25 Johnson, p. 53.

26 This author can write with some authority on the confusion resulting from the sudden unexpected loss of a mast. Whilst carrying out maintenance work on a square

rigged ship in early 2007 the mizzen mast fell. Although there was no battle going on at the time the loss of the mast, which remained attached to the ship by about half its rigging, left the working party in a state of shock and confusion. Splintered wood and ropes littered the deck, and for a few minutes (which seemed like half an hour) nobody knew quite what to do. Thanks to safety procedures in place nobody was injured, but the crew then faced a race against the tide to get the mast free and dragged away from the ship before she settled down on the fallen spars, potentially damaging the hull. I can only add that it would have taken an incredibly disciplined and efficient crew to effectively deal with such a catastrophe while under fire from another ship and with the added imminent danger of hand-to-hand fighting.

[27] The fight between the *Gang-i-Sawai* and the pirate ships has been reconstructed from the depositions of John Dann, Jameson, pp. 168-9, and *CSPC* 1696-7, p. 262; the testimony of John Dann and Phillip Middleton, Trial, pp. 224-6; Phillips; the deposition of Phillip Middleton reprinted in Grey, p. 159; and the account of the battle by contemporary Indian historian Khufi Khan, also quoted at length in Grey, p. 160.

The figure of 180 men sharing the plunder is given by Dann, and may only refer to the men aboard the *Fancy*, especially considering that the men of the *Pearl* later forfeited their shares as related in the next chapter. However, since the *Fancy* had aboard some 230 men, even this would represent a loss of over one fifth. Assuming the *Pearl*, which took an active part in the battle and which was less suited to attacking such large ships, to have suffered a similar casualty rate the pirates must have suffered between sixty deaths at the lowest estimate and 110 at the highest. William Phillips stated the number of shares as 160, and seems to have been speaking of the total number, but one cannot be certain.

[28] Quoted in Grey, p. 161.

[29] *CSPC* 1696-7, p. 261.

[30] Jameson, pp. 158-9.

[31] For atrocities towards women see ibid; Grey, pp. 159-161; *CSPC* 1696-7, p. 261.

Chapter Five

[1] Quoted in Talboys-Wheeler, pp. 20-1.

[2] Quoted in ibid, pp. 28-9.

[3] Jameson, pp. 156-7.

[4] Annesley's life story, which is an interesting one, can be read in Wright's *Annesley of Surat*, London 1918.

[5] Jameson, p. 157.

[6] ibid.

[7] Quoted in Wright, p. 170.

[8] Grey, p. 110.

[9] Wright, pp. 170-1.

[10] ibid, pp. 166-7.

[11] Jameson, pp. 156-7.

[12] ibid, pp. 157-8.

[13] Wright, pp. 164-6.

[14] Quoted ibid, pp. 166-7.

[15] Jameson, p. 158.

[16] Quoted in Wright, p. 176.

[17] ibid, pp. 179-80.

[18] ibid, pp. 181-9.

[19] Jameson, p. 169; SP 63/358 fol. 127.

[20] *CSPC* 1696-7, p. 261.

[21] Grey, p. 162.

[22] *CSPC* 1696-7, pp. 261, 263; *The Examination of John Sparks*, 10 September 1696; *The Examination of William Bishop*, 15 October 1696; *The Information of Thomas Joy*, 16 August 1699.

[23] Trial, p. 225; *CSPC* 1696-7, p. 263.

[24] Grey, p 162; Rodger, pp. 620-1. According to the 1686 scale of pay, seamen received 19s per lunar month while able seamen were paid £1 4s. In my calculations I have simplified a 'man's' wages to £1 per month, or £13 per year.

[25] Johnson, pp. 54-5.

[26] *CSPC* 1696-7, p. 263; Rogozinski, pp. 74-5; SP 63/358 fol. 127. The conversion of pieces of eight into pounds sterling is based on *A Royal Proclamation regulating the value of foreign coins*, 18 June 1704, printed in Jensen, M. (ed.), *American Colonial Documents to 1776* (Eyre and Spottiswoode, 1955), pp. 426-7.

[27] Johnson, pp. 58, 439.

[28] Jameson, p. 184.

[29] ibid, p. 159; SP 63/358 fol. 127.

Chapter Six

[1] The Examination of John Dann, 3 August 1696, reprinted in Jameson, p. 169.

[2] Grey, p. 162.

[3] Narrative of Phillip Middleton, *CSPC* 1696-7, p. 261; Grey, pp. 163, 168.

[4] Rogozinski, p. 249.

[5] Quoted in Grey, p. 163.

[6] Affidavit of Phillip Middleton, 11 November 1696, reprinted in Jameson, p. 172.

[7] The case of Nicholas Trott, *CSPC* 1698, p. 506.

[8] ibid p. 507; *Affidavit of Phillip Middleton*, 11 November 1696, reprinted in Jameson, pp. 172-3; 'The examination of John Dann', 3 August 1696, *CSPC* 1696-7, p. 262-3; 'The Voluntary Confession and Discovery of William Phillips', fol. 130.

[9] *Affidavit of Phillip Middleton*, 11 November 1696, reprinted in Jameson, p. 172-3.

[10] *CSPC* 1698, p. 208; Jameson, pp. 178-80; Grey, p. 165.

[11] *CSPC* 1699-1700, pp. 128-9.

[12] Baer (1996), pp. 110-1.

[13] Trial pp. 217, 227; *The Examination of David Evans*, 27 January 1697; *The Information of George Trevithin*, 12 July 1699; *The Information of Zachary Pitman*, undated; *The Examination of Edward Carwitheris*, 12 July 1699.

[14] *The Examination of David Evans*, 27 January 1697; *HCA* 1/29, fols. 108-21.

[15] *CSPC* 1697-8, p. 288; Rogozinski, p. 249.

[16] *CSPC* 1696-97, pp. 613-5.

[17] The information on Every's men at Philadelphia comes principally from documents in the *Calendar of State Papers and Maryland State records*, namely *CSPC* 1696-97, pp. 613-615; *CSPC* 1697-98, pp. 211-5; *Proceedings of the Council of Maryland, 1698-1731* (Baltimore, 1905), vol. 25, pp. 564, 577-80; Proclamation, *CSPD* 1696, p. 337; Brown's arrest with Kidd's men, *HCA* 1/26, fol. 16.

[18] *CSPD* 1696, p. 331; Jameson, pp. 160, 170-1, 174; Grey, pp. 164-5.

[19] Jameson, pp. 161-5.

[20] *CSPD* 1696, p. 331; *CSPD* 1697, pp. 44, 237.

[21] *The Arraignment, Tryal, and Condemnation of Captain John Quelch, and others of his Company* (London, 1704), pp. 17-9.

[22] Jameson, pp. 161-5, 184; *CSPC* 1696-97, pp. 259-60.

[23] Phillips, fol. 331; Jameson, pp. 170-1; *The Examination of James Lewis*, 13 October 1696.

[24] *The Information of Thomas Joy*, 16 August 1699; *The Examination of James Cragget*, 16 November 1699; *CSPD* 1698, pp. 404, 430.

[25] *CSPD* 1696, p. 364.

Chapter Seven

[1] Trial pp. 217, 227; *CSPD* 1696, p. 331; Jameson, p. 160; *The Examination of William Bishop*.

[2] Jameson, pp. 170-171; *The Information of Phillip Middleton*, 13 October 1696.

[3] Trial p. 218.

[4] *The Examination of Joseph Dawson*, 7 October 1696.

[5] *The Examination of William May*, 10 September 1696; *The Examination of William Bishop*, 15 October 1696; *The Examination of James Lewis*, 13 October 1696; *The Examination of John Sparks*, 10 September 1696.

6 *CSPD* 1696, p. 480.

7 Baer 1996, p. 102, *CSPD* 1697, p. 28.

8 Baer 1996, p. 102.

9 *CSPD* 1698, p. 430

10 A fuller description of life in Newgate at the close of the seventeenth century would be out of place here. Readers interested in the nature of the days spent at Newgate by prisoners awaiting trial or execution are urged to turn to chapters 17-21 of Richard Zacks' *The Pirate Hunter* (Hyperion, USA. 2002).

11 Quoted in Grey, p. 161.

12 *Naval Songs and Ballads*, C.H. Firth (Navy Records Society, 1907), pp. 133-4.

Chapter Eight

1 Proceedings of the Council of Maryland, vol. 20, pp. 496-8.

2 Johnson, pp. 78-9.

3 ADM 106/487, fol. 267.

4 *History and Lives*, p. 14. It might be theorised that, for reasons unknown, the author of the *History and Lives* was deliberately trying to associate the earlier author Captain Charles Johnson with Henry Every in the minds of the reading public. If Henry Every had written the *General History*, he would have been sixty-five at the time of publication (in fact, the first copies went on sale almost exactly sixty-five years after Every's baptism). Daniel Defoe, who has also been (probably incorrectly) suggested as a candidate for the authorship of the *General History* was probably born in the same year as Every, and was still publishing as late as 1728 before his death in 1731.

However, it is unlikely in the extreme that Henry Every penned the *General History*, for the chapter on himself, and that of his associate Thomas Tew, are among the least factually accurate sections of the book. Apart from the apparent coincidence of the choice of aliases, there is nothing at all to connect Every to the *General History*.

5 Johnson, pp. 56-7.

6 Rogozinski, p. 81.

7 Grey, pp. 60-1.

8 Jameson, p. 170.

9 Phillips, fols. 130-1.

10 Jameson, p. 171

11 History and Lives, p. 15.

12 By the King, a proclamation. William R:

Whereas we being informed, by the frequent complaints of our good subjects trading to the East Indies, of several wicked practises committed on those seas, as well upon our own subjects as those of our allies, have therefore thought fit (for the security of the trade of those countries, by an utter extirpation of the pirates in all parts eastward of the Cape of Good Hope, as well beyond Cape Comorin as on this side of it, unless they shall forthwith surrender themselves, as in hereinafter directed) to send out a squadron of men-of-war, under the command of Captain Thomas Warren.

Now we, to the intent that such who have been guilty of any acts of piracy in those seas, may have notice of our most gracious intention, of extending our royal mercy to such of them as shall surrender themselves, and to cause the severest punishment according to law to be inflicted upon those who shall continue obstinate, have thought fit, by the advice of our privy council, to issue this proclamation; hereby requiring and commanding all persons who have been guilty of any act of piracy, or any ways aiding or assisting therein, in any place eastward of the Cape of Good Hope, to surrender themselves within the several respective times hereinafter limited, unto the said Captain Thomas Warren, and the commander-in-chief of the squadron for the time being, and to Israel Hayes, Peter Dellanoye, and Christopher Pollard, esquires, commissioners appointed by us for the said expedition, or to any three of them, or, in case of death, to the major part of the survivors of them.

And we do hereby declare, that we have been graciously pleased to empower the said Captain Thomas Warren, and the commander-in-chief of the said squadron for the time being, Israel Hayes, Peter Dellanoye, and Christopher Pollard, esquires, commissioners aforesaid, or any three of them, or in case of death, to the major part of the survivors of them, to give assurance of our most gracious pardon unto all such pirates in the East Indies, viz. all eastward of the Cape of Good Hope, who shall surrender themselves for piracies or robberies committed by them upon sea or land; except, nevertheless, such as they shall commit in any place whatsoever after notice of our grace and favour hereby declared; and also excepting all such piracies and robberies as shall be committed from the Cape of Good Hope eastward, to the longitude or meridian of Socatora eastward, to the longitude or meridian of Cape Comorin, after the last day of June 1699, and in any place whatsoever eastward of Cape Comorin after the last day of July, 1699; and also excepting Henry Every, alias Bridgman, and William Kidd.

Given at our court at Kensington, the 8th day of December, 1698, in the 10th year of our reign, God save the King.

[13] CSPC 1699, p. 117.

Epilogue

[1] For a good overview of the St Mary's pirates see Rogozinski.

[2] Probably the best history of William Kidd's life and piracies is Robert C. Ritchie's *Captain Kidd and the War against the Pirates* (Harvard University Press, 1986), though Richard Zacks' *The Pirate Hunter* (Hyperion, 2002) is also a readable account.

[3] Johnson, p. 343; *The Arraignment, Tryal, and Condemnation of Captain John Quelch, and*

others of his Company (London, 1704), pp. 17-19; *HCA* 1/53, fol. 59; *Lives of the Most Remarkable Criminals* (London, 1735).

⁴ Thomas Wake's subsequent career, and that of his crew, is reconstructed from Phillips; Jameson, pp. 184-7; Rogozinski, pp. 94–100.

⁵ Jameson, pp. 183-184; Grey, pp. 128-30.

⁶ Phillips; *CSPC* 1697-98, p. 205; Grey, pp. 130-1.

⁷ Johnson, pp. 58-62, 668.

⁸ The imprisonment of William Street and the subsequent events are drawn from *SP* 42/3, fol 698; *CSPD* 1694-95, p. 226.

⁹ Baer 1996, pp. 99-101; *HCA* 13/81, fol. 256; *HCA* 13/82, fols. 106-107.

¹⁰ Evelyn, J., Diary, 6 August 1698.

¹¹ Fox, E.T., *Pirates of the West Country*, pp. 94-102, 154-5; Baer 1996, pp. 106-112.

¹² Quoted in Wright, p. 190.

¹³ Wright, pp. 208-13; Ritchie, R.C., *Captain Kidd and the War against the Pirates* (Harvard University Press, 1986), pp. 132-4.

Appendices

¹ *CSPD* 1694-5, p. 226.

² Rogozinski, pp. xx-xxi.

³ Jensen, M. (ed.), *American Colonial Documents to 1776* (Eyre and Spottiswoode, 1955), pp. 426-7.

⁴ Rodger, p. 620; *ADM* 33/127; Every's wages in the Spanish Expedition estimated from *HCA* 13/82; *Naval Documents*, pp. 76-7.

⁵ Rodger, pp. 620-1; *HCA* 13/82; *Wives' Petition*, fol. 61.

⁶ Zacks, R., *The Pirate Hunter* (Review, 2003), p. 391; Jameson, p. 236.

⁷ Jameson, p. 205-6.

⁸ Cornwall Record Office, J22779.

⁹ *CSPD* 1700-1702, p. 216.

Index

Index

Index

Index

Other titles published by The History Press

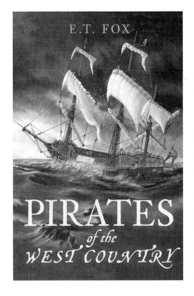

Pirates of the West Country
E.T. FOX

Discover the handful of true West Country pirates of the past and also those that voyaged from the West to the Caribbean and Indian Ocean in this compelling history. Herein lies a true account of piracy, often called the 'oldest trade afloat'. Indeed, it is older than the golden age represented in the literature of Stevenson and Barrie, and more widespread than portrayed by Hollywood. These true tales of pirates operating from places such as Lulworth Cove, Plymouth Hoe and Corfe Castle inspired the pirate fiction we know today.

978 0 7524 4377 5

Pirates
JOEL BAER

From Blackbeard to the pirates' pirate, Black Bart, this book encapsulates the true story of the 'golden age of piracy' and how it ended. The mythical hero of the golden age of piracy lived for the moment, so goes the myth, and 'the devil take the consequences'. Joel Baer shows how false a notion this really is and how aware freebooters were of the law. Joel Baer tells the story of this age through the lens of seven British freebooters. The author details their exuberant and murderous lives, their crimes, and 'prizes', and how the Admiralty forced new laws through Parliament that ultimately defeated them.

978 0 7524 4928 3

If you are interested in purchasing other books published by The History Press, or in case you have difficulty finding any History Press books in your local bookshop, you can also place orders directly through our website

www.thehistorypress.co.uk